MW01065912

THE LAST JOURNALS OF
DAVID LIVINGSTONE,
IN CENTRAL AFRICA,
FROM 1865 TO HIS DEATH

DAVID LIVINGSTONE

David Livingstone

THE LAST JOURNALS OF DAVID LIVINGSTONE, IN CENTRAL AFRICA, FROM 1865 TO HIS DEATH

Volume I
1866–1868

CONTINUED BY A NARRATIVE OF HIS LAST
MOMENTS AND SUFFERINGS, OBTAINED FROM
HIS FAITHFUL SERVANTS CHUMA AND SUSI,
BY HORACE WALLER, F.R.G.S.,
RECTOR OF TWYWELL, NORTHAMPTON.

WITH PORTRAIT, MAPS, AND ILLUSTRATIONS.

BIBLIOBAZAAR

THE LAST JOURNALS OF DAVID LIVINGSTONE, IN CENTRAL AFRICA, FROM 1865 TO HIS DEATH

INTRODUCTION.

In the midst of the universal sorrow caused by the intelligence that Dr. Livingstone had lost his life at the furthest point to which he had penetrated in his search for the true sources of the Nile, a faint hope was indulged that some of his journals might survive the disaster: this hope, I rejoice to say, has been realized beyond the most sanguine expectations.

It is due, in the first place, to his native attendants, whose faithfulness has placed his last writings at our disposal, and also to the reader, before he launches forth upon a series of travels and scientific geographical records of the most extraordinary character, to say that in the following narrative of seven years' continuous work and new discovery *no break whatever occurs.*

We have not to deplore the loss, by accident or carelessness, of a single entry, from the time of Livingstone's departure from Zanzibar in the beginning of 1866 to the day when his note-book dropped from his hand in the village of Ilala at the end of April, 1873.

I trust it will not be uninteresting if I preface the history with a few words on the nature of these journals and writings as they have come to hand from Central Africa.

It will be remembered that when Mr. Stanley returned to England in 1872, Dr. Livingstone entrusted to his care a very large Letts' diary, sealed up and consigned to the safe keeping of his daughter, Miss Agnes Livingstone. Upon the confirmation of the worst news, this book was examined and found to contain a considerable portion of the notes which her father made during his travels previous to the time of Mr. Stanley's meeting him.

The Doctor's custom was always to have metallic note-books in use, in which the day's jottings were recorded. When time and opportunity served, the larger volume was posted up with scrupulous care.

It seems, however, that in the last three or four years of his life this excellent rule had to give way to the toils of travel and the exhaustion of most distressing illnesses. Whilst in the Manyuema country he ran out of note-books, ink, and pencils, and had to resort to shifts which at first made it a very debateable point whether the most diligent attempt at deciphering would suceeed after all. Such pocket-books as remained at this period of his travels were utilized to the last inch of paper. In some of them we find lunar observations, the names of rivers, and the heights of hills advancing towards the middle from one end, whilst from the other the itinerary grows day by day, interspersed with map routes of the march, botanical notes, and carefully made drawings. But in the mean time the middle portion of the book was filling up with calculations, private memoranda, words intended for vocabularies, and extracts from books, whilst here and there the stain of a pressed flower causes indistinctness; yet the thread of the narrative runs throughout. Noting but his invariable habit of constantly repeating the month and year obviates hopeless confusion. Nor is this all; for pocket-books gave out at last, and old newspapers, yellow with African damp, were sewn together, and his notes were written across the type with a substitute for ink made from the juice of a tree. To Miss Livingstone and to the Rev. C.A. Alington I am very much indebted for help in the laborious task of deciphering this portion of the Doctor's journals. Their knowledge of his handwriting, their perseverance, coupled with good eyes and a strong magnifying-glass, at last made their task a complete success.

In comparing this great mass of material with the journal brought home by Mr. Stanley, one finds that a great deal of most interesting matter can be added. It would seem that in the hurry of writing and copying despatches previous to his companion's departure, the Doctor rapidly entered up as much from his note-books as time and space permitted.

Most fortunately, he still carried the greater part of these original notes till the time of his death, so that they were forthcoming when his effects were subsequently saved.

This brings us to the second instalment of the journals, for we have thus acknowledged the first to have reached us on Mr. Stanley's return.

When the battered tin travelling-case, which was with Livingstone to the last, was opened at the Foreign Office in the spring of this year, not only were these valuable papers disclosed which I have mentioned, but it was found also that Livingstone had kept a copious journal during his stay at Unyanyembé in some copy-books, and that when his stock of note-books was replenished a daily record of his subsequent travels had been made.

It was with fear and trembling that one looked to see whether all had been saved or only part, but with satisfaction and thankfulness I have subsequently discovered that his men preserved every single line, besides his maps, which now come to light for the first time.

Thus much on the material of the diaries: it remains to say a few words on the Map which accompanies these journals. It has been compiled from Dr. Livingstone's original drawings and note-books, with the corrections and additions he made from time to time as the work of exploration progressed, and the details of physical geography became clearer to him. The compiler, Mr. John Bolton[1], implicitly following the original outline of the drawing as far as possible, has honestly endeavoured to give such a rendering of the entire work, as the Doctor would have done had he lived to return home, and superintend the construction; and I take this opportunity of expressing my sincere gratification that Mr. Bolton's rare technical skill, scientific knowledge, and unwearying labour have been available for the purpose.

Amongst almost the last words that Livingstone wrote, I find an unfinished letter to myself, in which he gives me very clear and explicit directions concerning the geographical notes he had previously sent home, and I am but carrying out the sacred duty which is attached to a last wish when I call attention to the fact, that he particularly desired in this letter that *no positions gathered from his observations for latitude and longitude, nor for the levels of the Lakes, &c., should be considered correct till Sir Thomas Maclear had examined them.* The position of Casembe's town, and of a point near Pambetté at the S.E., and of Lake Liemba (Tanganyika), have been computed and corrected by Sir T. Maclear and Dr. Mann. The observations for latitude were taken at short intervals, and where it has been possible to test them they have been found very correct, but I repeat that until the imprimatur of his old friend at the Cape of Good Hope stands over the whole of Livingstone's work, the map must be accepted as open to further corrections.

The journey from Kabwabwata to Mparru has been inserted *entirely* from notes, as the traveller was too ill to mark the route: this is the only instance in all his wanderings where he failed to give some indication on his map of the nature of the ground over which he passed. The journey front Mikindany Bay to Lake Nyassa has also been laid down from his journal and latitudes in consequence of the section of this part of his route (which he left at Ujiji) not having arrived in England at this date.[2] It will be observed that the outline of Lake Nyassa differs from that on any published map: it has been drawn from the original exploratory survey of its southern shores made by Dr. Livingstone in 1861-3. For some reason this original plan was not adhered to by a former draughtsman, but the Lake has here been restored to a more accurate bearing and position.

How often shall we see in the pages of this concluding chapter of his life, that unwavering determination which was pre-eminently the great characteristic of David Livingstone!

Naturally endowed with unusual endurance, able to concentrate faculties of no ordinary kind upon whatever he took in hand, and with a dread of exaggeration which at times almost militated against the importance of some of his greatest discoveries, it may be doubted if ever Geographer went forth strengthened with so much true power. Let us add to these a sincere trust that slavery, the "great open sore of the world," as he called it, might under God's good guidance receive healing at his hands; a fervent hope that others would follow him after he had removed those difficulties which are comprised in a profound ignorance of the physical features of a new country, and we have the marching orders of him who left us in August 1865 never to return alive.

Privileged to enjoy his near personal friendship for a considerable period in Africa, and also at home, it has been easy to trace—more especially from correspondence with him of late years—that Livingstone wanted just some such gigantic problem as that which he attacked at the last to measure his strength against: that he finally overrated and overtaxed it I think all must admit.

He had not sufficiently allowed for an old wound which his constitution received whilst battling with dysentery and fever, on his celebrated journey across Africa, and this finally sapped his vital powers, and, through the irritation of exhaustion, insidiously clouded much of his happiness.

Many of his old friends were filled with anxiety when they found that he intended to continue the investigation of the Nile sources, for the letters sent home by Mr. Stanley raised the liveliest apprehensions, which, alas! soon proved themselves well grounded.

The reader must be warned that, however versed in books of African travel he may be, the very novelty of his situation amongst these pages will render him liable perhaps to a danger which a timely word may avert. Truly it may be said he has an *embarras de richesses!* To follow an explorer who by his individual exertions has filled up a great space in the map of Africa, who has not only been the first to set foot on the shores of vast inland seas, but who, with the simple appliances of his bodily stature for a sounding pole and his stalwart stride for a measuring tape, lays down new rivers by the hundreds, is a task calculated to stagger him. It may be provoking to find Livingstone busily engaged in bargaining for a canoe upon the shores of Bangweolo, much as he would have secured a boat on his own native Clyde; but it was not in his nature to be subject to those paroxysms in which travellers too often indite their discoveries and descriptions.

At the same time these journals will be found to contain innumerable notes on the habits of animals, birds, and fishes, many of them probably new species, and on phenomena in every direction which the keen eye searched out as the great traveller moved amongst some of the grandest scenes of this beautiful world: it may be doubted if ever eye so keen was backed by so much perseverance to shield it from a mere superficial habit of noticing. Let his adventures speak for themselves.

Amongst the greatest facts recorded here the Geographer will perceive that the Doctor has placed it beyond doubt that Lake Nyassa belongs to a totally distinct system of waters to that which holds Lake Tanganyika, and the rivers running north and west. He was too sagacious to venture the surmise that Tanganyika has a subterranean outlet without having duly weighed the probabilities in the scale with his elaborate observations: the idea gathers force when we remember that in the case of limestone cliffs, water so often succeeds in breaking bounds by boring through the solid rock. No more interesting problem is left to solve, and we shall yet learn whether, through the caverns of Western Kabogo, this Lake adds its waters to the vast northerly flow of rivers we now read of for the first time, and which are undoubtedly amongst the largest in the world.

I cannot close these remarks without stating how much obliged I am to Mr. James Young, F.R.S., of Kelly, for having ensured the presence of the Doctor's men, Chuma and Susi. Ever ready to serve his old friend Livingstone, he took care that they should be at my elbow so long as I required them to help me amidst the pile of MSS. and maps. Their knowledge of the countries they travelled in is most remarkable, and from constantly aiding their master by putting questions to the natives respecting the course of rivers, &c., I found them actual geographers of no mean attainments. In one instance, when in doubt concerning a particular watershed, to my surprise Susi returned a few hours afterwards with a plan of the whole system of rivers in the region under examination, and I found his sketch tally well with the Doctor's map. Known to me previously for years on the Zambesi and Shiré it was a pleasure to have them with me for four months. Amongst other good services they have aided the artist by reproducing the exact facsimile of the hut in which Dr. Livingstone expired, besides making models of the "kitanda" on which he was carried, and of the village in which his body lay for fourteen days.

I need not add what ready and valuable assistance I have derived from the Doctor's old companion Dr. Kirk wherever I have found it necessary to apply to him; some of the illustrations are more particularly owing to his kindness.

It only remains to say that it has been thought advisable to retain all the strictly scientific matter found in Dr. Livingstone's journals for future publication. When one sees that a register of the daily rainfall was kept throughout, that the temperature was continually recorded, and that barometrical and hypsometrical observations were made with unflagging thoroughness of purpose year in and year out, it is obvious that an accumulated mass of information remains for the meteorologist to deal with separately, which alone must engross many months of labour.

A constant sense of great responsibility has been mine throughout this task, for one cannot doubt that much of the future welfare of distant tribes and races depends upon Livingstone obtaining through these records a distinct hearing for their woes, their misery, and above all for their willingness to welcome men drawn towards them by motives like his.

At the same time memory and affection have not failed to bring back vividly the man, the traveller, and the friend. May that which he has said in his journals suffer neither loss of interest nor depth of meaning at the compiler's hands.

HORACE WALLER.

TWYWELL RECTORY, THRAPSTON,
NORTHAMPTONSHIRE.
Nov. 2, 1874.

FOOTNOTES:

1. Attached to Mr. Stanford's staff.
2. In February last this section of the map (as we suppose), together with some of the Doctor's papers, was sent off from Ujiji by Lieutenant Cameron. Nothing, however, had arrived on the 22nd September at Zanzibar, and H.M. Consul, Captain Prideaux, entertained serious doubts at that time whether they would ever come to hand. All Livingstone's journals were saved through other instrumentality, as I have shown.

* * * * *

CONTENTS.

cattle. Life with the chief. Beauty of country and healthiness of climate. The Waiyau people and their peculiarities. Regrets at the abandonment of Bishop Mackenzie's plans.

Geology and description of the Waiyau land. Leaves Mataka's. The Nyumbo plant. Native iron-foundry. Blacksmiths. Makes for the Lake Nyassa. Delight at seeing the Lake once more. The Manganja or Nyassa tribe. Arab slave crossing. Unable to procure passage across. The Kungu fly. Fear of the English amongst slavers. Lake shore. Blue ink. Chitané changes colour. The Nsaka fish. Makalaosé drinks beer. The Sanjika fish. London antiquities. Lake rivers. Mukaté's. Lake Pamalombé. Mponda's. A slave gang. Wikatani discovers his relatives and remains.

Crosses Cape Maclear. The havildar demoralised. The discomfited chief. Reaches Marenga's town. The earth-sponge. Description of Marenga's town. Rumours of Mazitu. Musa and the Johanna men desert. Reaches Kimsusa's. His delight at seeing the Doctor once more. The fat ram. Kimsusa relates his experience of Livingstone's advice. Chuma finds relatives. Kimsusa solves the transport difficulty nobly. Another old fishing acquaintance. Description of the people and country on the west of the Lake. The Kanthundas. Kauma. Iron-smelting. An African Sir Colin Campbell. Milandos.

Progress northwards. An African forest. Destruction by Mazitu. Native salutations. A disagreeable chief. On the watershed between the Lake and the Loangwa River. Extensive iron-workings. An old Nimrod. The Bua River. Lovely scenery. Difficulties of transport. Chilobé. An African Pythoness. Enlists two Waiyou bearers. Ill. The Chitella bean. Rains set in. Arrives at the Loangwa.

Crosses the Loangwa. Distressing march. The king-hunter. Great hunger. Christmas feast necessarily postponed. Loss of goats. Honey-hunters. A meal at last. The Babisa. The Mazitu again. Chitembo's. End of 1866. The new year. The northern brim of the great Loangwa Valley. Accident to chronometers. Meal gives out. Escape from a Cobra capella. Pushes for the Chambezé. Death of Chitané. Great pinch for food. Disastrous loss of medicine chest. Bead currency. Babisa. The Chambezé. Reaches Chitapangwa's town. Meets Arab traders from Zanzibar. Sends off letters. Chitapangwa and his people. Complications.

Chitapangwa's parting oath. Course laid for Lake Tanganyika. Moamba's village. Another watershed. The Babemba tribe. Ill with fever. Threatening attitude of Chibué's people. Continued illness. Reaches cliffs overhanging Lake Liemba. Extreme beauty of the scene. Dangerous fit of insensibility. Leaves the Lake. Pernambuco cotton. Rumours of war between Arabs and Nsama. Reaches Chitimba's village. Presents Sultan's letter to principal Arab, Hamees. The war in Itawa. Geography of the Arabs. Ivory traders and slave-dealers. Appeal to the Koran. Gleans intelligence of the Wasongo, to the eastward, and their chief, Méréré. Hamees sets out against Nsama. Tedious sojourn. Departure for Ponda. Native cupping.

Peace negotiations with Nsama. Geographical gleanings. Curious spider. Reaches the River Lofu. Arrives at Nsama's. Hamees marries the daughter of Nsama. Flight of the bride. Conflagration in Arab quarters. Anxious to visit Lake Moero. Arab burial. Serious illness. Continues journey. Slave-traders on the march. Reaches Moero. Description of the Lake. Information concerning the Chambezé and Luapula. Hears of Lake Bemba. Visits spot of Dr. Lacerda's death. Casembe apprised of Livingstone's approach. Meets Mohamad Bogharib. Lakelet Mofwé. Arrives at Casembe's town.

Grand reception of the traveller. Casembe and his wife. Long stay in the town. Goes to explore Moero. Despatch to Lord Clarendon, with notes on recent travels. Illness at the end of

1867. Further exploration of Lake Moero. Flooded plains. The River Luao. Visits Kabwabwata. Joy of Arabs at Mohamad bin Salleh's freedom. Again ill with fever. Stories of underground dwellings.

Riot in the camp. Mohamad's account of his long imprisonment. Superstitions about children's teeth. Concerning dreams. News of Lake Chowambé. Life of the Arab slavers. The Katanga gold supply. Muabo. Ascent of the Rua Mountains. Syde bin Habib. Birthday, 19th March, 1868. Hostility of Mpwéto. Contemplates visiting Lake Bemba. Nile sources. Men desert. The shores of Moero. Visits Fungafunga. Return to Casembe's. Obstructiveness of "Cropped-ears." Accounts of Pereira and Dr. Lacerda. Major Monteiro. The line of Casembes. Casembe explains the connection of the Lakes and the Luapula. Queen Moäri. Arab sacrifice. Kapika gets rid of his wife.

Prepares to examine Lake Bemba. Starts from Casembe's 11th June, 1868. Dead leopard. Moenampanda's reception. The River Luongo. Weird death-song of slaves. The forest grave. Lake Bemba changed to Lake Bangweolo. Chikumbi's. The Imbozhwa people. Kombokombo's stockade. Mazitu difficulties. Discovers Lake Bangweolo on 18th July, 1868. The Lake Chief Mapuni. Description of the Lake. Prepares to navigate it. Embarks for Lifungé Island. Immense size of Lake. Reaches Mpabala Island. Strange dream. Fears of canoe men. Return to shore. March back. Sends letters. Meets Banyamwezi. Reviews recent explorations at length. Disturbed state of country.

Cataracts of the Kalongosi. Passage of the river disputed. Leeches and method of detaching them. Syde bin Habib's slaves escape. Enormous collection of tusks. Ill. Theory of the Nile sources. Tribute to Miss Tinné. Notes on climate. Separation of Lake Nyassa from the Nile system. Observations on Victoria Nyanza. Slaves dying. Repentant deserters.

Mohamad Bogharib. Enraged Imbozhwa. An attack. Narrow escape. Renewed attack. A parley. Help arrives. Bin Juma. March from the Imbozhwa country. Slaves escape. Burial of Syde bin Habib's brother. Singular custom. An elephant killed. Native game-laws. Rumour of Baker's Expedition. Christmas dinners.

LIST OF ILLUSTRATIONS.

[DR. LIVINGSTONE, though no artist, had acquired a practice of making rude sketches of scenes and objects, which have furnished material for the Engravers in the Illustrations for this book.]

CHAPTER I.

Arrival at Zanzibar. Hearty reception by Said Majid, the Sultan. Murder of Baron van der Decken. The slave-market. Preparations for starting to the interior. Embarkation in H.M.S. *Penguin* and dhow. Rovuma Bay impracticable. Disembarks at Mikindany. Joy at travelling once more. Trouble with sepoys. Camels attacked by tsetse fly, and by sepoys. Jungle sappers. Meets old enemies. The Makondé. Lake Nangandi. Gum-copal diggings.

ZANZIBAR, *28th January, 1866.*—After a passage of twenty-three days from Bombay we arrived at this island in the *Thule*, which was one of Captain Sherard Osborne's late Chinese fleet, and now a present from the Bombay Government to the Sultan of Zanzibar. I was honoured with the commission to make the formal presentation, and this was intended by H.E. the Governor-in-Council to show in how much estimation I was held, and thereby induce the Sultan to forward my enterprise. The letter to his Highness was a commendatory epistle in my favour, for which consideration on the part of Sir Bartle Frere I feel deeply grateful. It runs as follows:—

TO HIS HIGHNESS SEJUEL MAJID, SULTAN OF ZANZIBAR.

(*Copy.*)
"YOUR HIGHNESS,—I trust that this will find you in the enjoyment of health and happiness.

"I have requested my friend, Dr. David Livingstone, who is already personally well and favourably known to your Highness, to convey to you the assurance of the continual friendship and goodwill of Her Majesty's Government in India.

"Your Highness is already aware of the benevolent objects of Dr. Livingstone's life and labours, and I feel assured that your Highness will continue to him the favour and protection which you have already shown to him on former occasions, and that your Highness will direct every aid to be given him within your Highness's dominions which may tend to further the philanthropic designs to which he has devoted himself, and which, as your Highness is aware, are viewed with the warmest interest by Her Majesty's Government both in India and England.

"I trust your Highness will favour me with continued accounts of your good health and welfare.

"I remain, your Highness's sincere friend,
(Signed) "H.B.E. FRERE.
"BOMBAY CASTLE, *2nd January, 1866.*"

When we arrived Dr. Seward, the Acting Consul, was absent at the Seychelles on account of serious failure of health: Mr. Schultz, however, was representing him, but he too was at the time away. Dr. Seward was expected back daily, and he did arrive on the 31st. I requested a private interview with the Sultan, and on the following day (29th) called and told him the nature of my commission to his Highness. He was very gracious, and seemed pleased with the gift, as well he might, for the *Thule* is fitted up in the most gorgeous manner. We asked a few days to put her in perfect order, and this being the Ramadân, or fasting month, he was all the more willing to defer a visit to the vessel.

Dr. Seward arranged to have an audience with the Sultan, to carry out his instructions, which were to present me in a formal manner; Captain Bradshaw of the *Wasp*, with Captain Leatham of the *Vigilant*, and Bishop Tozer, were to accompany us in full dress, but the Sultan had a toothache and gumboil, and could not receive us; he, however, placed one of his houses at my disposal, and appointed a man who speaks English to furnish board for my men and me, and also for Captain Brebner, of the *Thule*, and his men.

Livingstone's House, Zanzibar.

6th February, 1866.—The Sultan being still unable to come, partly on account of toothache and partly on account of Ramadân, he sent his commodore, Captain Abdullah, to receive the *Thule*. When the English flag was hauled down in the *Thule*, it went up to the mainmast of the *Iskander Shah*, and was saluted by twenty-one guns; then the *Wasp* saluted the Arab flag with an equal number, which honour being duly acknowledged by a second royal salute from the *Iskander Shah*, Captain Abdullah's frigate, the ceremony ended.

Next day, the 7th, we were received by the Sultan, and through his interpreter, I told him that his friend, the Governor of Bombay, had lately visited the South Mahratta Princes, and had pressed on them the necessity of education; the world was moving on, and those who neglected to acquire knowledge would soon find that power slipped through their fingers, and that the Bombay Government, in presenting his Highness with a portion of steam power, showed its desire to impart one of the greatest improvements of modern times, not desiring to monopolize power, but hoping to lift up others with themselves, and I wished him to live a hundred years and enjoy all happiness. The idea was borrowed partly from Sir

Bartle Frere's addresses, because I thought it would have more weight if he heard a little from that source than if it emanated from myself. He was very anxious that Captain Brebner and his men, in returning to India, should take a passage from him in the *Nadir Shah*, one of his men-of-war, and though he had already placed his things aboard the *Vigilant*, to proceed to Seychelles, and thence to Bombay, we persuaded Captain Brebner to accept his Highness's hospitality. He had evidently set his heart on sending them back with suitable honours, and an hour after consent was given to go by the *Nadir Shah*, he signed an order for the money to fit her out.

11th February, 1866.—One of the foremost subjects that naturally occupied my mind here was the sad loss of the Baron van der Decken, on the River Juba, or Aljib. The first intimation of the unfortunate termination of his explorations was the appearance of Lieutenant von Schich at this place, who had left without knowing whether his leader were dead or alive, but an attack had been made on the encampment which had been planned after the steamer struck the rocks and filled, and two of the Europeans were killed. The attacking party came from the direction in which the Baron and Dr. Link went, and three men of note in it were slain. Von Schich went back from Zanzibar to Brava to ascertain the fate of the Baron, and meanwhile several native sailors from Zanzibar had been allowed to escape from the scene of confusion to Brava.

18th February, 1866.—All the Europeans went to pay visits of congratulation to his Highness the Sultan upon the conclusion of the Ramadân, when sweetmeats were placed before us. He desired me to thank the Governor of Bombay for his magnificent gift, and to state that although he would like to have me always with him, yet he would show me the same favour in Africa which he had done here: he added that the *Thule* was at my service to take me to the Rovuma whenever I wished to leave. I replied that nothing had been wanting on his part; he had done more than I expected, and I was sure that his Excellency the Governor would be delighted to hear that the vessel promoted his health and prosperity; nothing would delight him more than this. He said that he meant to go out in her on Wednesday next (20th): Bishop Tozer, Captain Fraser, Dr. Steere, and all the English were present. The sepoys came in and did obeisance; and I pointed out the Nassick lads as those who had been rescued from slavery, educated, and sent back to their own country by the Governor. Surely he must see that some people in the world act from other than selfish motives.

In the afternoon Sheikh Sulieman, his secretary, came with a letter for the Governor, to be conveyed by Lieutenant Brebner, I.N., in the *Nadir Shah*, which is to sail to-morrow. He offered money to the lieutenant, but this could not be heard of for a moment.

The translation of the letter is as follows, and is an answer to that which I brought.

TO HIS EXCELLENCY THE GOVERNOR OF BOMBAY.

[After compliments.]

" . . . The end of my desire is to know ever that your Excellency's health is good. As for me—your friend—I am very well.

"Your honoured letter borne by Dr. Livingstone duly reached me, and all that you said about him I understood.

"I will show him respect, give him honour, and help him in all his affairs; and that I have already done this, I trust he will tell you.

"I hope you will let me rest in your heart, and that you will send me many letters.

"If you need anything I shall be glad, and will give it.

"Your sincere friend,
"MAJID BIN SAID.
"Dated 2nd Shaul, 1282 (18th February, 1866)."

2nd March, 1866.—A northern dhow came in with slaves; when this was reported to the Sultan he ordered it to be burned, and we saw this done from the window of the Consulate; but he has very little power over Northern Arabs. He has shown a little vigour of late. He wished to raise a revenue by a charge of 10 per cent. on all articles brought into town for sale, but this is clearly contrary to treaty, which provides that no monopoly shall be permitted, and no dues save that of 5 per cent. import duty. The French Consul bullies him: indeed the French system of dealing with the natives is well expressed by that word; no wonder they cannot gain influence among them: the greatest power they exercise is by lending their flag to slaving dhows, so that it covers that nefarious traffic.

The stench arising from a mile and a half or two square miles of exposed sea beach, which is the general depository of the filth of the town, is quite horrible. At night it is so gross or crass one might cut out a slice and manure a garden with it: it might be called Stinkibar rather than Zanzibar. No one can long enjoy good health here.

On visiting the slave-market I found about 300 slaves exposed for sale, the greater part of whom came from Lake Nyassa and the Shiré River; I am so familiar with the peculiar faces and markings or tattooings, that I expect them to recognize me. Indeed one woman said that she had heard of our passing up Lake Nyassa in a boat, but she did not see me: others came from Chipéta, S.W. of the Lake. All who have grown up seem ashamed at being hawked about for sale. The teeth are examined, the cloth lifted up to examine the lower limbs, and a stick is thrown for the slave to bring, and thus exhibit his paces. Some are dragged through the crowd by the hand, and the price called out incessantly: most of the purchasers were Northern Arabs and Persians. This is the period when the Sultan's people may not carry slaves coastwise; but they simply cannot, for the wind is against them. Many of the dhows leave for Madagascar, and thence come back to complete their cargoes.

The Arabs are said to treat their slaves kindly, and this also may be said of native masters; the reason is, master and slave partake of the general indolence, but the lot of the slave does not improve with the general progress in civilization. While no great disparity of rank exists, his energies are little tasked, but when society advances, wants multiply; and to supply these the slave's lot grows harder. The distance between master and man increases as the lust of gain is developed, hence we can hope for no improvement in the slave's condition, unless the master returns to or remains in barbarism.

6th March, 1866.—Rains have begun now that the sun is overhead. We expect the *Penguin* daily to come from Johanna, and take us to the Rovuma. It is an unwholesome place; six of my men have fever; few retain health long, and considering the lowness of the island, and the absence of sanitary regulations in the town, it is not to be wondered at. The Sultan has little power, being only the successor to the captain of the horde of Arabs who came down and overran the island and maritime coasts of the adjacent continent. He is called only Said or Syed, never Sultan; and they can boast of choosing a new one if he does not suit them. Some coins were found in digging here which have Cufic inscriptions, and are about 900 years old. The island is low; the highest parts may not be more than 150 feet above the sea; it is of a coral formation, with sandstone conglomerate. Most of the plants are African, but clove-trees, mangoes, and cocoa-nut groves give a luxuriant South Sea Island look to the whole scenery.

We visited an old man to-day, the richest in Zanzibar, who is to give me letters to his friends at Tanganyika, and I am trying to get a depôt of goods for provisions formed there, so that when I reach it I may not be destitute.

18th March, 1866.—I have arranged with Koorje, a Banian, who farms the custom-house revenue here, to send a supply of beads, cloth, flour, tea, coffee, and sugar, to Ujiji, on Lake Tanganyika. The Arab there, with whom one of Koorje's people will remain in charge of the goods, is called Thani bin Suelim.

Yesterday we went to take leave of the Sultan, and to thank him for all his kindness to me and my men, which has indeed been very great. He offered me men to go with me, and another letter if I wished it. He looks very ill.

I have received very great kindness during my stay from Dr. and Mrs. Seward. They have done everything for me in their power: may God Almighty return it all abundantly into their bosoms, in the way that He best can. Dr. Seward's views of the policy pursued here I have no doubt are the right ones; in fact, the only ones which can be looked back to with satisfaction, or that have probability of success among a race of Pariah Arabs.

The *Penguin* came a few days ago, and Lieutenant Garforth in command agrees to take me down to the Rovuma River, and land me there. I have a dhow to take my animals: six camels, three buffaloes, and a calf, two mules, and four donkeys. I have thirteen Sepoys, ten Johanna men, nine Nassick boys, two Shupanga men, and two Wayaus, Wekatani and Chuma.[3]

[It may be well to point out that several of these men had previously been employed by Dr. Livingstone on the Zambesi and Shiré; thus Musa, the Johanna man, was a sailor on the *Lady Nyassa*, whilst Susi and Amoda were engaged at Shupanga to cut wood for the *Pioneer*. The two Waiyau lads, Wakatani and Chuma, were liberated from the slavers by the Doctor and Bishop Mackenzie in 1861, and lived for three years with the Mission party at Chibisa's before they were engaged by Livingstone. The Nassick lads were entire strangers, and were trained in India.]

19th March, 1866.—We start this morning at 10 A.M. I trust that the Most High may prosper me in this work, granting me influence in the eyes of the heathen, and helping me to make my intercourse beneficial to them.

22nd March, 1866.—We reached Rovuma Bay to-day, and anchored about two miles from the mouth of the river, in five fathoms. I went up the left bank to see if the gullies which formerly ran into the bay had altered, so as to allow camels to cross them: they seemed to have become shallower. There was no wind for the dhow, and as for the man-of-war towing her, it was out of the question. On the 23rd the cutter did try to tow the dhow, but without success, as a strong tide runs constantly out of the river at this season. A squall came up from the S.E., which would have taken the dhow in, but the master was on board the *Penguin*, and said he had no large sail. I got him off to his vessel, but the wind died away before we could reach the mouth of the river.

24th March, 1866.—I went to the dhow, and there being no wind I left orders with the captain to go up the right bank should a breeze arise. Mr. Fane, midshipman, accompanied me up the left bank above, to see if we could lead the camels along in the water. Near the point where the river first makes a little bend to the north, we landed and found three formidable gullies, and jungle so thick with bush, date-palms, twining bamboo, and hooked thorns, that one could scarcely get along. Further inland it was sticky mud, thickly planted over with mangrove roots and gullies in whose soft banks one sank over the ankles. No camels could have moved, and men with extreme difficulty might struggle through; but we never could have made an available road. We came to a she-hippopotamus lying in a ditch, which did not cover her; Mr. Fane fired into her head, and she was so upset that she nearly fell backward in plunging up the opposite bank: her calf was killed, and was like sucking-pig, though in appearance as large as a full-grown sow.

We now saw that the dhow had a good breeze, and she came up along the right bank and grounded at least a mile from the spot where the mangroves ceased. The hills, about two hundred feet high, begin about two or three miles above that, and they looked invitingly green and cool. My companion and I went from the dhow inland, to see if the mangroves gave way, to a more walkable country, but the swamp covered over thickly with mangroves only became worse the farther we receded from the river. The whole is flooded at high tides, and had we landed all the men we should have been laid up with fever ere we could have attained the higher land, which on the right bank bounds the line of vision, and the first part of which lies so near. I thought I had better land on the sand belt on the left of Rovuma Bay, and then explore and get information from the natives, none of whom had as yet come near us, so I ordered the dhow to come down to the spot next day, and went on board the *Penguin*. Lieutenant Garforth was excessively kind, and though this is his best time for cruising in the North, he most patiently agreed to wait and help me to land.

24th March, 1866.—During the night it occurred to me that we should be in a mess if after exploration and information from the natives we could find no path, and when I mentioned this, Lieutenant Garforth suggested that we should proceed to Kilwa, so at 5 A.M. I went up to the dhow with Mr. Fane, and told the captain that we were going there. He was loud in his protestations against this, and strongly recommended the port of Mikindany, as quite near to Rovuma, Nyassa, and the country I wished to visit, besides being a good landing-place, and the finest port on the coast. Thither we went, and on the same evening landed all our animals in Mikindany bay, which lies only twenty-five miles N. of Rovuma. The *Penguin* then left.

The Rovuma is quite altered from what it was when first we visited it. It is probable that the freshets form banks inside the mouth, which are washed out into the deep bay, and this periodical formation probably has prevented the Arabs from using the Rovuma as a port of shipment. It is not likely that Mr. May[4] would have made a mistake if the middle were as shoal as now: he found soundings of three fathoms or more.

Dhow used for Transport of Dr. Livingstone's Camels.

25th March, 1866.—I hired a house for four dollars a month and landed all our goods from the dhow. The bay gives off a narrow channel, about 500 yards wide and 200 yards long, the middle is deep, but the sides are coral reefs and shoal: the deep part seems about 100 yards wide. Outside in the Bay of Mikindany there is no anchorage except on the edge of the reef where the *Penguin* got seven fathoms, but further in it was only two fathoms. The inner bay is called Pemba, not Pimlea, as erroneously printed in the charts of Owen. It is deep and quite sheltered; another of a similar round form lies somewhat to the south: this bay may be two miles square.

The cattle are all very much the worse for being knocked about in the dhow. We began to prepare saddles of a very strong tree called Ntibwé, which is also used for making the hooked spear with which hippopotami are killed—the hook is very strong and tough; I applied also for twenty carriers and a Banian engaged to get them as soon as possible. The people have no cattle here, they are half-caste Arabs mostly, and quite civil to us.

26th March, 1866.—A few of the Nassick boys have the slave spirit pretty strongly; it goes deepest in those who have the darkest skins. Two Gallah men are the most intelligent and hardworking among them; some look on work with indifference when others are the actors.

Now that I am on the point of starting on another trip into Africa I feel quite exhilarated: when one travels with the specific object in view of ameliorating the condition of the natives every act becomes ennobled.

Whether exchanging the customary civilities, or arriving at a village, accepting a night's lodging, purchasing food for the party, asking for information, or answering polite African enquiries as to our objects in travelling, we begin to spread a knowledge of that people by whose agency their land will yet become enlightened and freed from the slave-trade.

The mere animal pleasure of travelling in a wild unexplored country is very great. When on lands of a couple of thousand feet elevation, brisk exercise imparts elasticity to the muscles, fresh and healthy blood circulates through the brain, the mind works well, the eye is clear, the step is firm, and a day's exertion always makes the evening's repose thoroughly enjoyable.

We have usually the stimulus of remote chances of danger either from beasts or men. Our sympathies are drawn out towards our humble hardy companions by a community of interests, and, it may be, of perils, which make us all friends. Nothing but the most pitiable puerility would lead any manly heart to make their inferiority a theme for self-exaltation; however, that is often done, as if with the vague idea that we can, by magnifying their deficiencies, demonstrate our immaculate perfections.

The effect of travel on a man whose heart is in the right place is that the mind is made more self-reliant: it becomes more confident of its own resources—there is greater presence of mind. The body is soon well-knit; the muscles of the limbs grow as hard as a board, and seem to have no fat; the countenance is bronzed, and there is no dyspepsia. Africa is a most wonderful country for appetite, and it is only when one gloats over marrow bones or elephant's feet that indigestion is possible. No doubt much toil is involved, and fatigue of which travellers in the more temperate climes can form but a faint conception; but the sweat of one's brow is no longer a curse when one works for God: it proves a tonic to the system, and is actually a blessing. No one can truly appreciate the charm of repose unless he has undergone severe exertion.

27th March, 1866.—The point of land which on the north side of the entrance to the harbour narrows it to about 300 yards is alone called Pemba; the other parts have different names. Looking northwards from the point, the first hundred yards has ninety square houses of wattled daub; a ruin (a mosque) has been built of lime and coral. The whole point is coral, and the soil is red, and covered over with dense tropical vegetation, in which the baobab is conspicuous. Dhows at present come in with ease by the easterly wind which blows in the evening, and leave next morning, the land wind taking them out.

While the camels and other animals are getting over their fatigues and bad bruises, we are making camels' saddles, and repairing those of the mules and buffaloes. Oysters abound on all the rocks and on the trees over which the tide flows: they are small, but much relished by the people.

The Arabs here are a wretched lot physically—thin, washed-out creatures—many with bleared eyes.

29-30th March, 1866.—This harbour has somewhat the shape of a bent bow or the spade on a playing-card, the shaft of the arrow being the entrance in; the passage is very deep, but not more than 100 yards wide, and it goes in nearly S.W.; inside it is deep and quite secure, and protected from all winds. The lands westward rise at once to about 200 feet, and John, a hill, is the landmark by which it is best known in coming along the coast—so say the Arabs. The people have no cattle, but say there are no tsetse flies: they have not been long here, *i.e.* under the present system; but a ruin on the northern peninsula or face of the entrance, built of stone and lime—Arab-fashion, and others on the north-west, show that the place has been known and used of old. The adjacent country has large game at different water pools, and as the whole country is somewhat elevated it probably is healthy. There is very little mangrove, but another enclosed piece of water to the south of this probably has more. The language of the people here is Swaheli;

they trade a little in gum-copal and Orchilla weed. An agent of the Zanzibar custom-house presides over the customs, which are very small, and a jemidar acknowledging the Sultan is the chief authority; but the people are little superior to the natives whom they have displaced. The jemidar has been very civil to me, and gives me two guides to go on to Adondé, but no carriers can be hired. Water is found in wells in the coral rock which underlies the whole place.

4th April, 1866.—When about to start from Pemba, at the entrance to the other side of the bay one of our buffaloes gored a donkey so badly that he had to be shot: we cut off the tips of the offender's horns, on the principle of "locking the stable-door when the steed is stolen," and marched. We came to level spots devoid of vegetation, and hard on the surface, but a deposit of water below allowed the camels to sink up to their bodies through the crust. Hauling them out, we got along to the jemidar's house, which is built of coral and lime. Hamesh was profuse in his professions of desire to serve, but gave a shabby hut which let in rain and wind. I slept one night in it, and it was unbearable, so I asked the jemidar to allow me to sleep in his court-room, where many of the sepoys were: he consented, but when I went refused; then, being an excitable, nervous Arab, he took fright, mustered all his men, amounting to about fifteen, with matchlocks; ran off, saying he was going to kill a lion; came back, shook hands nervously with me, vowing it was a man who would not obey him, "it was not you."

Our goods were all out in the street, bound on the pack-saddles, so at night we took the ordinary precaution of setting a guard. This excited our dignitary, and after dark all his men were again mustered with matches lighted. I took no notice of him, and after he had spent a good deal of talk, which we could hear, he called Musa and asked what I meant. The explanations of Musa had the effect of sending him to bed, and in the morning, when I learned how much I had most unintentionally disturbed him, I told him that I was sorry, but it did not occur to me to tell him about an ordinary precaution against thieves. He thought he had given me a crushing reply when he said with vehemence, "But there are no thieves here." I did not know till afterwards that he and others had done me an ill turn in saying that no carriers could be hired from the independent tribes adjacent. They are low-coast Arabs, three-quarters African, and, as usual, possess the bad without the good qualities of both parents. Many of them came and begged brandy, and laughed when they remarked that they could drink it in secret but not openly; they have not, however, introduced it as an article of trade, as we Christians have done on the West Coast.

6th April, 1866.—We made a short march round to the south-west side of the Lake, and spent the night at a village in that direction. There are six villages dotted round the inner harbour, and the population may amount to 250 or 300 souls—coast Arabs and their slaves; the southern portion of the harbour is deep, from ten to fourteen fathoms, but the north-western part is shoal and rocky. Very little is done in the way of trade; some sorghum, sem-sem seed, gum-copal, and orchilla weed, constitute the commerce of the port: I saw two Banian traders settled here.

7th April, 1866.—Went about south from Kindany with a Somalie guide, named Ben Ali or Bon Ali, a good-looking obliging man, who was to get twenty dollars to take us up to Ngomano. Our path lay in a valley, with well-wooded heights on each side, but the grass towered over our heads, and gave the sensation of smothering, whilst the sun beat down on our heads very fiercely, and there was not a breath of air stirring. Not understanding camels, I had to trust to the sepoys who overloaded them, and before we had accomplished our march of about seven miles they were knocked up.

8th April, 1866.—We spent the Sunday at a village called Nyañgedi. Here on the evening of the 7th April our buffaloes and camels were first bitten by the tsetse fly.[5] We had passed through some pieces of dense jungle which, though they offered no obstruction to foot-passengers, but rather an agreeable shade, had to be cut for the tall camels, and fortunately we found the Makondé of this village glad to engage themselves by the day either as woodcutters or carriers. We had left many things with the jemidar from an idea that no carriers could be procured. I lightened the camels, and had a party of woodcutters to heighten and widen the path in the dense jungle into which we now penetrated. Every now and then we emerged on open spaces, where the Makondé have cleared gardens for sorghum, maize, and cassava. The people were very much more taken up with the camels and buffaloes than with me. They are all independent of each other, and no paramount chief exists. Their foreheads may be called compact, narrow, and rather low; the *alae nasi* expanded laterally; lips full, not excessively thick;

limbs and body well formed; hands and feet small; colour dark and light-brown; height middle size, and bearing independent.

10th April, 1866.—We reached a village called Narri, lat. 10° 23' 14" S. Many of the men had touches of fever. I gave medicine to eleven of them, and next morning all were better. Food is abundant and cheap. Our course is nearly south, and in "wadys," from which, following the trade-road, we often ascend the heights, and then from the villages, which are on the higher land, we descend to another on the same wady. No running water is seen; the people depend on wells for a supply.

11th April, 1866.—At Tandahara we were still ascending as we went south; the soil is very fertile, with a good admixture of sand in it, but no rocks are visible. Very heavy crops of maize and sorghum are raised, and the cassava bushes are seven feet in height. The bamboos are cleared off them, spread over the space to be cultivated and burned to serve as manure. Iron is very scarce, for many of the men appear with wooden spears; they find none here, but in some spots where an ooze issued from the soil iron rust appeared. At each of the villages where we spent a night we presented a fathom of calico, and the headman always gave a fowl or two, and a basket of rice or maize. The Makondé dialect is quite different from Swaheli, but from their intercourse with the coast Arabs many of the people here have acquired a knowledge of Swaheli.

A Thorn-climber.

12th April, 1866.—On starting we found the jungle so dense that the people thought "there was no cutting it:" it continued upwards of three miles. The trees are not large, but so closely planted together that a great deal of labour was required to widen and heighten the path: where bamboos prevail they have starved out the woody trees. The reason why the trees are not large is because all the spaces we passed over were formerly garden ground before the Makondé had been thinned by the slave-trade. As soon as a garden is deserted, a thick crop of trees of the same sorts as those formerly cut down springs up, and here the process of woody trees starving out their fellows, and occupying the land without dense scrub below, has not had time to work itself out. Many are mere poles, and so intertwined with climbers as to present the appearance of a ship's ropes and cables shaken in among them, and many have woody stems as thick as an eleven-inch hawser. One species may be likened to the scabbard of a dragoon's sword, but along the middle of the flat side runs a ridge, from which springs up every few inches a bunch of inch-long straight sharp thorns. It hangs straight for a couple of yards, but as if it could not give its thorns a fair chance of mischief, it suddenly bends on itself, and all its cruel points are now at right angles to what they were before. Darwin's observation shows a great deal of what looks like instinct in these climbers. This species seems to be eager for mischief; its tangled limbs hang out ready to inflict injury on all passers-by. Another climber is so tough it is not to be broken by the fingers; another appears at its root as a young tree, but it has the straggling habits of its class, as may be seen by its cords stretched some fifty or sixty feet off; it is often two inches in diameter; you cut it through at one part and find it reappear forty yards off.

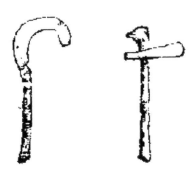

Tomahawk and Axe.

Another climber is like the leaf of an aloe, but convoluted as strangely as shavings from the plane of a carpenter. It is dark green in colour, and when its bark is taken off it is beautifully striated beneath, lighter and darker green, like the rings of growth on wood; still another is a thin string with a succession of large knobs, and another has its bark pinched up all round at intervals so as to present a great many cutting edges. One sort need scarcely be mentioned, in which all along its length are strong bent hooks, placed in a way that will hold one if it can but grapple with him, for that is very common and not like those mentioned, which the rather seem to be stragglers from the carboniferous period of geologists, when Pachydermata wriggled unscathed among tangled masses worse than these. We employed about ten jolly young Makondé to deal with these prehistoric plants in their own way, for they are accustomed to clearing spaces for gardens, and went at the work with a will, using tomahawks well adapted for the work. They whittled away right manfully, taking an axe when any trees had to be cut. Their pay, arranged beforehand, was to be one yard of calico per day: this is not much, seeing we are still so near the sea-coast. Climbers and young trees melted before them like a cloud before the sun! Many more would have worked than we employed, but we used the precaution of taking the names of those engaged. The tall men became exhausted soonest, while the shorter men worked vigorously still—but a couple of days' hard work seemed to tell on the best of them. It is doubtful if any but meat-eating people can stand long-continued labour without exhaustion: the Chinese may be an exception. When French navvies were first employed they could not do a tithe of the work of our English ones; but when the French were fed in the same style as the English, they performed equally well. Here the Makondé have rarely the chance of a good feed of meat: it is only when one of them is fortunate enough to spear a wild hog or an antelope that they know this luxury; if a fowl is eaten they get but a taste of it with their porridge.

13th April, 1866.—We now began to descend the northern slope down to the Rovuma, and a glimpse could occasionally be had of the country; it seemed covered with great masses of dark green forest, but the undulations occasionally looked like hills, and here and there a Sterculia had put on yellow foliage in anticipation of the coming winter. More frequently our vision was circumscribed to a few yards till our merry woodcutters made for us the pleasant scene of a long vista fit for camels to pass: as a whole, the jungle would have made the authors of the natty little hints to travellers smile at their own productions, good enough, perhaps, where one has an open country with trees and hills; by which to take bearings, estimate distances, see that one point is on the same latitude, another on the same longitude with such another, and all to be laid down fair and square with protractor and compass, but so long as we remained within the vegetation, that is fed by the moisture from the Indian Ocean, the steamy, smothering air, and dank, rank, luxuriant vegetation made me feel, like it, struggling for existence,—and no more capable of taking bearings than if I had been in a hogshead and observing through the bunghole!

An old Monyiñko headman presented a goat and asked if the sepoys wished to cut its throat: the Johannees, being of a different sect of Mahometans, wanted to cut it in some other way than their Indian co-religionists: then ensued a fierce dispute as to who was of the right sort of Moslem! It was interesting to see that not Christians alone, but other nations feel keenly on religious subjects.

I saw rocks of grey sandstone (like that which overlies coal) and the Rovuma in the distance. Didi is the name of a village whose headsman, Chombokëa, is said to be a doctor; all the headmen pretend or are really doctors; however one, Fundindomba, came after me for medicine for himself.

14th April, 1866.—To-day we succeeded in reaching the Rovuma, where some very red cliffs appear on the opposite heights, and close by where it is marked on the map that the *Pioneer* turned back in 1861. Here we rested on Sunday 15th.

16th April, 1866.—Our course now lay westwards, along the side of that ragged outline of table-land, which we had formerly seen from the river as flanking both sides. There it appeared a range of hills shutting in Rovuma, here we had spurs jutting out towards the river, and valleys retiring from a mile to three miles inland. Sometimes we wended our way round them, sometimes rose over and descended their western sides, and then a great deal of wood-cutting was required. The path is not straight, but from one village to another. We came perpetually on gardens, and remarked that rice was sown among the other grain; there must be a good deal of moisture at other times to admit of this succeeding: at present the crops were suffering for want of rain. We could purchase plenty of rice for the sepoys, and well it was so, for the supply which was to last till we arrived at Ngomano was finished on the 13th. An old doctor, with our food awaiting, presented me with two large bags of rice and his wife husked it for us.

17th April, 1866.—I had to leave the camels in the hands of the sepoys: I ordered them to bring as little luggage as possible, and the Havildar assured me that two buffaloes were amply sufficient to carry all they would bring. I now find that they have more than full loads for two buffaloes, two mules, and two donkeys; but when these animals fall down under them, they assure me with so much positiveness that they are not overloaded, that I have to be silent, or only, as I have several times done before, express the opinion that they will kill these animals. This observation on my part leads them to hide their things in the packs of the camels, which also are over-burdened. I fear that my experiment with the tsetse will be vitiated, but no symptoms yet occur in any of the camels except weariness.[6] The sun is very sharp; it scorches. Nearly all the sepoys had fever, but it is easily cured; they never required to stop marching, and we cannot make over four or five miles a day, which movement aids in the cure. In all cases of fever removal from the spot of attack should be made: after the fever among the sepoys, the Nassick boys took their turn along with the Johannees.

18th April, 1866.—Ben Ali misled us away up to the north in spite of my protest, when we turned in that direction; he declared that was the proper path. We had much wood-cutting, and found that our course that day and next was to enable him to visit and return from one of his wives—a comely Makondé woman! He brought her to call on me, and I had to be polite to the lady, though we lost a day by the zigzag. This is one way by which the Arabs gain influence; a great many very light-coloured people are strewed among the Makondé, but only one of these had the Arab hair. On asking Ali whether any attempts had been made by Arabs to convert those with whom they enter into such intimate relationships, he replied that the Makondé had no idea of a Deity—no one could teach them, though Makondé slaves when taken to the coast and elsewhere were made Mahometans. Since the slave-trade was introduced this tribe has much diminished in numbers, and one village makes war upon another and kidnaps, but no religious teaching has been attempted. The Arabs come down to the native ways, and make no efforts to raise the natives to theirs; it is better that it is so, for the coast Arab's manners and morals would be no improvement on the pagan African!

19th April, 1866.—We were led up over a hill again, and on to the level of the plateau (where the evaporation is greater than in the valley), and tasted water of an agreeable coldness for the first time this journey. The people, especially the women, are very rude, and the men very eager to be employed as woodcutters. Very merry they are at it, and every now and then one raises a cheerful shout, in which all join. I suppose they are urged on by a desire to please their wives with a little clothing. The higher up the Rovuma we ascend the people are more and more tattooed on the face, and on all parts of the body. The teeth are filed to points, and huge lip-rings are worn by the women; some few Mabeha men from the south side of the river have lip-rings too.

20th April, 1866.—A Johanna man allowed the camels to trespass and destroy a man's tobacco patch: the owner would not allow us after this to pass through his rice-field, in which the route lay. I examined the damage, and made the Johanna man pay a yard of calico for it, which set matters all right.

Tsetse are biting the buffaloes again. Elephants, hippopotami, and pigs are the only game here, but we see none: the tsetse feed on them. In the low meadow land, from one to three miles broad, which lies along both banks, we have brackish pools, and one, a large one, which we passed, called Wrongwé, had much fish, and salt is got from it.

21st April, 1866.—After a great deal of cutting we reached the valley of Mehambwé to spend Sunday, all glad that it had come round again. Here some men came to our camp from Ndondé, who report that an invasion of Mazitu had three months ago swept away all the food out of the country, and they are now obliged to send in every direction for provisions. When saluting, they catch each other's hands and say, "Ai! Ai!" but the general mode (introduced, probably by the Arabs) is to take hold of the right hand, and say, "Marhaba" (welcome).

A wall-eyed ill-looking fellow, who helped to urge on the attack on our first visit in 1861, and the man to whom I gave cloth to prevent a collision, came about us disguised in a jacket. I knew him well, but said nothing to him.[7]

23rd April, 1866.—When we marched this morning we passed the spot where an animal had been burned in the fire, and on enquiry I found that it is the custom when a leopard is killed to take off the skin and consume the carcase thus, because the Makondé do not eat it. The reason they gave for not eating flesh which is freely eaten by other tribes, is that the leopard devours men; this shows the opposite of an inclination to cannibalism.

All the rocks we had seen showed that the plateau consists of grey sandstone, capped by a ferruginous sandy conglomerate. We now came to blocks of silicified wood lying on the surface; it is so like recent wood, that no one who has not handled it would conceive it to be stone and not wood: the outer surface preserves the grain or woody fibre, the inner is generally silica.

Buffaloes bitten by tsetse again show no bad effects from it: one mule is, however, dull and out of health; I thought that this might be the effect of the bite till I found that his back was so strained that he could not stoop to drink, and could only eat the tops of the grasses. An ox would have been ill in two days after the biting on the 7th.

A carrier stole a shirt, and went off unsuspected; when the loss was ascertained, the man's companions tracked him with Ben Ali by night, got him in his hut, and then collected the headmen of the village, who fined him about four times the value of what had been stolen. They came back in the morning without seeming to think that they had done aught to be commended; this was the only case of theft we had noticed, and the treatment showed a natural sense of justice.

24th April, 1866.—We had showers occasionally, but at night all the men were under cover of screens. The fevers were speedily cured; no day was lost by sickness, but we could not march more than a few miles, owing to the slowness of the sepoys; they are a heavy drag on us, and of no possible use, except when acting as sentries at night.

When in the way between Kendany and Rovuma, I observed a plant here, called *Mandaré*, the root of which is in taste and appearance like a waxy potato; I saw it once before at the falls below the Barotsé Valley, in the middle of the continent; it had

43

been brought there by an emigrant, who led out the water for irrigation, and it still maintained its place in the soil. Would this not prove valuable in the soil of India? I find that it is not cultivated further up the country of the Makondé, but I shall get Ali to secure some for Bombay.

25th April, 1866.—A serpent bit Jack, our dog, above the eye, the upper eyelid swelled very much, but no other symptoms appeared, and next day all swelling was gone; the serpent was either harmless, or the quantity of poison injected very small. The pace of the camels is distressingly slow, and it suits the sepoys to make it still slower than natural by sitting down to smoke and eat. The grass is high and ground under it damp and steamy.

26th April, 1866.—On the 25th we reached Narri, and resolved to wait the next day and buy food, as it is not so plentiful in front; the people are eager traders in meal, fowls, eggs, and honey; the women are very rude. Yesterday I caught a sepoy, Pando, belabouring a camel with a big stick as thick as any part of his arm, the path being narrow, it could not get out of his way; I shouted to him to desist; he did not know I was in sight, to-day the effect of the bad usage is seen in the animal being quite unable to move its leg: inflammation has set up in the hip-joint. I am afraid that several bruises which have festered on the camels, and were to me unaccountable, have been wilfully bestowed. This same Pando and another left Zanzibar drunk: he then stole a pair of socks from me, and has otherwise been perfectly useless, even a pimple on his leg was an excuse for doing nothing for many days. We had to leave this camel at Narri under charge of the headman.

28th April, 1866.—The hills on the north now retire out of our sight. A gap in the southern plateau gives passage to a small river, which arises in a lakelet of some size, eight or ten miles inland: the river and lakelet are both called Nangadi; the latter is so broad that men cannot be distinguished, even by the keen eyes of the natives on the other side: it is very deep, and abounds in large fish; the people who live there are Mabiha. A few miles above this gap the southern highland falls away, and there are lakelets on marshes, also abounding in fish, an uninhabited space next succeeds, and then we have the Matambwé country, which extends up to Ngomano. The Matambwé seem to be a branch of the Makondé, and a very large one: their country extends a long way south, and is well stocked with elephants and gum-copal trees.

They speak a language slightly different from that of the Makondé, but they understand them. The Matambwé women are, according to Ali, very dark, but very comely, though they do wear the lip-ring. They carry their ivory, gum-copal, and slaves to Ibo or Wibo.

29th April, 1866.—We spend Sunday, the 29th, on the banks of the Rovuma, at a village called Nachuchu, nearly opposite Konayumba, the first of the Matambwé, whose chief is called Kimbembé. Ali draws a very dark picture of the Makondé. He says they know nothing of a Deity, they pray to their mothers when in distress or dying; know nothing of a future state, nor have they any religion except a belief in medicine; and every headsman is a doctor. No Arab has ever tried to convert them, but occasionally a slave taken to the coast has been circumcised in order to be clean; some of them pray, and say they know not the ordeal or muavi. The Nassick boys failed me when I tried to communicate some knowledge through them. They say they do not understand the Makondé language, though some told me that they came from Ndondé's, which is the head-quarters of the Makondé. Ali says that the Makondé blame witches for disease and death; when one of a village dies, the whole population departs, saying "that is a bad spot." They are said to have been notorious for fines, but an awe has come over them, and no complaints have been made, though our animals in passing the gardens have broken a good deal of corn. Ali says they fear the English. This is an answer to my prayer for influence on the minds of the heathen. I regret that I cannot speak to them that good of His name which I ought.

I went with the Makondé to see a specimen of the gum-copal tree in the vicinity of this village. The leaves are in pairs, glossy green, with the veins a little raised on both face and back; the smaller branches diverge from the same point: the fruit, of which we saw the shells, seems to be a nut; some animal had in eating them cut them through. The bark of the tree is of a light ash colour; the gum was oozing from the bark at wounded places, and it drops on the ground from branches; it is thus that insects are probably imbedded in the gum-copal. The people dig in the vicinity of modern trees in the belief that the more ancient trees which dropped their gum before it became an article of commerce must have stood there. "In digging, none may be found on one day but God (Mungu) may give it to us on the next." To this all the Makondé present assented, and showed me the consciousness of His existence was present in their minds. The Makondé get the gum in large quantities, and this attracts the coast Arabs, who remain a long time in the country purchasing it. Hernia humoralis abounds; it is ascribed to beer-drinking.

30th April, 1866.—Many ulcers burst forth on the camels; some seem old dhow bruises. They come back from pasture, bleeding in a way that no rubbing against a tree would account for. I am sorry to suspect foul play: the buffaloes and mules are badly used, but I cannot be always near to prevent it.

Bhang[8] is not smoked, but tobacco is: the people have no sheep or goats; only fowls, pigeons, and Muscovy ducks are seen. Honey is very cheap; a good large pot of about a gallon, with four fowls, was given for two yards of calico. Buffaloes again bitten by tsetse, and by another fly exactly like the house-fly, but having a straight hard proboscis instead of a soft one; other large flies make the blood run. The tsetse does not disturb the buffaloes, but these others and the smaller flies do. The tsetse seem to like the camel best; from these they are gorged with blood—they do not seem to care for the mules and donkeys.

Carved Door, Zanzibar.

FOOTNOTES:

3. Dhow is the name given to the coasting vessel of East Africa and the Indian Ocean.

4. The Commander of H.M.S. *Pioneer* in 1861.

5. Those who have read the accounts given by African travellers will remember that the bites inflicted by two or three of these small flies will visually lay the foundation of a sickness which destroys oxen, horses, and dogs in a few weeks.

6. Dr. Livingstone was anxious to try camels and Indian buffaloes in a tsetse country to see the effect upon them.

7. This refers to an attack made upon the boats of the *Pioneer* when the Doctor was exploring the River Rovuma in 1861.

8. A species of hemp.

* * * * *

CHAPTER II.

Effect of *Pioneer's* former visit. The poodle Chitané. Result of tsetse bites. Death of camels and buffaloes. Disaffection of followers. Disputed right of ferry. Mazitu raids. An old friend. Severe privations. The River Loendi. Sepoys mutiny. Dr. Roscher. Desolation. Tattooing. Ornamental teeth. Singular custom. Death of the Nassick boy, Richard. A sad reminiscence.

1st May, 1866.—We now came along through a country comparatively free of wood, and we could move on without perpetual cutting and clearing. It is beautiful to get a good glimpse out on the surrounding scenery, though it still seems nearly all covered with great masses of umbrageous foliage, mostly of a dark green colour, for nearly all of the individual trees possess dark glossy leaves like laurel. We passed a gigantic specimen of the Kumbé, or gum-copal tree. Kumba means to dig. Changkumbé, or things dug, is the name of the gum; the Arabs call it "sandarusé." Did the people give the name Kumbé to the tree after the value of the gum became known to them? The Malolé, from the fine grained wood of which all the bows are made, had shed its fruit on the ground; it looks inviting to the eye—an oblong peach-looking thing, with a number of seeds inside, but it is eaten by maggots only.

When we came to Ntandé's village, we found it enclosed in a strong stockade, from a fear of attack by Mabiha, who come across the river and steal their women when going to draw water: this is for the Ibo market. They offered to pull down their stockade and let us in if we would remain over-night, but we declined. Before reaching Ntandé we passed the ruins of two villages; the owners were the attacking party when we ascended the Rovuma in 1862. I have still the old sail, with four bullet-holes through it, made by the shots which they fired after we had given cloth and got assurances of friendship. The father and son of this village were the two men seen by the second boat preparing to shoot; the fire of her crew struck the father on the chin and the son on the head. It may have been for the best that the English are thus known as people who can hit hard when unjustly attacked, as we on this occasion most certainly were: never was a murderous assault more unjustly made or less provoked. They had left their villages and gone up over the highlands away from the river to their ambush whilst their women came to look at us.

2nd May, 1866.—Mountains again approach us, and we pass one which was noticed in our first ascent from its resemblance to a table mountain. It is 600 or 800 feet high, and called Liparu: the plateau now becomes mountainous, giving forth a perennial stream which comes down from its western base and forms a lagoon on the meadow-land that flanks the Rovuma. The trees which love these perpetual streams spread their roots all over the surface of the boggy banks, and make a firm surface, but at spots one may sink a yard deep. We had to fill up these deep ditches with branches and leaves, unload the animals, and lead them across. We spent the night on the banks of the Liparu,[9] and then proceeded on our way.

3rd May, 1866.—We rested in a Makoa village, the head of which was an old woman. The Makoa or Makoané are known by a half-moon figure tattooed on their foreheads or elsewhere. Our poodle dog Chitané chased the dogs of this village with unrelenting fury, his fierce looks inspired terror among the wretched pariah dogs of a yellow and white colour, and those looks were entirely owing to its being difficult to distinguish at which end his head or tail lay. He enjoyed the chase of the yelping curs immensely, but if one of them had turned he would have bolted the other way.

A motherly-looking woman came forward and offered me some meal; this was when we were in the act of departing: others had given food to the men and no return had been made. I told her to send it on by her husband, and I would purchase it, but it would have been better to have accepted it: some give merely out of kindly feeling and with no prospect of a return.

Many of the Makoa men have their faces thickly tattooed in double, raised lines of about half an inch in length. After the incisions are made charcoal is rubbed in and the flesh pressed out, so that all the cuts are raised above the level of the surface. It gives them rather a hideous look, and a good deal of that fierceness which our kings and chiefs of old put on whilst having their portraits taken.

4th May, 1866.—The stream, embowered in perpetual shade and overspread with the roots of water-loving, broad-leaved trees, we found to be called Nkonya. The spot of our encampment was an island formed by a branch of it parting and re-entering it again: the owner had used it for rice.

The buffaloes were bitten again by tsetse on 2nd, and also to-day, from the bites of other flies (which look much more formidable than tsetse), blood of arterial colour flows down; this symptom I never saw before, but when we slaughtered an ox which had been tsetse bitten, we observed that the blood had the arterial hue. The cow has inflammation of one eye, and a swelling on the right lumbar portion of the pelvis: the grey buffalo has been sick, but this I attribute to unmerciful loading; for his back is hurt: the camels do not seem to feel the fly, though they get weaker from the horrid running sores upon them and hard work. There are no symptoms of tsetse in mules or donkeys, but one mule has had his shoulder sprained, and he cannot stoop to eat or drink.

We saw the last of the flanking range on the north. The country in front is plain, with a few detached granitic peaks shot up. The Makoa in large numbers live at the end of the range in a place called Nyuchi. At Nyamba, a village where we spent the night of the 5th, was a doctoress and rain-maker, who presented a large basket of soroko, or, as they call it in India, "mung," and a fowl. She is tall and well made, with fine limbs and feet, and was profusely tattooed all over; even her hips and buttocks had their elaborate markings: no shame is felt in exposing these parts.

A good deal of salt is made by lixiviation of the soil and evaporating by fire. The head woman had a tame khanga tolé or tufted guinea-fowl, with bluish instead of white spots.

In passing along westwards after leaving the end of the range, we came first of all on sandstone hardened by fire; then masses of granite, as if in that had been contained the igneous agency of partial metamorphosis; it had also lifted up the sandstone, so as to cause a dip to the east. Then the syenite or granite seemed as if it had been melted, for it was all in striae, which striae, as they do elsewhere, run east and west. With the change in geological structure we get a different vegetation. Instead of the laurel-leaved trees of various kinds, we have African ebonies, acacias, and mimosae: the grass is shorter and more sparse, and we can move along without wood-cutting. We were now opposite a hill on the south called Simba, a lion, from its supposed resemblance to that animal. A large Mabiha population live there, and make raids occasionally over to this side for slaves.

6th May, 1866.—Tsetse again. The animals look drowsy. The cow's eye is dimmed; when punctured, the skin emits a stream of scarlet blood. The people hereabouts seem intelligent and respectful. At service a man began to talk, but when I said, "Ku soma Mlungu,"—"we wish to pray to God," he desisted. It would be interesting to know what the ideas of these men are, and to ascertain what they have gained in their communings with nature during the ages past. They do not give the idea of that boisterous wickedness and disregard of life which we read of in our own dark ages, but I have no one to translate, although I can understand much of what is said on common topics chiefly from knowing other dialects.

7th May, 1866.—A camel died during the night, and the grey buffalo is in convulsions this morning. The cruelty of these sepoys vitiates my experiment, and I quite expect many camels, one buffalo, and one mule to die yet; they sit down and smoke and eat, leaving the animals loaded in the sun. If I am not with them, it is a constant dawdling; they are evidently unwilling to exert themselves, they cannot carry their belts and bags, and their powers of eating and vomiting are astounding. The Makondé villages are remarkably clean, but no sooner do we pass a night in one than the fellows make it filthy. The climate does give a sharp appetite, but these sepoys indulge it till relieved by vomiting and purging. First of all they breakfast, then an hour afterwards they are sitting eating the pocketfuls of corn maize they have stolen and brought for the purpose, whilst I have to go ahead, otherwise we may be misled into a zigzag course to see Ali's friends; and if I remain behind to keep the sepoys on the move, it deprives me of all the pleasure of travelling. We have not averaged four miles a day in a straight line, yet the animals have often been kept in the sun for eight hours at a stretch. When we get up at 4 A.M. we cannot get under weigh before 8 o'clock. Sepoys are a mistake.

7th May, 1866.—We are now opposite a mountain called Nabungala, which resembles from the north-east an elephant lying down. Another camel, a very good one, died on the way: its shiverings and convulsions are not at all like what we observed in horses and oxen killed by tsetse, but such may lie the cause, however. The only symptom pointing to the tsetse is the arterial-looking blood, but we never saw it ooze from the skin after the bite of the gad-fly as we do now.

8th May, 1866.—We arrived at a village called Jpondé, or Lipondé, which lies opposite a granitic hill on the other-side of the river (where we spent a night on our boat trip), called Nakapuri; this is rather odd, for the words are not Makondé but Sichuana, and signify goat's horn, from the projections jutting out from the rest of the mass. I left the havildar, sepoys, and Nassick boys here in order to make a forced march forward, where no food is to be had, and send either to the south or westwards for supplies, so that after they have rested the animals and themselves five days they may come. One mule is very ill; one buffalo drowsy and exhausted; one camel a mere skeleton from bad sores; and another has an enormous hole at the point of the pelvis, which sticks out at the side. I suspect that this was made maliciously, for he came from the field bleeding profusely; no tree would have perforated a round hole in this way. I take all the goods and leave only the sepoys' luggage, which is enough for all the animals now.

9th May, 1866.—I went on with the Johanna men and twenty-four carriers, for it was a pleasure to get away from the sepoys and Nassick boys; the two combined to overload the animals. I told them repeatedly that they would kill them, but no sooner had I adjusted the burdens and turned my back than they put on all their things. It was however such continual vexation to contend with the sneaking spirit, that I gave up annoying myself by seeing matters, though I felt certain that the animals would all be killed. We did at least eight miles pleasantly well, and slept at Moedaa village. The rocks are still syenite. We passed a valley with the large thorny acacias of which canoes are often made, and a euphorbiaceous tree, with seed-vessels as large as mandarin oranges, with three seeds inside. We were now in a country which, in addition to the Mazitu invasion, was suffering from one of those inexplicable droughts to which limited and sometimes large portions of this country are subject. It had not been nearly so severe on the opposite or south side, and thither too the Mazitu had not penetrated. Rushes, which plagued us nearer the coast, are not observed now; the grass is all crisp and yellow; many of the plants are dead, and leaves are fallen off the trees as if winter had begun. The ground is covered with open forest, with here and there thick jungle on the banks of the streams. All the rivulets we have passed are mere mountain torrents filled with sand, in which the people dig for water.

We passed the spot where an Arab called Birkal was asked payment for leave to pass. After two and a half days' parley he fought, killed two Makondé, and mortally wounded a headman, which settled the matter; no fresh demand has been made. Ali's brother also resisted the same sort of demand, fought several times, or until three Makondé and two of his people were killed; they then made peace, and no other exactions have been made.

11th May, 1866.—We now found a difficulty in getting our carriers along, on account of exhaustion from want of food. In going up a sand stream called Nyédé, we saw that all moist spots had been planted with maize and beans, so the loss caused by the Mazitu, who swept the land like a cloud of locusts, will not be attended by much actual starvation. We met a runaway woman: she was seized by Ali, and it was plain that he expected a reward for his pains. He thought she was a slave, but a quarter of a mile off was the village she had left, and it being doubtful if she were a runaway at all, the would-be fugitive slave-capture turned out a failure.

12th May, 1866.—About 4' E.N.E. of Matawatawa, or Nyamatololé, our former turning point.

13th May, 1866.—We halted at a village at Matawatawa. A pleasant-looking lady, with her face profusely tattooed, came forward with a bunch of sweet reed, or *Sorghum saceliaratum*, and laid it at my feet, saying, "I met you here before," pointing to the spot on the river where we turned. I remember her coming then, and that I asked the boat to wait while she went to bring us a basket of food, and I think it was given to Chiko, and no return made. It is sheer kindliness that prompts them sometimes, though occasionally people do make presents with a view of getting a larger one in return: it is pleasant to find that it is not always so. She had a quiet, dignified manner, both in talking and walking, and I now gave her a small looking-glass, and she went and brought me her only fowl and a basket of cucumber-seeds, from which oil is made; from the amount of oily matter they contain thov are nutritious when roasted and eaten as nuts. She made an apology, saying they were hungry times at present. I gave her a cloth, and so parted with Kanañgoné, or, as her name may be spelled, Kanañoné. The carriers were very useless from hunger, and we could not buy anything for them; for the country is all dried up, and covered sparsely with mimosas and thorny acacias.

14th May, 1866.—I could not get the carriers on more than an hour and three-quarters: men tire very soon on empty stomachs. We had reached the village of Hassané, opposite to a conical hill named Chisulwé, which is on the south side of the river, and evidently of igneous origin. It is tree-covered, while the granite always shows lumps of naked rock. All about lie great patches of beautiful dolomite. It may have been formed by baking of the tufa, which in this country seems always to have been poured out with water after volcanic action. Hassané's daughter was just lifting a pot of French beans, boiled in their pods, off the fire when we entered the village, these he presented to me, and when I invited him to partake, he replied that he was at home and would get something, while I was a stranger on a journey. He, like all the other headmen, is a reputed doctor, and his wife, a stout old lady, a doctoress; he had never married any wife but this one, and he had four children, all of whom lived with their parents. We employed one of his sons to go to the south side and purchase food, sending at the same time some carriers to buy for themselves. The siroko and rice bought by Hassané's son we deposited with him for the party behind, when they should arrive. The amount of terror the Mazitu inspire cannot be realized by us. They shake their shields and the people fly like stricken deer. I observed that a child would not go a few yards for necessary purposes unless grandmother stood in sight. Matumora, as the Arabs call the chief at Ngomano, gave them a warm reception, and killed several of them: this probably induced them to retire.

15th and 16th May, 1866.—Miserably short marches from hunger, and I sympathise with the poor fellows. Those sent to buy food for themselves on the south bank were misled by a talkative fellow named Chikungu, and went off north, where we knew nothing could be had. His object was to get paid for three days, while they only loitered here. I suppose hunger has taken the spirit out of them; but I told them that a day in which no work was done did not count: they admitted this. We pay about two feet of calico per day, and a fathom or six feet for three days' carriage.

17th May, 1866.—With very empty stomachs they came on a few miles and proposed to cross to the south side; as this involved crossing the Luendi too, I at first objected, but in hopes that we might get food for them we consented, and were taken over in two very small canoes. I sent Ali and Musa meanwhile to the south to try and get some food. I got a little green sorghum for them and paid them off. These are the little troubles of travelling, and scarce worth mentioning. A granitic peak now appears about 15' off, to the W.S.W. It is called Chihoka.

18th May, 1866.—At our crossing place metamorphic rocks of a chocolate colour stood on edge; and in the country round we have patches of dolomite, sometimes as white as marble. The country is all dry: grass and leaves crisp and yellow. Though so arid now, yet the great abundance of the dried stalks of a water-loving plant, a sort of herbaceous acacia, with green pea-shaped flowers, proves that at other times it is damp enough. The marks of people's feet floundering in slush, but now baked, show that the country can be sloppy.

The headman of the village where we spent the night of 17th is a martyr to rheumatism. He asked for medicine, and when I gave some he asked me to give it to him out of my own hand. He presented me with a basket of siroko and of green sorghum as a fee, of which I was very glad, for my own party were suffering, and I had to share out the little portion of flour I had reserved to myself.

19th May, 1866.—Coming on with what carriers we could find at the crossing place, we reached the confluence without seeing it; and Matumora being about two miles up the Loendi, we sent over to him for aid. He came over this morning early,—a tall, well-made man, with a somewhat severe expression of countenance, from a number of wrinkles on his forehead. He took us over the Loendi, which is decidedly the parent stream of the Rovuma, though that as it comes from the west still retains the name Loendi from the south-west here, and is from 150 to 200 yards wide, while the Rovuma above Matawatawa is from 200 to 250, full of islands, rocks, and sandbanks. The Loendi has the same character. We can see the confluence from where we cross about 2' to the north. Both rivers are rapid, shoal, and sandy; small canoes are used on them, and the people pride themselves on their skilful management: in this the women seem in no way inferior to the men.

In looking up the Loendi we see a large granitic peak called Nkanjé, some 20 miles off, and beyond it the dim outline of distant highlands, in which seams of coal are exposed. Pieces of the mineral are found in Loendi's sands.

Matumora has a good character in the country, and many flee to him from oppression. He was very polite; sitting on the right bank till all the goods were carried over, then coming in the same canoe wifn me himself, he opened a fish basket in a weir and gave me the contents, and subsequently a little green sorghum. He literally has lost all his corn, for he was obliged to flee with his people to Marumba, a rocky island in Rovuma, about six miles above Matawatawa. He says that both Loendi and Rovuma come out of Lake Nyassa; a boat could not ascend, however, because many waterfalls are in their course: it is strange if all this is a myth. Matumora asked if the people through whose country I had come would preserve the peace I wished. He says he has been assailed on all sides by slave-hunters: he alone has never hunted for captives: if the people in front should attack me he would come and fight them: finally he had never seen a European before (Dr. Roscher travelled as an Arab), nor could I learn where Likumbu at Ngomano lives; it was with him that Roscher is said to have left his goods.

The Mazitu had women, children, oxen and goats with them. The whole tribe lives on plundering the other natives by means of the terror their shields inspire; had they gone further down the Rovuma, no ox would have survived the tsetse.

20th May, 1866.—I paid Ali to his entire satisfaction, and entrusted him with a despatch, "No. 2 Geographical," and then sent off four men south to buy food. Here we are among Matambwé. Two of Matumora's men act as guides. We are about 2' south and by west of the confluence Ngomano. Lat. 11° 26' 23" S.; long. 37° 40' 52" E.

Abraham, one of the Nassick boys, came up and said he had been sent by the sepoys, who declared they would come no further. It was with the utmost difficulty they had come so far, or that the havildar had forced them on, they would not obey him—would not get up in the mornings to march; lay in the paths, and gave their pouches and muskets to the natives to carry: they make themselves utterly useless. The black buffalo is dead; one camel ditto, and one mule left behind ill. Were I not aware of the existence of the tsetse, I should say they died from sheer bad treatment and hard work.

I sent a note to be read to the sepoys stating that I had seen their disobedience, unwillingness, and skulking, and as soon as I received the havildar's formal evidence, I would send them back. I regretted parting with the havildar only.

A leopard came a little after dark while the moon was shining, and took away a little dog from among us; it is said to have taken off a person a few days ago.

22nd May, 1866.—The men returned with but little food in return for much cloth. Matumora is very friendly, but he has nothing to give save a little green sorghum, and that he brings daily.

A south wind blows strongly every afternoon. The rains ceased about the middle of May, and the temperature is lowered. A few heavy night showers closed the rainy season.

23rd—24th May, 1866.—I took some Lunar observations.

25th May, 1866.—Matumora is not Ndondé. A chief to the south-west of this owns that name and belongs to the Matumbwé tribe.

26th May, 1866.—I sent Musa westwards to buy food, and he returned on the evening of 27th without success; he found an Arab slave-dealer waiting in the path, who had bought up all the provisions. About 11 P.M. we saw two men pass our door with two women in a chain; one man carried fire in front, the one behind, a musket. Matumora admits that his people sell each other.

27th May, 1866.—The havildar and Abraham came up. Havildar says that all I said in my note was true, and when it was read to the sepoys they bewailed their folly, he adds that if they were all sent away disgraced, no one would be to blame but themselves. He brought them to Hassané's, but they were useless, though they begged to be kept on: I may give them another trial, but at present they are a sad incumbrance. South-west of this the Manganja begin; but if one went by them, there is a space beyond in the south-west without people.

The country due west of this is described by all to be so mountainous and beset by Mazitu, that there is no possibility of passing that way. I must therefore make my way to the middle of the Lake, cross over, and then take up my line of 1863.

2nd June, 1866.—The men sent to the Matambwé south-east of this returned with a good supply of grain. The sepoys won't come; they say they cannot,—a mere excuse, v because they tried to prevail on the Nassick boys to go slowly like them, and wear my patience out. They killed one camel with the butt ends of their muskets, beating it till it died. I thought of going down disarming them all, and taking five or six of the willing ones, but it is more trouble than profit, so I propose to start westwards on Monday the 4th, or Tuesday the 5th. My sepoys offered Ali eight rupees to take them to the coast, thus it has been a regularly organized conspiracy.

From the appearance of the cow-buffalo, I fear the tsetse is its chief enemy, but there is a place like a bayonet wound on its shoulder, and many of the wounds or bruises on the camels were so probed that I suspect the sepoys.

Many things African are possessed of as great vitality in their line as the African people. The white ant was imported accidentally into St. Helena from the coast of Guinea, and has committed such ravages in the town of St. James, that numerous people have been ruined, and the governor calls out for aid against them. In other so-called new countries a wave of English weeds follows the tide of English emigration, and so with insects; the European house-fly chases away the blue-bottle fly in New Zealand. Settlers have carried the house-fly in bottles and boxes for their new locations, but what European insect will follow us and extirpate the tsetse? The Arabs have given the Makondé bugs, but we have the house-fly wherever we go, the blue-bottle and another like the house-fly, but with a sharp proboscis; and several enormous gad-flies. Here there is so much room for everything. In New Zealand the Norwegian rat is driven off by even the European mouse; not to mention the Hanoverian rat of Waterton, which is lord of the land. The Maori say that "as the white man's rat has driven away the native rat, so the European fly drives away our own; and as the clover kills our fern, so will the Maori disappear before the white man himself." The hog placed ashore by Captain Cook has now overrun one side of the island, and is such a nuisance that a large farmer of 100,000 acres has given sixpence per head for the destruction of some 20,000, and without any sensible diminution; this would be no benefit here, for the wild hogs abound and do much damage, besides affording food for the tsetse: the brutes follow the ewes with young, and devour the poor lambs as soon as they make their appearance.

3rd June, 1866.—The cow-buffalo fell down foaming at the mouth, and expired. The meat looks fat and nice, and is relished by the people, a little glariness seemed to be present on the foreleg, and I sometimes think that, notwithstanding the dissimilarity of the symptoms observed in the camels and buffaloes now, and those we saw in oxen and horses, the evil may be the tsetse, after all, but they have been badly used, without a doubt. The calf has a cut half an inch deep, the camels have had large ulcers, and at last a peculiar smell, which portends death. I feel perplexed, and not at all certain as to the real causes of death.

I asked Matumora if the Matambwé believed in God, he replied, that he did not know Him, and I was not to ask the people among whom I was going if they prayed to Him, because they would imagine that I wished them to be killed. I told him that we loved to speak about Him, &c. He said, when they prayed they offered a little meal and then prayed, but did not know much about Him.

They have all great reverence for the Deity, and the deliberate way in which they say "We don't know Him" is to prevent speaking irreverently, as that may injure the country. The name is "Mulungu": Makochera afterwards said, that "He was not good, because He killed so many people."

4th June, 1866.—Left Ngomano. I was obliged to tell the Nassick boys that they must either work or return, it was absurd to have them eating up our goods, and not even carrying their own things, and I would submit to it no more: five of them carry bales, and two the luggage of the rest. Abraham and Richard are behind. I gave them bales to carry, and promised them ten rupees per month, to begin on this date. Abraham has worked hard all along, and his pay may be due from 7th April, the day we started from Kindany.

5th June, 1866.—We slept at a village called Lamba, on the banks of the Rovuma, near a brawling torrent of 150 yards, or 200 perhaps, with many islands and rocks in it. The country is covered with open forest, with patches of cultivation everywhere, but all dried up at present and withered, partly from drought and partly from the cold of winter. We passed a village with good ripe sorghum cut down, and the heads or ears all laid neatly in a row, this is to get it dried in the sun, and not shaken out by the wind, by waving to and fro; besides it is also more easily watched from being plundered by birds. The sorghum occasionally does not yield seed, and is then the *Sorghum saccharatum,* for the stalk contains abundance of sugar, and is much relished by the natives. Now that so much has failed to yield seed, being indeed just in flower, the stalks are chewed as if sugar-cane, and the people are fat thereon; but the hungry time is in store when these stalles are all done. They make the best provision in their power against famine by planting beans and maize in moist spots. The common native pumpkin forms a bastard sort in the same way, but that is considered very inferior.

6th June, 1866.—Great hills of granite are occasionally in sight towards the north, but the trees, though scraggy, close in the view. We left a village, called Mekosi, and goon came to a slaving party by a sand stream. They said that they had bought two slaves, but they had run away from them, and asked us to remain with them; more civil than inviting. We came on to Makochera, the principal headman in this quarter, and found him a merry laughing mortal, without any good looks to recommend his genial smile,—low forehead, covered with deep wrinkles; flat nose, somewhat of the Assyrian shape; a big mouth and lean body. He complained of the Machinga (a Waiyau tribe north of him and the Rovuma) stealing his people. Lat. of village, 11° 22' 49" S. The river being about 2' north, still shows that it makes a trend to the north after we pass Ngomano. Makochera has been an elephant hunter. Few acknowledge as a reason for slaving that sowing and spinning cotton for clothing is painful. I waited some days for the Nassick boys, who are behind, though we could not buy any food except at enormous prices and long distances off.

7th June, 1866.—The havildar and two sepoys came up with Abraham, but Richard, a Nassick boy, is still behind from weakness. I sent three off to help him with the only cordials we could muster. The sepoys sometimes profess inability to come on, but it is unwillingness to encounter hardship: I must move on whether they come or not, for we cannot obtain food here. I sent the sepoys some cloth, and on the 8th proposed to start, but every particle of food had been devoured the night before, so we despatched two parties to scour the country round, and give any price rather than want.

I could not prevail on Makochera to give me a specimen of poetry; he was afraid, neither he nor his forefathers had ever seen an Englishman. He thought that God was not good because He killed so many people. Dr. Roscher must have travelled as an Arab if he came this way, for he was not known.[10]

9th June, 1866.—We now left and marched through the same sort of forest, gradually ascending in altitude as we went west, then we came to huge masses of granite, or syenite, with flakes peeling off. They are covered with a plant with grassy-looking leaves and rough stalk which strips into portions similar to what are put round candles as ornaments. It makes these hills look light grey, with patches of black rock at the more perpendicular parts; the same at about ten miles off look dark blue. The ground is often hard and stony, but all covered over with grass and plants: looking down at it, the grass is in tufts, and like that on the Kalahari desert. Trees show uplands. One tree of which bark cloth is made, pterocarpus, is abundant. Timber-trees appear here and there, but for the most part the growth is stunted, and few are higher than thirty feet. We spent the night by a hill of the usual rounded form, called Njeñgo. The Rovuma comes close by, but leaves us again to wind among similar great masses. Lat. 11° 20' 05" S.

10th June, 1866.—A very heavy march through the same kind of country, no human habitation appearing; we passed a dead body—recently, it was said, starved to death. The large tract between Makochera's and our next station at Ngozo hill is without any perennial stream; water is found often by digging in the sand streams which we several times crossed; sometimes it was a trickling rill, but I suspect that at other seasons all is dry, and people are made dependent on the Rovuma alone. The first evidence of our being near the pleasant haunts of man was a nice little woman drawing water at a well. I had become separated from the rest: on giving me water she knelt down, and, as country manners require, held it up to me with *both* hands. I had been misled by one of the carriers, who got confused, though the rounded mass of Ngozo was plainly visible from the heights we crossed east of it.

An Arab party bolted on hearing of our approach: they don't trust the English, and this conduct increases our importance among the natives. Lat. 11° 18' 10" S.

11th June, 1866.—Our carriers refuse to go further, because they say that they fear being captured here on their return.

12th June, 1866.—I paid off the carriers, and wait for a set from this. A respectable man, called Makoloya, or Impandé, visited me, and wished to ask some questions as to where I was going, and how long I should be away. He had heard from a man who came from Ibo, or Wibo, about the Bible, a large book which was consulted.

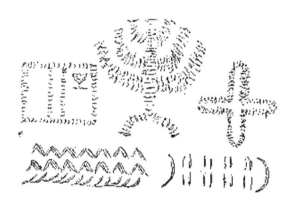

Tattoo of Matambwé.

13th June, 1866.—Makoloya brought his wife and a little corn, and says that his father told him that there is a God, but nothing more. The marks on their foreheads and bodies are meant only to give beauty in the dance, they seem a sort of heraldic ornament, for they can at once tell by his tattoo to what tribe or portion of tribe a man belongs. The tattoo or tembo of the Matambwé and Upper

Makondé very much resembles the drawings of the old Egyptians; wavy lines, such as the ancients made to signify water, trees and gardens enclosed in squares, seem to have been meant of old for the inhabitants who lived on the Rovuma, and cultivated also, the son takes the tattoo of his father, and thus it has been perpetuated, though the meaning now appears lost. The Makoa have the half or nearly full moon, but it is, they say, all for ornament. Some blue stuff is rubbed into the cuts (I am told it is charcoal), and the ornament shows brightly in persons of light complexion, who by the bye are common. The Makondé and Matambwé file their front teeth to points; the Machinga, a Waiyan tribe, leave two points on the sides of the front teeth, and knock out one of the middle incisors above and below.

14th June, 1866.—I am now as much dependent on carriers as if I had never bought a beast of burden—but this is poor stuff to fill a journal with. We started off to Metaba to see if the chief there would lend some men. The headman, Kitwanga, went a long way to convoy us; then turned, saying he was going to get men for Musa next day. We passed near the base of the rounded masses Ngozo and Mekanga, and think, from a near inspection, that they are over 2000 feet above the plain, possibly 3000 feet, and nearly bare, with only the peculiar grassy plant on some parts which are not too perpendicular. The people are said to have stores of grain on them, and on one the chief said there is water; he knows of no stone buildings of the olden time in the country. We passed many masses of ferruginous conglomerate, and I noticed that most of the gneiss dips westwards. The striae seem as if the rock had been partially molten: at times the strike is north and south, at others east and west; when we come to what may have been its surface, it is as if the striae had been stirred with a rod while soft.

We slept at a point of the Rovuma, above a cataract where a reach of comparatively still water, from 150 to 200 yards wide, allows a school of hippopotami to live: when the river becomes fordable in many places, as it is said to do in August and September, they must find it difficult to exist.

15th June, 1866.—Another three hours' march brought us from the sleeping-place on the Rovuma to Metaba, the chief of which, Kinazombé, is an elderly man, with a cunning and severe cast of countenance, and a nose Assyrian in type; he has built a large reception house, in which a number of half-caste Arabs have taken up their abode. A great many of the people have guns, and it is astonishing to see the number of slave-taming sticks abandoned along the road as the poor wretches gave in, and professed to have lost all hope of escape. Many huts have been built by the Arabs to screen themselves from the rain as they travelled. At Kinazombé's the second crop of maize is ready, so the hunger will not be very much felt.

16th June, 1866.—We heard very sombre accounts of the country in front:—four or five days to Mtarika, and then ten days through jungle to Mataka's town: little food at Mtarika's, but plenty with Mataka, who is near the Lake. The Rovuma trends southerly after we leave Ngozo, and Masusa on that river is pointed out as south-west from Metaba, so at Ngozo the river may be said to have its furthest northing. Masusa is reported to be five days, or at least fifty miles, from Metaba. The route now becomes south-west.

The cattle of Africa are like the Indian buffalo, only partially tamed; they never give their milk without the presence of the calf or its stuffed skin, the "fulchan." The women adjacent to Mozambique partake a little of the wild animal's nature, for, like most members of the inferior races of animals, they refuse all intercourse with their husbands when enceinte and they continue this for about three years afterwards, or until the child is weaned, which usually happens about the third year. I was told, on most respectable authority, that many fine young native men marry one wife and live happily with her till this period; nothing will then induce her to continue to cohabit with him, and, as the separation is to continue for three years, the man is almost compelled to take up with another wife: this was mentioned to me as one of the great evils of society. The same absurdity prevails on the West Coast, and there it is said that the men acquiesce from ideas of purity.

It is curious that trade-rum should form so important an article of import on the West Coast while it is almost unknown on the East Coast, for the same people began the commerce in both instances. If we look north of Cape Delgado, we might imagine that the religious convictions of the Arabs had something to do with the matter, but the Portuguese south of Cape Delgado have no scruples in the matter, and would sell their grandfathers as well as the rum if they could make money by the transaction, they have even erected distilleries to furnish a vile spirit from the fruit of the cashew and other fruits and grain, but the trade does not succeed. They give their slaves also rewards of spirit, or "maata bicho" ("kill the creature," or "craving within"), and you may meet a man who, having had much intercourse with Portuguese, may beg spirits, but the trade does not pay. The natives will drink it if furnished gratis. The indispensable "dash" of rum on the West Coast in every political transaction with independent chiefs is, however, quite unknown. The Moslems would certainly not abstain from trading in spirits were the trade profitable. They often asked for brandy from me in a sly way—as medicine; and when reminded that their religion forbade it, would say, "Oh, but we can drink it in secret."

It is something in the nature of the people quite inexplicable, that throughout the Makondé country hernia humoralis prevails to a frightful extent; it is believed by the natives to be the result of beer drinking, so they cannot be considered as abstemious.

18th June, 1866.—Finding that Musa did not come up with the goods I left in his charge, and fearing that all was not right, we set off with all our hands who could carry, after service yesterday morning, and in six hours' hard tramp arrived here just in time, for a tribe of Wanindi, or Manindi, who are either Ajawas (Waiyau),[11] or pretended Mazitu, had tried to cross the Rovuma from the north bank. They came as plunderers, and Musa having received no assistance was now ready to defend the goods. A shot or two from the people of Kitwanga made the Wanindi desert after they had entered the water.

Six sepoys and Simon had come up this length; Reuben and Mabruki reported Richard to be dead. This poor boy was left with the others at Lipondé, and I never saw him again. I observed him associating too much with the sepoys; and often felt inclined to reprove him, as their conversation is usually very bad, but I could not of my own knowledge say so. He came on with the others as far as Hassané or Pachassané: there he was too weak to come further, and as the sepoys were notoriously skulkers, I feared that poor Richard was led away by them, for I knew that they had made many attempts to draw away the other Nassick boys from their duty. When, however, Abraham came up and reported Richard left behind by the sepoys, I became alarmed, and sent off three boys with cordials to help him on: two days after Abraham left he seems to have died, and I feel very sorry that I was not there to do what I could. I am told now that he never consented to the sepoy temptation: he said to Abraham that he wished he were dead, he was so much troubled. The people where he died were not v$ry civil to Simon.

The sepoys had now made themselves such an utter nuisance that I felt that I must take the upper hand with them, so I called them up this morning, and asked if they knew the punishment they had incurred by disobeying orders, and attempting to tamper with the Nassick boys to turn them back. I told them they not only remained in the way when ordered to march, but offered eight rupees to Ali to lead them to the coast, and that the excuse of sickness was nought, for they had eaten heartily three meals a day while pretending illness. They had no excuse to offer, so I disrated the naik or corporal, and sentenced the others to carry loads; if they behave well, then they will get fatigue pay for doing fatigue duty, if ill, nothing but their pay. Their limbs are becoming contracted from sheer idleness; while all the other men are well and getting stronger they alone are disreputably slovenly and useless-looking. Their filthy habits are to be reformed, and if found at their habit of sitting down and sleeping for hours on the march, or without their muskets and pouches, they are to be flogged. I sent two of them back to bring up two comrades, left behind yesterday. All who have done work are comparatively strong.

[We may venture a word in passing on the subject of native recruits, enlisted for service in Africa, and who return thither after a long absence. All the Nassick boys were native-born Africans, and yet we see one of them succumb immediately. The truth is that natives; under these circumstances, are just as liable to the effects of malaria on landing as Europeans, although it is not often that fever assumes a dangerous form in such cases. The natives of the interior have the greatest dread of the illnesses which they say are sure to be in store for them if they visit the coast.]

19th June, 1866.—I gave the sepoys light loads in order to inure them to exercise and strengthen them, and they carried willingly so long as the fright was on them, but when the fear of immediate punishment wore off they began their skulking again. One, Perim, reduced his load of about 20 lbs. of tea by throwing away the lead in which it was rolled, and afterwards about 15 lbs. of the tea, thereby diminishing our stock to 5 lbs.

[Dr. Livingstone's short stay in England in 1864-5 was mainly taken up with compiling an account of his travels on the Zambesi and Shiré: during this time his mother expired in Scotland at a good old age. When he went back to Africa he took with him, as part of his very scanty travelling equipment, a number of letters which he received from friends at different times in England, and he very often quoted them when he had an opportunity of sending letters home. We come to an entry at this time which shows that in these reminiscences he had not thus preserved an unmixed pleasure. He says:—]

I lighted on a telegram to-day:—"Your mother died at noon on the 18th June."

This was in 1865: it affected me not a little.

FOOTNOTES:

9. Further on we found it called Nkonya.

10. It will be remembered that this German traveller was murdered near Lake Nyassa. The native chiefs denounced his assassins, and sent them to Zanzibar, where they were executed.—ED.

11. Further westward amongst the Manganja or Nyassa people the Waiyan tribe is called "Ajawa," and we find Livingstone always speaking of them as Ajawas in his previous explorations on the River Rovuma. (See 'The Zambesi and its Tributaries.')—ED.

* * * * *

Slavers revenging their Losses.

CHAPTER III.

Horrors of the slave-trader's track. System of cultivation. Pottery. Special exorcising. Death of the last mule. Rescue of Chirikaloma's wife. Brutalities of the slave-drivers. Mtarika's. Desperate march to Mtaka's. Meets Arab caravans. Dismay of slavers. Dismissal of sepoys. Mataka. The Waiyan metropolis. Great hospitality and good feeling. Mataka restores stolen cattle. Life with the chief. Beauty of country and healthiness of climate. The Waiyan people and their peculiarities. Regrets at the abandonment of Bishop Mackenzie's plans.

19th June, 1866.—We passed a woman tied by the neck to a tree and dead, the people of the country explained that she had been unable to keep up with the other slaves in a gang, and her master had determined that she should not become the property of anyone else if she recovered after resting for a time. I may mention here that we saw others tied up in a similar manner, and one lying in the path shot or stabbed[12], for she was in a pool of blood. The explanation we got invariably was that the Arab who owned these victims was enraged at losing his money by the slaves becoming unable to march, and vented his spleen by murdering them; but I have nothing more than common report in support of attributing this enormity to the Arabs.

20th June, 1866.—Having returned to Metaba, we were told by Kinazombé, the chief, that no one had grain to sell but himself. He had plenty of powder and common cloth from the Arabs, and our only chance with him was parting with our finer cloths and other things that took his fancy. He magnified the scarcity in front in order to induce us to buy all we could from him, but he gave me an ample meal of porridge and guinea-fowl before starting.

21st June, 1866.—We had difficulties about carriers, but on reaching an island in the Rovuma, called Chimiki, we found the people were Makoa and more civil and willing to work than the Waiyau: we sent men back to bring up the havildar to a very civil headman called Chirikaloma.

22nd June, 1866.—A poor little boy with prolapsus ani was carried yesterday by his mother many a weary mile, lying over her right shoulder—the only position he could find ease in,—an infant at the breast occupied the left arm, and on her head were carried two baskets. The mother's love was seen in binding up the part when we halted, whilst the coarseness of low civilization was evinced in the laugh with which some black brutes looked at the sufferer.

23rd June, 1866.—The country is covered with forest, much more open than further east. We are now some 800 feet above the sea. The people all cultivate maize near the Rovuma, and on islands where moisture helps them, nearly all possess guns, and plenty of powder and fine beads,—red ones strung on the hair, and fine blue ones in rolls on the neck, fitted tightly like soldiers' stocks. The lip-ring is universal; teeth filed to points.

24th June, 1866.—Immense quantities of wood are cut down, collected in heaps, and burned to manure the land, but this does not prevent the country having an appearance of forest. Divine service at 8.30 A.M.; great numbers looking on. They have a clear idea of the Supreme Being, but do not pray to Him.. Cold south winds prevail; temp. 55°. One of the mules is very ill—it was left with the havildar when we went back to Ngozo, and probably remained uncovered at night, for as soon as we saw it, illness was plainly visible. Whenever an animal has been in their power the sepoys have abused it. It is difficult to feel charitably to fellows whose scheme seems to have been to detach the Nassick boys from me first, then, when the animals were all killed, the Johanna men, afterwards they could rule me as they liked, or go back and leave me to perish; but I shall try to feel as charitably as I can in spite of it all, for the mind has a strong tendency to brood over the ills of travel. I told the havildar when I came up to him at Metaba what I had done, and that I was very much displeased with the sepoys for compassing my failure, if not death; an unkind word had never passed my lips to them: to this he could bear testimony. He thought that they would only be a plague and trouble to me, but he "would go on and die with me."

Stone boiling is unknown in these countries, but ovens are made in anthills. Holes are dug in the ground for baking the heads of large game, as the zebra, feet of elephants, humps of rhinoceros, and the production of fire by drilling between the palms of the hands is universal. It is quite common to see the sticks so used attached to the clothing or bundles in travelling; they wet the blunt end of the upright stick with the tongue, and dip it in the sand to make some particles of silica adhere before inserting it in the horizontal piece. The wood of a certain wild fig-tree is esteemed as yielding fire readily.

In wet weather they prefer to carry fire in the dried balls of elephants' dung which are met with—the male's being about eight inches in diameter and about a foot long: they also employ the stalk of a certain plant which grows on rocky places for the same purpose.

We bought a senzé, or *Aulacaudatus Swindernianus*, which had been dried over a slow fire. This custom of drying fish, flesh, and fruits, on stages over slow fires, is practised very generally: the use of salt for preservation is unknown. Besides stages for drying, the Makondé use them about six feet high for sleeping on instead of the damp ground: a fire beneath helps to keep off the mosquitoes, and they are used by day as convenient resting-places and for observation.

Pottery seems to have been known to the Africans from the remotest times, for fragments are found everywhere, even among the oldest fossil bones in the country. Their pots for cooking, holding water and beer, are made by the women, and the form is preserved by the eye alone, for no sort of machine is ever used. A foundation or bottom is first laid, and a piece of bone or bamboo used to scrape the clay or to smooth over the pieces which are added to increase the roundness; the vessel is then left a night: the next morning a piece is added to the rim—as the air is dry several rounds may be added—and all is then carefully smoothed off; afterwards it is thoroughly sun-dried. A light fire of dried cow-dung, or corn-stalks, or straw, and grass with twigs, is made in a hole in the ground for the final baking. Ornaments are made on these pots of black lead, or before being hardened by the sun they are ornamented for a couple or three inches near the rim, all the tracery being in imitation of plaited basket work.

Chirikaloma says that the surname of the Makoa, to whom he belongs, is Mirazi—others have the surname Melola or Malola—Chimposola. All had the half-moon mark when in the south-east, but now they leave it off a good deal and adopt the Waiyau marks, because of living in their country. They show no indications of being named after beasts and birds. Mirazi was an ancestor; they eat all clean animals, but refuse the hyaena, leopard, or any beast that devours dead men.[13]

25th June, 1866.—On leaving Chirikaloma we came on to Namalo, whose village that morning had been deserted, the people moving off in a body towards the Matambwé country, where food is more abundant. A poor little girl was left in one of the huts from being too weak to walk, probably an orphan. The Arab slave-traders flee from the path as soon as they hear of our approach. The Rovuma is from 56 to 80 yards wide here. No food to be had for either love or money.

Near many of the villages we observe a wand bent and both ends inserted into the ground: a lot of medicine, usually the bark of trees, is buried beneath it. When sickness is in a village, the men proceed to the spot, wash themselves with the medicine and water, creep through beneath the bough, then bury the medicine and the evil influence together. This is also used to keep off evil spirits, wild beasts, and enemies.

Chirikaloma told us of a child in his tribe which was deformed from his birth. He had an abortive toe where his knee should have been; some said to his mother, "Kill him;" but she replied, "How can I kill my son?" He grew up and had many fine sons and daughters, but none deformed like himself: this was told in connection with an answer to my question about the treatment of Albinoes: he said they did not kill them, but they never grew to manhood. On inquiring if he had ever heard of cannibals, or people with tails, he replied, "Yes, but we have always understood that these and other monstrosities are met with only among you sea-going people." The other monstrosities he referred to were those who are said to have eyes behind the head as well as in front: I have heard of them before, but then I was near Angola, in the west.

The rains are expected here when the Pleiades appear in the east soon after sunset; they go by the same name here as further south—Lemila or the "hoeings."

In the route along the Rovuma, we pass among people who are so well supplied with white calico by the slave-trade from Kilwa, that it is quite a drug in the market: we cannot get food for it. If we held on westwards we should cross several rivers flowing into the Rovuma from the southward, as the Zandulo, the Sanjenzé, the Lochiringo, and then, in going round the north end of Nyassa, we should pass among the Nindi, who now inhabit the parts vacated by the Mazitu, and imitate them in having shields and in marauding. An Arab party went into their country, and got out again only by paying a whole bale of calico; it would not be wise in me to venture there at present, but if we return this way we may; meanwhile we shall push on to Mataka, who is only a few days off from the middle of the Lake, and has abundance of provisions.

26th June, 1866.—My last mule died. In coming along in the morning we were loudly accosted by a well-dressed woman who had just had a very heavy slave-taming stick put on her neck; she called in such an authoritative tone to us to witness the flagrant injustice of which she was the victim that all the men stood still and went to hear the case. She was a near relative of Chirikaloma, and was going up the river to her husband, when the old man (at whose house she was now a prisoner) caught her, took her servant away from her, and kept her in the degraded state we saw. The withes with which she was bound were green and sappy. The old man said in justification that she was running away from Chirikaloma, and he would be offended with him if he did not secure her.

I asked the officious old gentleman in a friendly tone what he expected to receive from Chirikaloma, and he said, "Nothing." Several slaver-looking fellows came about, and I felt sure that the woman had been seized in order to sell her to them, so I gave the captor a cloth to pay to Chirikaloma if he were offended, and told him to say that I, feeling ashamed to see one of his relatives in a slave-stick, had released her, and would, take her on to her husband.

She is evidently a lady among them, having many fine beads and some strung on elephant's hair: she has a good deal of spirit too, for on being liberated she went into the old man's house and took her basket and calabash. A virago of a wife shut the door and tried to prevent her, as well as to cut off the beads from her person, but she resisted like a good one, and my men thrust the door open and let her out, but minus her slave. The other wife— for old officious had two—joined her sister in a furious tirade of abuse, the elder holding her sides in regular fishwife fashion till I burst into a laugh, in which the younger wife joined. I explained to the different headmen in front of this village what I had done, and sent messages to Chirikaloma explanatory of my friendly deed to his relative, so that no misconstruction should be put on my act.

Slaves abandonned.

We passed a slave woman shot or stabbed through the body and lying on the path: a group of mon stood about a hundred yards off on one side, and another of women on the other side, looking on; they said an Arab who passed early that morning had done it in anger at losing the price he had given for her, because she was unable to walk any longer.

27th June, 1866.—To-day we came upon a man dead from starvation, as he was very thin. One of our men wandered and found a number of slaves with slave-sticks on, abandoned by their master from want of food; they were too weak to be able to speak or say where they had come from; some were quite young.

We crossed the Tulosi, a stream coming from south, about twenty yards wide.

At Chenjewala's the people are usually much startled when I explain that the numbers of slaves we see dead on the road have been killed partly by those who sold them, for I tell them that if they sell their fellows, they are like the man who holds the victim while the Arab performs the murder.

Chenjewala blamed Machemba, a chief above him on the Rovuma, for encouraging the slave-trade; I told him I had travelled so much among them that I knew all the excuses they could make, each headman blamed some one else.

"It would be better if you kept your people and cultivated more largely," said I, "Oh, Machemba sends his men and robs our gardens after we have cultivated," was the reply. One man said that the Arabs who come and tempt them with fine clothes are the cause of their selling: this was childish, so I told them they would very soon have none to sell: their country was becoming jungle, and all their people who did not die in the road would be making gardens for Arabs at Kilwa and elsewhere.

28th June, 1866.—When we got about an hour from Chenjewala's we came to a party in the act of marauding; the owners of the gardens made off for the other side of the river, and waved to us to go against the people of Machemba, but we stood on a knoll with all our goods on the ground, and waited to see how matters would turn out. Two of the marauders came to us and said they had captured five people. I suppose they took us for Arabs, as they addressed Musa. They then took some green maize, and so did some of my people, believing that as all was going, they who were really starving might as well have a share.

I went on a little way with the two marauders, and by the footprints thought the whole party might amount to four or five with guns; the gardens and huts were all deserted. A poor woman was sitting, cooking green maize, and one of the men ordered her to follow him. I said to him, "Let her alone, she is dying." "Yes," said he, "of hunger," and went'on without her.

We passed village after village, and gardens all deserted! We were now between two contending parties. We slept at one garden; and as we were told by Chenjewala's people to take what we liked, and my men had no food, we gleaned what congo beans, bean leaves, and sorghum stalks we could,—poor fare enough, but all we could get.

29th June, 1866.—We came onto Machemba's brother, Chimseia, who gave us food at once. The country is now covered with deeper soil, and many large acacia-trees grow in the rich loam: the holms too are large, and many islands afford convenient maize grounds. One of the Nassiek lads came up and reported his bundle, containing 240 yards of calico, had been stolen; he went aside, leaving it on the path (probably fell asleep), and it was gone when he came back. I cannot impress either on them or the sepoys that it is wrong to sleep on the march.

Akosakoné, whom we had liberated, now arrived at the residence of her husband, who was another brother of Machemba. She behaved like a lady all through, sleeping at a fire apart from the men. The ladies of the different villages we passed condoled with her, and she related to them the indignity that had been done to her. Besides this she did us many services: she bought food for us, because, having a good address, we saw that she could get double what any of our men could purchase for the same cloth; she spoke up for us when any injustice was attempted, and, when we were in want of carriers, volunteered to carry a bag of beads on her head. On arriving at Machemba's brother, Chimseia, she introduced me to him, and got him to be liberal to us in food on account of the service we had rendered to her. She took leave of us all with many expressions of thankfulness, and we were glad that we had not mistaken her position or lavished kindness on the undeserving.

One Johanna man was caught stealing maize, then another, after I had paid for the first. I sent a request to the chief not to make much of a grievance about it, as I was very much ashamed at my men stealing; he replied that he had liked me from the first, and I was not to fear, as whatever service he could do he would most willingly in order to save me pain and trouble. A sepoy now came up having given his musket to a man to carry, who therefore demanded payment. As it had become a regular nuisance for the sepoys to employ people to carry for them, telling them that I would pay, I demanded why he had promised in my name. "Oh, it was but a little way he carried the musket," said he. Chimseia warned us next morning, 30th June, against allowing any one to straggle or steal in front, for stabbing and plundering were the rule. The same sepoy who had employed a man to carry his musket now came forward, with his eyes fixed and shaking all over. This, I was to understand, meant extreme weakness; but I had accidentally noticed him walking quite smartly before this exhibition, so I ordered him to keep close to the donkey that carried the havildar's luggage, and on no account to remain behind the party. He told the havildar that he would sit down only for a little while; and, I suppose, fell asleep, for he came up to us in the evening as naked as a robin.

I saw another person bound to a tree and dead—a sad sight to see, whoever was the perpetrator. So many slave-sticks lie along our path, that I suspect the people here-about make a practice of liberating what slaves they cian find abandoned on the march, to sell them again.

A large quantity of maize is cultivated at Chimsaka's, at whose place we this day arrived. We got a supply, but being among thieves, we thought it advisable to move on to the next place (Mtarika's). When starting, we found that fork, kettle, pot, and shot-pouch had been taken. The thieves, I observed, kept up a succession of jokes with Chuma and Wikatani and when the latter was enjoying them, gaping to the sky, they were busy putting the things of which he had charge under their cloths! I spoke to the chief, and he got the three first articles back for me.

A great deal if not all the lawlessness of this quarter is the result of the slave-trade, for the Arabs buy whoever is brought to them and in a country covered with forest as this is, kidnapping can be prosecuted with the greatest ease; elsewhere the people are honest, and have a regard for justice.

1st July, 1866.—As we approach Mtarika's place, the country becomes more mountainous and the land sloping for a mile down to the south bank of the Rovuma supports a large population. Some were making new gardens by cutting down trees and piling the branches for burning; others had stored tip large quantities of grain and were moving it to a new locality, but they were all so well supplied with calico (Merikano) that they would not look at ours: the market was in fact glutted by slavers from (Quiloa) Kilwa. On asking why people were seen tied to trees to die as we had seen them, they gave the usual answer that the Arabs tie them thus and leave them to perish, because they are vexed, when the slaves can walk no further, that they have lost their money by them. The path is almost strewed with slave-sticks, and though the people denied it, I suspect that they make a practice of following slave caravans and cutting off the sticks from those who fall out in the march, and thus stealing them. By selling them again they get the quantities of cloth we see. Some asked for gaudy prints, of which we had none, because we knew that the general taste of the Africans of the Interior is for strength rather than show in what they buy.

The Rovuma here is about 100 yards broad, and still keeps up its character of a rapid stream, with sandy banks and islands: the latter are generally occupied, as being defensible when the river is in flood.

2nd July, 1866.—We rested at Mtarika's old place; and though we had to pay dearly with our best table-cloths[14] for it, we got as much as made one meal a day. At the same dear rate we could give occasionally only two ears of maize to each man; and if the sepoys got their comrades' corn into their hands, they eat it without shame. We had to bear a vast amount of staring, for the people, who are Waiyau, have a great deal of curiosity, and are occasionally rather rude. They have all heard of our wish to stop the slave-trade, and are rather taken aback when told that by selling they are part and part guilty of the mortality of which we had been unwilling spectators. Some were dumbfounded when shown that in the eye of their Maker they are parties to the destruction of human life which accompanies this traffic both by sea and land. If they did not sell, the Arabs would not come to buy. Chuma and Wakatani render what is said very eloquently in Chiyau, most of the people being of their tribe, with only a sprinkling of slaves. Chimseia, Chimsaka, Mtarika, Mtendé, Makanjela, Mataka, and all the chiefs and people in our route to the Lake, are Waiyau, or Waiau.[15]

On the southern slope down to the river there are many oozing springs and damp spots where rice has been sown and reaped. The adjacent land has yielded large crops of sorghum, congo-beans, and pumpkins. Successive crowds of people came to gaze. My appearance and acts often cause a burst of laughter; sudden standing up produces a flight of women and children. To prevent peeping into the hut which I occupy, and making the place quite dark, I do my writing in the verandah. Chitané, the poodle dog, the buffalo-calf, and our only remaining donkey are greeted with the same amount of curiosity and laughter-exciting comment as myself.

Every evening a series of loud musket reports is heard from the different villages along the river; these are imitation evening guns. All copy the Arabs in dress and chewing tobacco with "nora" lime, made from burnt river shells instead of betel-nut and lime. The women are stout, well-built persons, with thick arms and legs; their heads incline to the bullet shape; the lip-rings are small; the tattoo a mixture of Makoa and Waiyau. Fine blue and black beads are in fashion, and so are arm-coils of thick brass wire. Very nicely inlaid combs are worn in the hair; the inlaying is accomplished by means of a gum got from the root of an orchis called *Nangazu.*

3rd July, 1866.—A short march brought us to Mtarika's new place. The chief made his appearance only after he had ascertained all he could about us. The population is immense; they are making new gardens, and the land is laid out by straight lines about a foot broad, cut with the hoe; one goes miles without getting beyond the marked or surveyed fields.

Mtarika came at last; a big ugly man, with large mouth and receding forehead. He asked to see all our curiosities, as the watch, revolver, breech-loading rifle, sextant. I gave him a lecture on the evil of selling his people, and he wished me to tell all the other chiefs the same thing.

They dislike the idea of guilt being attached to them for having sold many who have lost their lives on their way down to the sea-coast. We had a long visit from Mtarika next day; he gave us meal, and meat of wild hog, with a salad made of bean-leaves. A wretched Swaheli Arab, ill with rheumatism, came for aid, and got a cloth. They all profess to me to be buying ivory only.

5th July, 1866.—We left for Mtendé, who is the last chief before we enter on a good eight days' march to Mataka's; we might have gone to Kandulo's, who is near the Rovuma, and more to the north, but all are so well supplied with everything by slave-traders that we have difficulty in getting provisions at all. Mataka has plenty of all kinds of food. On the way we passed the burnt bones of a person Avho was accused of having eaten human flesh; he had been poisoned, or, as they said, killed by poison (muave?), and then burned. His clothes were hung, up on trees by the wayside as a warning to others. The country was covered with scraggy forest, but so undulating that one could often see all around from the crest of the waves. Great mountain masses appear in the south and south-west. It feels cold, and the sky is often overcast.

6th July, 1866.—I took lunars yesterday, after which Mtendé invited us to eat at his house where he had provided a large mess of rice porridge and bean-leaves as a relish. He says that many Arabs pass him and many of them die in their journeys. He knows no deaf or dumb person in the country. He says that he cuts the throats of all animals to be eaten, and does not touch lion or hyaena.

7th July, 1866.—We got men from Mtendé to carry loads and show the way. He asked a cloth to ensure his people going to the journey's end and behaving properly; this is the only case of anything like tribute being demanded in this journey: I gave him a cloth worth 5s. 6d. Upland vegetation prevails; trees are dotted here and there among bushes five feet high, and fine blue and yellow flowers are common. We pass over a succession of ridges and valleys as in Londa; each valley has a running stream or trickling rill; garden willows are in full bloom, and also a species of sage with variegated leaves beneath the flowers.

When the sepoy Perim threw away the tea and the lead lining, I only reproved him and promised him punishment if he committed any other wilful offence, but now he and another skulked behind and gave their loads to a stranger to carry, with a promise to him that I would pay. We waited two hours for them; and as the havildar said that they would not obey him, I gave Perim and the other some smart cuts with a cane, but I felt that I was degrading myself, and resolved not to do the punishment myself again.

8th July, 1866.—Hard travelling through a depopulated country. The trees are about the size of hop-poles with abundance of tall grass; the soil is sometimes a little sandy, at other times that reddish, clayey sort which yields native grain so well. The rock seen uppermost is often a ferruginous conglomerate, lying on granite rocks. The gum-copal tree is here a mere bush, and no digging takes place for the gum: it is called Mchenga, and yields gum when wounded, as also bark, cloth, and cordage when stripped. Mountain masses are all around us; we sleep at Linata mountain.

9th July, 1866.—The Masuko fruit abounds: the name is the same here as in the Batoka country; there are also rhododendrons of two species, but the flowers white. We slept in a wild spot, near

Mount Leziro, with many lions roaring about us; one hoarse fellow serenaded us a long time, but did nothing more. Game is said to be abundant, but we saw none, save an occasional diver springing away from the path. Some streams ran to the north-west to the Lismyando, which flows N. for the Rovuma; others to the south-east for the Loendi.

10th and 11th July, 1866.—Nothing to interest but the same weary trudge: our food so scarce that we can only give a handful or half a pound of grain to each person per day. The Masuko fruit is formed, but not ripe till rains begin; very few birds are seen or heard, though there is both food and water in the many grain-bearing grasses and running streams, which we cross at the junction of every two ridges. A dead body lay in a hut by the wayside; the poor thing had begun to make a garden by the stream, probably in hopes of living long enough (two months or so) on wild fruits to reap a crop of maize.

12th July, 1866.—A drizzling mist set in during the night and continued this morning, we set off in the dark, however, leaving our last food for the havildar and sepoys who had not yet come up. The streams are now of good size. An Arab brandy bottle was lying broken in one village called Msapa. We hurried on as fast as we could to the Luatizé, our last stage before getting to Mataka's; this stream is rapid, about forty yards wide, waist deep, with many podostemons on the bottom. The country gets more and more undulating and is covered with masses of green foliage, chiefly Masuko trees, which have large hard leaves. There are hippopotami further down the river on its way to the Loendi. A little rice which had been kept for me I divided, but some did not taste food.

13th July, 1866.—A good many stragglers behind, but we push on to get food and send it back to them. The soil all reddish clay, the roads baked hard by the sun, and the feet of many of us are weary and sore: a weary march and long, for it is perpetually up and down now. I counted fifteen running streams in one day: they are at the bottom of the valley which separates the ridges. We got to the brow of a ridge about an hour from Mataka's first gardens, and all were so tired that we remained to sleep; but we first invited volunteers to go on and buy food, and bring it back early next morning: they had to be pressed to do this duty.

14th July, 1866.—As our volunteers did not come at 8 A.M., I set off to see the cause, and after an hour of perpetual up and down march, as I descended the steep slope which overlooks the first gardens, I saw my friends start up at the apparition—they were comfortably cooking porridge for themselves! I sent men of Mataka back with food to the stragglers behind and came on to his town.

An Arab, Sef Rupia or Rubea, head of a large body of slaves, on his way to the coast, most kindly came forward and presented an ox, bag of flour, and some cooked meat, all of which were extremely welcome to half-famished men, or indeed under any circumstances. He had heard of our want of food and of a band of sepoys, and what could the English think of doing but putting an end to the slave-trade? Had he seen our wretched escort, all fear of them would have vanished! He had a large safari or caravan under him. This body is usually divided into ten or twelve portions, and all are bound to obey the leader to á certain extent: in this case there were eleven parties, and the traders numbered about sixty or seventy, who were dark coast Arabs. Each underling had his men under him, and when I saw them they were busy making the pens of branches in which their slaves and they sleep. Sef came on with me to Mataka's, and introduced me in due form with discharges of gunpowder. I asked him to come back next morning, and presented three cloths with a request that he would assist the havildar and sepoys, if he met them, with food: this he generously did.

We found Mataka's town situated in an elevated valley surrounded by mountains; the houses numbered at least 1000, and there were many villages around. The mountains were pleasantly green, and had many trees which the people were incessantly cutting down. They had but recently come here: they were besieged by Mazitu at their former location west of this; after fighting four days they left unconquered, having beaten the enemy off.

Mataka kept us waiting some time in the verandah of his large square house, and then made his appearance, smiling with his good-natured face. He is about sixty years of age, dressed as an Arab, and if we may judge from the laughter with which his remarks were always greeted, somewhat humorous. He had never seen any but Arabs before. He gave me a square house to live in, indeed the most of the houses here are square, for the Arabs are imitated in everything: they have introduced the English pea, and we were pleased to see large patches of it in full bearing, and ripe in moist hollows which had been selected for it. The numerous springs which come out at various parts are all made use of. Those parts which are too wet are drained, whilst beds are regularly irrigated by watercourses and ridges: we had afterwards occasion to admire the very extensive draining which has been effected among the hills. Cassava is cultivated on ridges along all the streets in the town, which give it a somewhat regular and neat appearance. Peas and tobacco were the chief products raised by irrigation, but batatas and maize were often planted too: wheat would succeed if introduced. The altitude is about 2700 feet above the sea: the air at this time is cool, and many people have coughs.

Mataka soon sent a good mess of porridge and cooked meat (beef); he has plenty of cattle and sheep: and the next day he sent abundance of milk. We stand a good deal of staring unmoved, though it is often accompanied by remarks by no means complimentary; they think that they are not understood, and probably I do misunderstand sometimes. The Waiyau jumble their words as I think, and Mataka thought that I did not enunciate anything, but kept my tongue still when I spoke.

Town of Matak, Moembé. *15th July, 1866.*—The safari under Sef set off this morning for Kilwa. Sef says that about 100 of the Kilwa people died this year, so slaving as well as philanthropy is accompanied with loss of life: we saw about seven of their graves; the rest died on the road up.

There are two roads from this to the Lake, one to Loséwa, which is west of this, and opposite Kotakota; the other, to Makatu, is further south: the first is five days through deserted country chiefly; but the other, seven, among people and plenty of provisions all the way.

It struck me after Sef had numbered up the losses that the Kilwa people sustained by death in their endeavours to «nslave people, similar losses on the part of those who go to "proclaim liberty to the captives, the opening of the prison to them that are bound,"—to save and elevate, need not be made so very much of as they sometimes are.

Soon after our arrival we heard that a number of Mataka's Waiyau had, without his knowledge, gone to Nyassa, and in a foray carried off cattle and people: when they came home with the spoil, Mataka ordered all to be sent back whence they came. The chief came up to visit me soon after, and I told him that his decision was the best piece of news I had heard in the country: he was evidently pleased with my approbation, and, turning to his people, asked if they heard what I said. He repeated my remark, and said, "You silly fellows think me wrong in returning the captives, but all wise men will approve of it," and he then scolded them roundly.

I was accidentally spectator of this party going back, for on going out of the town I saw a meat market opened, and people buying with maize and meal. On inquiring, I was told that the people and cattle there were the Nyassas, and they had slaughtered an ox, in order to exchange meat for grain as provisions on the journey. The women and children numbered fifty-four, and about a dozen boys were engaged in milking the cows: the cattle were from twenty-five to thirty head.

The change from hard and scanty fare caused illness in several of our party. I had tasted no animal food except what turtle-doves and guinea-fowls could be shot since we passed Matawatawa,—true, a fowl was given by Mtendé. The last march was remarkable for the scarcity of birds, so eight days were spent on porridge and rice without relish.

I gave Mataka a trinket, to be kept in remembrance of his having sent back the Nyassa people: he replied that he would always act in a similar manner. As it was a spontaneous act, it was all the more valuable.

The sepoys have become quite intolerable, and if I cannot get rid of them we shall all starve before we accomplish what we wish. They dawdle behind picking up wild fruits, and over our last march (which we accomplished on the morning of the eighth day) they took from fourteen to twenty-two days. Retaining their brutal feelings to the last they killed the donkey which I lent to the havildar to carry his things, by striking it on the head when in boggy places into which they had senselessly driven it loaded; then the havildar came on (his men pretending they could go no further from weakness), and killed the young buffalo and eat it when they thought they could hatch up a plausible story. They said it had died, and tigers came and devoured it—they saw them. "Did you see the stripes of the tiger?" said I. All declared that they saw the stripes distinctly. This gave us an idea of their truthfulness, as there is no striped tiger in all Africa. All who resolved on skulking or other bad behaviour invariably took up with the sepoys; their talk seemed to suit evil-doers, and they were such a disreputable-looking lot that I was quite ashamed of them. The havildar had no authority, and all bore the sulky dogged look of people going where they were forced but hated to go. This hang-dog expression of countenance was so conspicuous that I many a time have heard the country people remark, "These are the slaves of the party." They have neither spirit nor pluck as compared with the Africans, and if one saw a village he turned out of the way to beg in the most abject manner, or lay down and slept, the only excuse afterwards being, "My legs were sore." Having allowed some of them to sleep at the fire in my house, they began a wholesale plunder of everything they could sell, as cartridges, cloths, and meat, so I had to eject them. One of them then threatened to shoot my interpreter Simon if he got him in a quiet place away from the English power. As this threat had been uttered three times, and I suspect that something of the kind had prevented the havildar exerting his authority, I resolved to get rid of them by sending them back to the coast by the first trader. It is likely that some sympathizers will take their part, but I strove to make them useful. They had but poor and scanty fare in a part of the way, but all of us suffered alike. They made themselves thoroughly disliked by their foul talk and abuse, and if anything tended more than another to show me that theirs was a moral unfitness for travel, it was the briskness assumed when they knew they were going back to the coast. I felt inclined to force them on, but it would have been acting from revenge, and to pay them out, so I forbore. I gave Mataka forty-eight yards of calico, and to the sepoys eighteen yards, and arranged that he should give them food till Suleiman, a respectable trader, should arrive. He was expected every day, and we passed him near the town. If they chose to go and get their luggage, it was of course all safe for them behind. The havildar begged still to go on with me, and I consented, though he is a drag on the party, but he will count in any difficulty.

Abraham recognised his uncle among the crowds who came to see us. On making himself known he found that his mother and two sisters had been sold to the Arabs after he had been enslaved. The uncle pressed him to remain, and Mataka urged, and so did another uncle, but in vain. I added my voice, and could have given him goods to keep him afloat a good while, but he invariably replied, "How can I stop where I have no mother and no sister?" The affection seems to go to the maternal side. I suggested that he might come after he had married a wife, but I fear very much that unless some European would settle, none of these Nassick boys will come to this country. It would be decidedly better if they were taught agriculture in the simplest form, as the Indian. Mataka would have liked to put his oxen to use, but Abraham could not help him with that. He is a smith, or rather a nothing, for unless he could smelt iron he would be entirely without materials to work with.

14th-28th July, 1866.—One day, calling at Mataka's, I found as usual a large crowd of idlers, who always respond with a laugh to everything he utters as wit. He asked, if he went to Bombay what ought he to take to secure some gold? I replied, "Ivory," he rejoined, "Would slaves not be a good speculation?" I replied that, "if he took slaves there for sale, they would put him in prison." The idea of the great Mataka in "chokee" made him wince, and the laugh turned for once against him. He said that as all the people from the coast crowd to him, they ought to give him something handsome for being here to supply their wants. I replied, if he would fill the fine well-watered country we had passed over with people instead of sending them off to Kilwa, he would confer a benefit on visitors, but we had been starved on the way to him; and I then told him what the English would do in road-making in a fine country like this. This led us to talk of railways, ships, ploughing with oxen—the last idea struck him most. I told him that I should have liked some of the Nassick boys to remain and teach this and other things, but they might be afraid to venture lest they should be sold again. The men who listened never heard such decided protests against selling each other into slavery before!

The idea of guilt probably floated but vaguely in their minds, but the loss of life we have witnessed (in the guilt of which the sellers as well as the buyers participate) comes home very forcibly to their minds.

Mataka has been an active hand in slave wars himself, though now he wishes to settle down in quiet. The Waiyau generally are still the most active agents the slave-traders have. The caravan leaders from Kilwa arrive at a Waiyau village, show the goods they have brought, are treated liberally by the elders, and told to wait and enjoy themselves, slaves enough to purchase all will be procured: then a foray is made against the Manganja, who have few or no guns. The Waiyau who come against them are abundantly supplied with both by their coast guests. Several of the low coast Arabs, who differ in nothing from the Waiyau, usually accompany the foray, and do business on their own account: this is the usual way in which a safari is furnished with slaves.

Makanjela, a Waiyau chief about a third of the way from Mtendé's to Mataka, has lost the friendship of all his neighbours by kidnapping and selling their people; if any of Mataka's people are found in the district between Makanjela and Moembé, they are considered fair game and sold. Makanjela's people cannot piss Mataka to go to the Manganja, so they do what they can by kidnapping and plundering all who fall into their hands.

When I employed two of Mataka's people to go back on the 14th with food to the havildar and sepoys, they went a little way and relieved some, but would not venture as far as the Luatizé, for fear of losing their liberty by Makanjela's people. I could not get the people of the country to go back; nor could I ask the Nassick boys, who had been threatened by the sepoys with assassination,—and it was the same with the Johanna men, because, though Mahometans, the sepoys had called them Caffirs, &c., and they all declared, "We are ready to do anything for you, but we will do nothing for these Hindis." I sent back a sepoy, giving him provisions; he sat down in the first village, ate all the food, and returned.

An immense tract of country lies uninhabited. To the north-east of Moembé we have at least fifty miles of as fine land as can be seen anywhere, still bearing all the marks of having once supported a prodigious iron-smelting and grain-growing population. The clay pipes which are put on the nozzles of their bellows and inserted into the furnace are met with everywhere—often vitrified. Then the ridges on which they planted maize, beans, cassava, and sorghum, and which they find necessary to drain off the too abundant moisture of the rains, still remain unlevelled to attest the industry of the former inhabitants; the soil being clayey, resists for a long time the influence of the weather. These ridges are very regular, for in crossing the old fields, as the path often compels us to do, one foot treads regularly on the ridge, and the other in the hollow, for a considerable distance. Pieces of broken pots, with their rims ornamented with very good imitations of basket-work, attest that the lady potters of old followed the example given them by their still more ancient mothers,—their designs are rude, but better than we can make them without referring to the original.

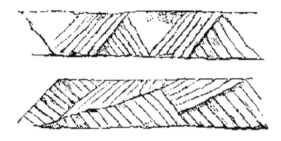

Imitation of basket-work in Pottery.

No want of water has here acted to drive the people away, as has been the case further south. It is a perpetual succession of ridge and valley, with a running stream or oozing bog, where ridge is separated from ridge: the ridges become steeper and narrower as we approach Mataka's.

I counted fifteen running burns of from one to ten yards wide in one day's march of about six hours; being in a hilly or rather mountainous region, they flow rapidly and have plenty of water-power. In July any mere torrent ceases to flow, but these were brawling burns with water too cold (61°) for us to bathe in whose pores were all open by the relaxing regions nearer the coast. The sound, so un-African, of gushing water dashing over rocks was quite familiar to our ears.

This district, which rises up west of Mataka's to 3400 feet above the sea, catches a great deal of the moisture brought up by the easterly winds. Many of the trees are covered with lichens. While here we had cold southerly breezes, and a sky so overcast every day after 10 A.M., that we could take no astronomical observations: even the latitude was too poor to be much depended on. 12° 53' S. may have been a few miles from this.

The cattle, rather a small breed, black and white in patches, and brown, with humps, give milk which is duly prized by these

Waiyau. The sheep are the large-tailed variety, and generally of a black colour. Fowls and pigeons are the only other domestic animals we see, if we except the wretched village dogs which our-poodle had immense delight in chasing.

The Waiyau are far from a handsome race, but they are not the prognathous beings one sees on the West Coast either. Their heads are of a round shape; compact foreheads, but not particularly receding; the alae nasi are flattened out; lips full, and with the women a small lip-ring just turns them up to give additional thickness. Their style of beauty is exactly that which was in fashion when the stone deities were made in the caves of Elephanta and Kenora near Bombay. À favourite mode of dressing the hair into little knobs, which was in fashion there, is more common in some tribes than in this. The mouths of the women would not be so hideous with a small lip-ring if they did not file their teeth to points, but they seem strong and able for the work which falls to their lot. The men are large, strong-boned fellows, and capable of enduring great fatigue, they undergo a rite which once distinguished the Jews about the age of puberty, and take a new name on the occasion; this was not introduced by the Arabs, whose advent is a recent event, and they speak of the time before they were inundated with European manufactures in exchange for slaves, as quite within their memory.

Young Mataka gave me a dish of peas, and usually brought something every time he made a visit, he seems a nice boy, and his father, in speaking of learning to read, said he and his companions could learn, but he himself was too old. The soil seems very fertile, for the sweet potatoes become very large, and we bought two loads of them for three cubits and two needles; they quite exceeded 1 cwt. The maize becomes very large too; one cob had 1600 seeds. The abundance of water, the richness of soil, the available labour for building square houses, the coolness of the climate, make this nearly as desirable a residence as Magomero; but, alas! instead of three weeks' easy sail up the Zambesi and Shiré, we have spent four weary months in getting here: I shall never cease bitterly to lament the abandonment of the Magomero mission.

Moaning seems a favourite way of spending the time with some sick folk. For the sake of the warmth, I allowed a Nassick boy to sleep in my house; he and I had the same complaint, dysentery, and I was certainly worse than he, but did not moan, while he played at it as often as he was awake. I told him that people moaned only when too ill to be sensible of what they were doing; the groaning ceased, though he became worse.

Three sepoys played at groaning very vigorously outside my door; they had nothing the matter with them, except perhaps fatigue, which we all felt alike; as these fellows prevented my sleeping, I told them quite civilly that, if so ill that they required to groan, they had better move off a little way, as I could not sleep; they preferred the verandah, and at once forbore.

The abundance of grain and other food is accompanied by great numbers of rats or large mice, which play all manner of pranks by night; white ants have always to be guarded against likewise. Anyone who would find an antidote to drive them away would confer a blessing; the natural check is the driver ant, which when it visits a house is a great pest for a time, but it clears the others out.

FOOTNOTES:

12. There is a double purpose in these murders; the terror inspired in the minds of the survivors spurs them on to endure the hardships of the march: the Portuese drivers are quite alive to the merits of this stimulus.—ED.

13. A tribal distinction turns on the customs prevailing with respect to animal food, *e.g.* one tribe will eat the elephant, the next looks on such flesh as unclean, and so with other meat. The neighbouring Manganja gladly eat the leopard and hyaena.—ED.

14. A coloured cloth manufactured expressly for barter in East Africa.

15. This is pronounced "Y-yow."—ED.

* * * * *

CHAPTER IV.

Geology and description of the Waiyau land. Leaves Mataka's. The Nyumbo plant. Native iron-foundry. Blacksmiths. Makes for the Lake Nyassa. Delight at seeing the Lake once more. The Manganja or Nyassa tribe. Arab slave crossing. Unable to procure passage across. The Kungu fly. Fear of the English amongst slavers. Lake shore. Blue ink. Chitané changes colour. The Nsaka fish. Makalaosé drinks beer. The Sanjika fish. London antiquities. Lake rivers. Mukaté's. Lake Pamalombé. Mponda's. A slave gang. Wikatani discovers his relatives and remains.

28th July, 1866.—We proposed to start to-day, but Mataka said that he was not ready yet: the flour had to be ground, and he had given us no meat. He had sent plenty of cooked food almost every day. He asked if we would slaughter the ox he would give here, or take it on; we preferred to kill it at once. He came on the 28th with a good lot of flour for us, and men to guide us to Nyassa, telling us that this was Moembé, and his district extended all the way to the Lake: he would not send us to Loséwa, as that place had lately been plundered and burned.

In general the chiefs have shown an anxiety to promote our safety. The country is a mass of mountains. On leaving Mataka's we ascended considerably, and about the end of the first day's march, near Magola's village, the barometer showed our greatest altitude, about 3400 feet above the sea. There were villages of these mountaineers everywhere, for the most part of 100 houses or more each. The springs were made the most use of that they knew; the damp spots drained, and the water given a free channel for use in irrigation further down: most of these springs showed the presence of iron by the oxide oozing out. A great many patches of peas are seen in full bearing and flower. The trees are small, except in the hollows: there is plenty of grass and flowers near streams and on the heights. The mountain-tops may rise 2000 or 3000 feet above their flanks, along which we wind, going perpetually up and down the steep ridges of which the country is but a succession.

Looking at the geology of the district, the plateaux on each side of the Rovuma are masses of grey sandstone, capped with masses of ferruginous conglomerate; apparently an aqueous deposit. When we ascend the Rovuma about sixty miles, a great many pieces and blocks of silicified wood appear on the surface of the soil at the bottom of the slope up the plateaux. This in Africa is a sure indication of the presence of coal beneath, but it was not observed cropping out; the plateaux are cut up in various directions by wadys well supplied with grass and trees on deep and somewhat sandy soil: but at the confluence of the Loendi highlands they appear in the far distance. In the sands of the Loendi pieces of coal are quite common.[16]

Before reaching the confluence of the Rovuma and Loendi, or say about ninety miles from the sea, the plateau is succeeded by a more level country, having detached granitic masses shooting up some 500 or 700 feet. The sandstone of the plateau has at first been hardened, then quite metamorphosed into a chocolate-coloured schist. As at Chilolé hill, we have igneous rocks, apparently trap, capped with masses of beautiful white dolomite. We still ascend in altitude as we go westwards, and come upon long tracts of gneiss with hornblende. The gneiss is often striated, all the striae looking one way—sometimes north and south, and at other times east and west. These rocks look as if a stratified rock had been nearly melted, and the strata fused together by the heat. From these striated rocks have shot up great rounded masses of granite or syenite, whose smooth sides and crowns contain scarcely any trees, and are probably from 3000 to 4000 feet above the sea. The elevated plains among these mountain masses show great patches of ferruginous conglomerate, which, when broken, look like yellow haematite with madrepore holes in it: this has made the soil of a red colour.

On the watershed we have still the rounded granitic hills jutting above the plains (if such they may be called) which are all ups and downs, and furrowed with innumerable running rills, the sources of the Rovuma and Loendi. The highest rock observed with mica schist was at an altitude of 3440 feet. The same uneven country prevails as we proceed from the watershed about forty miles down to the Lake, and a great deal of quartz in small fragments renders travelling-very difficult. Near the Lake, and along its eastern shore, we have mica schist and gneiss foliated, with a great deal of hornblende; but the most remarkable feature of it is that the rocks are all tilted on edge, or slightly inclined to the Lake. The active agent in effecting this is not visible. It looks as if a sudden rent had been made, so as to form the Lake, and tilt all these rocks nearly over. On the east side of the lower part of the Lake we have two ranges of mountains, evidently granitic: the nearer one covered with small trees and lower than the other; the other jagged and bare, or of the granitic forms. But in all this country no fossil-yielding rock was visible except the grey sandstone referred to at the beginning of this note. The rocks are chiefly the old crystalline forms.

One fine straight tall tree in the hollows seemed a species of fig: its fruit was just forming, but it was too high for me to ascertain its species. The natives don't eat the fruit, but they eat the large grubs which come out of it. The leaves were fifteen inches long by five broad: they call it Unguengo.

29th July, 1866.—At Magola's village. Although we are now rid of the sepoys, we cannot yet congratulate ourselves on being rid of the lazy habits of lying down in the path which they introduced. A strong scud comes up from the south bringing much moisture with it: it blows so hard above, this may be a storm on the coast. Temperature in mornings 55°.

30th July, 1866.—A short march brought us to Pezimba's village, which consists of 200 houses and huts. It is placed very nicely on a knoll between two burns, which, as usual, are made use of for irrigating peas in winter time. The headman said that if we left now we had a good piece of jungle before us, and would sleep twice in it before reaching Mbanga. We therefore remained. An Arab party, hearing of our approach, took a circuitous route among the mountains to avoid coming in contact with us. In travelling to Pezimba's we had commenced our western descent to the Lake, for we were now lower than Magola's by 300 feet. We crossed many rivulets and the Lochesi, a good-sized stream. The watershed parts some streams for Loendi and some for Rovuma. There is now a decided scantiness of trees. Many of the hill-tops are covered with grass or another plant; there is pleasure now in seeing them bare. Ferns, rhododendrons, and a foliaged tree, which looks in the distance like silver-fir, are met with.

The Mandaré root is here called Nyumbo, when cooked it has a slight degree of bitterness with it which cultivation may remove. Mica schist crowned some of the heights on the watershed, then gneiss, and now, as we descend further, we have igneous rocks of more recent eruption, porphyry and gneiss, with hornblende. A good deal of ferruginous conglomerate, with holes in it, covers many spots; when broken, it looks like yellow haematite, with black linings to the holes: this is probably the ore used in former times by the smiths, of whose existence we now find still more evidence than further east.

31st July, 1866.—I had presented Pezimba with a cloth, so he cooked for us handsomely last night, and this morning desired us to wait a little as he had not yet sufficient meal made to present: we waited and got a generous present.

It was decidedly milder here than at Mataka's, and we had a clear sky. In our morning's march we passed the last of the population, and went on through a fine well-watered fruitful country, to sleep near a mountain called Mtéwiré, by a stream called Msapo. A very large Arab slave-party was close by our encampment, and I wished to speak to them; but as soon as they knew of our being near they set off in a pathless course across country, and were six days in the wilderness.[17]

1st August, 1866.—We saw the encampment of another Arab party. It consisted of ten pens, each of which, from the number of fires it contained, may have held from eighty to a hundred slaves. The people of the country magnified the numbers, saying that they would reach from this to Mataka's; but from all I can learn, I think that from 300 to 800 slaves is the commoner gang. This second party went across country very early this morning. We saw the fire-sticks which the slaves had borne with them. The fear they feel is altogether the effect of the English name, for we have done nothing to cause their alarm.

2nd August, 1866.—There was something very cheering to me in the sight at our encampment of yellow grass and trees dotted over it, as in the Bechuana country. The birds were singing merrily too, inspired by the cold, which was 47°, and by the vicinity of some population. Gum-copal trees and bushes grow here as well as all over the country; but gum is never dug for, probably because the trees were never large enough to yield the fossil gum. Marks of smiths are very abundant and some furnaces are still standing. Much cultivation must formerly have been where now all is jungle.

We arrived at Mbanga, a village embowered in trees, chiefly of the euphorbia, so common in the Manganja country further south. Kandulo, the headman, had gone to drink beer at another village, but sent orders to give a hut and to cook for us. We remained next day. Took lunars.

We had now passed through, at the narrowest part, the hundred miles of depopulated country, of which about seventy are on the N.E. of Mataka. The native accounts differ as to the cause. Some say slave wars, and assert that the Makoa from the vicinity of Mozambique played an important part in them; others say famine; others that the people have moved to and beyond Nyassa.[18] Certain it is, from the potsherds strewed over the country, and the still remaining ridges on which beans, sorghum, maize, and cassava, were planted, that the departed population was prodigious. The Waiyau, who are now in the country, came from the other side of the Rovuma, and they probably supplanted the Manganja, an operation which we see going on at the present day.

4th August, 1866.—An hour and a half brought us to Miulé, a village on the same level with Mbanga; and the chief pressing us to stay, on the plea of our sleeping two nights in the jungle, instead of one if we left early next morning, we consented. I asked him what had become of the very large iron-smelting population of this region; he said many had died of famine, others had fled to the west of Nyassa: the famine is the usual effect of slave wars, and much death is thereby caused—probably much more than by the journey to the coast. He had never heard any tradition of stone hatchets having been used, nor of stone spear-heads or arrowheads of that material, nor had he heard of any being turned up by the women in hoeing. The Makondé, as we saw, use wooden spears where iron is scarce. I saw wooden hoes used for tilling the soil in the Bechuana and Bataka countries, but never stone ones. In 1841 I saw a Bushwoman in the Cape Colony with a round stone and a hole through it; on being asked she showed me how it was used by inserting the top of a digging-stick into it, and digging a root. The stone was to give the stick weight.

Digging-stick weighted with round Stone.

The stones still used as anvils and sledge-hammers by many of the African smiths, when considered from their point of view, show sounder sense than if they were burdened with the great weights we use. They are unacquainted with the process of case-hardening, which, applied to certain parts of our anvils, gives them their usefulness, and an anvil of their soft iron would not do so well as a hard stone. It is true a small light one might be made, but let any one see how the hammers of their iron bevel over and round in the faces with a little work, and he will perceive that only a wild freak would induce any sensible native smith to make a mass equal to a sledge-hammer, and burden himself with a weight for what can be better performed by a stone. If people are settled, as on the coast, then they gladly use any mass of cast iron they may find, but never where, as in the interior, they have no certainty of remaining any length of time in one spot.

5th August, 1866.—We left Miulé, and commenced our march towards Lake Nyassa, and slept at the last of the streams that flow to the Loendi. In Mataka's vicinity, N.E., there is a perfect brush of streams flowing to that river: one forms a lake in its course, and the sources of the Rovuma lie in the same region. After leaving Mataka's we crossed a good-sized one flowing to Loendi, and, the day after leaving Pezimba's, another going to the Chiringa or Lochiringa, which is a tributary of the Rovuma.

6th August, 1866.—We passed two cairns this morning at the beginning of the very sensible descent to the Lake. They are very common in all this Southern Africa in the passes of the mountains, and are meant to mark divisions of countries, perhaps burial-places, but the Waiyau who accompanied us thought that they were merely heaps of stone collected by some one making a garden. The cairns were placed just about the spot where the blue waters of Nyassa first came fairly into view.

We now came upon a stream, the Misinjé, flowing into the Lake, and we crossed it five times; it was about twenty yards wide, and thigh deep. We made but short stages when we got on the lower plateau, for the people had great abundance of food, and gave large presents of it if we rested. One man gave four fowls, three large baskets of maize, pumpkins, eland's fat—a fine male, as seen by his horns,—and pressed us to stay, that he might see our curiosities as well as others. He said that at one day's distance south of him all sorts of animals, as buffaloes, elands, elephants, hippopotami, and antelopes, could be shot.

8th August, 1866.—We came to the Lake at the confluence of the Misinjé, and felt grateful to That Hand which had protected us thus far on our journey. It was as if I had come back to an old home I never expected again to see; and pleasant to bathe in the delicious waters again, hear the roar of the sea, and dash in the rollers. Temp. 71° at 8 A.M., while the air was 65°. I feel quite exhilarated.

The headman here, Mokalaosé, is a real Manganja, and he and all his people exhibit the greater darkness of colour consequent on being in a warm moist climate; he is very friendly, and presented millet, porridge, cassava, and hippopotamus meat boiled and asked if I liked milk, as he had some of Mataka's cattle here. His people bring sanjika the best Lake fish, for sale; they are dried on stages over slow fires, and lose their fine flavour by it, but they are much prized inland. I bought fifty for a fathom of calico; when fresh, they taste exactly like the best herrings, *i.e.* as we think, but voyagers' and travellers' appetites are often so whetted as to be incapable of giving a true verdict in matters of taste.

[It is necessary to explain that Livingstone knew of an Arab settlement on the western shore of the Lake, and that he hoped to induce the chief man Jumbé to give him a passage to the other side.]

10th August, 1866.—I sent Seyed Majid's letter up to Jumbé, but the messenger met some coast Arabs at the Loangwa, which may be seven miles from this, and they came back with him, haggling a deal about the fare, and then went off, saying that they would bring the dhow here for us. Finding that they did not come, I sent Musa, who brought back word that they had taken the dhow away over to Jumbé at Kotakota, or, as they pronounce it, Ngotagota. Very few of the coast Arabs can read; in words they are very polite, but truthfulness seems very little regarded. I am resting myself and people—working up journal, lunars, and altitudes—but will either move south or go to the Arabs towards the north soon.

Mokalaosé's fears of the Waiyau will make him welcome Jumbé here, and then the Arab will some day have an opportunity of scattering his people as he has done those at Kotakota. He has made Loséwa too hot for himself. When the people there were carried off by Mataka's people, Jumbé seized their stores of grain, and now has no post to which he can go there. The Loangwa Arabs give an awful account of Jumbé's murders and selling the people, but one cannot take it all in; at the mildest it must have been bad. This is all they ever do; they cannot form a state or independent kingdom: slavery and the slave-trade are insuperable obstacles to any permanence inland; slaves can escape so easily, all therefore that the Arabs do is to collect as much money as they can by hook and by crook, and then leave the country.

We notice a bird called namtambwé, which sings very nicely with a strong voice after dark here at the Misinjé confluence.

11th August, 1866.—Two headmen came down country from villages where we slept, bringing us food, and asking how we are treated; they advise our going south to Mukaté's, where the Lake is narrow.

12th-14th August, 1866.—Map making; but my energies were sorely taxed by the lazy sepoys, and I was usually quite tired out at night. Some men have come down from Mataka's, and report the arrival of an Englishman with cattle for me, "he has two eyes behind as well as two in front:" this is enough of news for awhile!

Mokalaosé has his little afflictions, and he tells me of them. A wife ran away, I asked how many he had; he told me twenty in all: I then thought he had nineteen too many. He answered with the usual reason, "But who would cook for strangers if I had but one?"

We saw clouds of "kungu" gnats on the Lake; they are not eaten here. An ungenerous traveller coming here with my statement in his hand, and finding the people denying all knowledge of how to catch and cook them, might say that I had been romancing in saying I had seen them made into cakes in the northern part of the Lake; when asking here about them, a stranger said, "They know how to use them in the north; we do not."

Mokalaosé thinks that the Arabs are afraid that I may take their dhows from them and go up to the north. He and the other headmen think that the best way will be to go to Mukaté's in the south. All the Arabs flee from me, the English name being in their minds inseparably connected with recapturing slavers: they cannot conceive that I have any other object in view; they cannot read Seyed Majid's letter.

21st August, 1866.—Started for the Loangwa, on the east side of the Lake; hilly all the way, about seven miles. This river may be twenty yards wide near its confluence; the Misinjé is double that: each has accumulated a promontory of deposit and enters the Lake near its apex. We got a house from a Waiyau man on a bank about forty feet above the level of Nyassa, but I could not sleep for the manoeuvres of a crowd of the minute ants which infested it. They chirrup distinctly; they would not allow the men to sleep either, though all were pretty tired by the rough road up.

22nd August, 1866.—We removed to the south side of the Loangwa, where there are none of these little pests.

23rd August, 1866.—Proposed to the Waiyau headman to send a canoe over to call Jumbé, as I did not believe in the assertions of the half-caste Arab here that he had sent for his. All the Waiyau had helped me, and why not he? He was pleased with this, but advised waiting till a man sent to Loséwa should return.

24th August, 1866.—A leopard took a dog out of a house next to ours; he had bitten a man before, but not mortally. *29th August,*

1866.—News come that the two dhows have come over to Loséwa (Loséfa). The Mazitu had chased Jumbé up the hills: had they said, on to an island, I might have believed them.

30th August,1866.—The fear which the English have inspired in the Arab slave-traders is rather inconvenient. All flee from me as if I had the plague, and I cannot in consequence transmit letters to the coast, or get across the Lake. They seem to think that if I get into a dhow I will be sure to burn it. As the two dhows on the Lake are used for nothing else but the slave-trade, their owners have no hope of my allowing them to escape, so after we have listened to various lies as excuses, we resolve to go southwards, and cross at the point of departure of the Shiré from the Lake. I took lunars several times on both sides of the moon, and have written a despatch for Lord Clarendon, besides a number of private letters.

3rd September, 1866.—Went down to confluence of the Misinjé and came to many of the eatable insect "kungu,"—they are caught by a quick motion of the hand holding a basket. We got a cake of these same insects further down; they make a buzz like a swarm of bees, and are probably the perfect state of some Lake insect.

I observed two beaches of the Lake: one about fifteen feet above the present high-water mark, and the other about forty above that; but between the two the process of disintegration, which results from the sudden cold and heat in these regions, has gone on so much that seldom is a well-rounded smoothed one seen; the lower beach is very well marked.

The strike of large masses of foliated gneiss is parallel with the major axis of the Lake, and all are tilted on edge. Some are a little inclined to the Lake, as if dipping to it westwards, but others are as much inclined the opposite way, or twisted.

I made very good blue ink from the juice of a berry, the fruit of a creeper, which is the colour of port wine when expressed. A little ferri carb. ammon., added to this is all that is required.

The poodle dog Chitané is rapidly changing the colour of its hair. All the parts corresponding to the ribs and neck are rapidly becoming red; the majority of country dogs are of this colour.

The Manganja, or Wa-nyassa, are an aboriginal race; they have great masses of hair, and but little, if any, of the prognathous in the profile. Their bodies and limbs are very well made, and the countenance of the men is often very pleasant. The women are very plain and lumpy, but exceedingly industrious in their gardens from early morning till about 11 A.M., then from 3 P.M. till dark, or pounding corn and grinding it: the men make twine or nets by day, and are at their fisheries in the evenings and nights. They build the huts, the women plaster them.

A black fish, the Nsaka, makes a hole, with raised edges, which, with the depth from which they are taken, is from fifteen to eighteen inches, and from two to three feet broad. It is called by the natives their house. The pair live in it for some time, or until the female becomes large for spawning; this operation over, the house is left.

I gave Mokalaosé some pumpkin seed and peas. He took me into his house, and presented a quantity of beer. I drank a little, and seeing me desist from taking more, he asked if I wished a servant-girl to "*pata mimba*." Not knowing what was meant, I offered the girl the calabash of beer, and told her to drink, but this was not the intention. He asked if I did not wish more; and then took the vessel, and as he drank the girl performed the operation on himself. Placing herself in front, she put both hands round his waist below the short ribs, and pressing gradually drew them round to his belly in front. He took several prolonged draughts, and at each she repeated the operation, as if to make the liquor go equally over the stomach. Our topers don't seem to have discovered the need for this.

5th September, 1866.—Our march is along the shore to Ngombo promontory, which approaches so near to Senga or Tsenga opposite, as to narrow the Lake to some sixteen or eighteen miles. It is a low sandy point, the edge fringed on the north-west and part of the south with a belt of papyrus and reeds; the central parts wooded. Part of the south side has high sandy dunes, blown up by the south wind, which strikes it at right angles there. One was blowing as we marched along the southern side eastwards, and was very tiresome. We reached Panthunda's village by a brook called Lilolé. Another we crossed before coming to it is named Libesa: these brooks form the favourite spawning grounds of the sanjika and mpasa, two of the best fishes of the Lake. The sanjika is very like our herring in shape and taste and size; the mpasa larger every way: both live on green herbage formed at the bottom of the Lake and rivers.

7th September, 1866.—Chirumba's village being on the south side of a long lagoon, we preferred sleeping on the mainland, though they offered their cranky canoes to ferry us over. This lagoon is called Pansangwa.

8th September, 1866.—In coming along the southern side of Ngombo promontory we look eastwards, but when we leave it we turn southwards, having a double range of lofty mountains on our left. These are granitic in form, the nearer range being generally the lowest, and covered with scraggy trees; the second, or more easterly, is some 6000 feet above the sea, bare and rugged, with jagged peaks shooting high into the air. This is probably the newest range. The oldest people have felt no earthquake, but some say that they have heard of such things from their elders.

We passed very many sites of old villages, which are easily known by the tree euphorbia planted round an umbelliferous one, and the sacred fig. One species here throws out strong buttresses in the manner of some mangroves instead of sending down twiners which take root, as is usually the ease with the tropical fig. These, with millstones—stones for holding the pots in cooking—and upraised clay benches, which have been turned into brick by fire in the destruction of the huts, show what were once the "pleasant haunts of men." No stone implements ever appear. If they existed they could not escape notice, since the eyes in walking are almost always directed to the ground to avoid stumbling on stones or stumps. In some parts of the world stone implements are so common they seem to have been often made and discarded as soon as formed, possibly by getting better tools; if, indeed, the manufacture is not as modern as that found by Mr. Waller. Passing some navvies in the City who were digging for the foundation of a house, he observed a very antique-looking vase, wet from the clay, standing on the bank. He gave ten shillings for it, and subsequently, by the aid of a scrubbing brush and some water, detected the hieroglyphics "Copeland late Spode" on the bottom of it!

Here the destruction is quite recent, and has been brought about by some who entertained us very hospitably on the Misinjé, before we came to the confluence. The woman chief, Ulenjelenjé, or Njelenjé, bore a part in it for the supply of Arab caravans. It was the work of the Masininga, a Waiyau tribe, of which her people form a part. They almost depopulated the broad fertile tract, of some three or four miles, between the mountain range and the Lake, along which our course lay. It was wearisome to see the skulls and bones scattered about everywhere; one would fain not notice them, but they are so striking as one trudges along the sultry path, that it cannot be avoided.

9th September, 1866.—We spent Sunday at Kandango's village. The men killed a hippopotamus when it was sleeping on the shore; a full-grown female, 10 feet 9 inches from the snout to the insertion of the tail, and 4 feet 4 inches high at the withers. The bottom here and all along southwards now is muddy. Many of the *Siluris Glanis* are caught equal in length to an eleven or a twelve-pound salmon, but a great portion is head; slowly roasted on a stick stuck in the ground before the fire they seemed to me much more savoury than I ever tasted them before. With the mud we have many shells: north of Ngombo scarcely one can be seen, and there it is sandy or rocky.

10th September, 1866.—In marching southwards we came close to the range (the Lake lies immediately on the other side of it), but we could not note the bays which it forms; we crossed two mountain torrents from sixty to eighty yards broad, and now only ankle deep. In flood these bring down enormous trees, which are much battered and bruised among the rocks in their course; they spread over the plain, too, and would render travelling here in the rains impracticable. After spending the night at a very civil headman's chefu, we crossed the Lotendé, another of these torrents: each very lofty mass in the range seemed to give rise to one. Nothing of interest occurred as we trudged along. A very poor headman, Pamawawa, presented a roll of salt instead of food: this was grateful to us, as we have been without that luxury some time.

12th September, 1866.—We crossed the rivulet Nguena, and then went on to another with a large village by it, it is called Pantoza Pangone. The headman had been suffering from sore eyes for four months, and pressed me to stop and give him medicine, which I did.

13th September, 1866.—We crossed a strong brook called Nkoré. My object in mentioning the brooks which were flowing at this time, and near the end of the dry season, is to give an idea of the sources of supply of evaporation. The men enumerate the following, north of the Misinjé. Those which are greater are marked thus +, and the lesser ones-.

1. Misinjé + has canoes.
2. Loangwa -
3. Leséfa -
4. Lelula -
5. Nchamanjé -
6. Musumba +
7. Fubwé +
8. Chia -
9. Kisanga +
10. Bweka -
11. Chifumero + has canoes.
12. Loangwa -
13. Mkoho -
14. Mangwelo -at N. end of Lake.

Including the above there are twenty or twenty-four perennial brooks and torrents which give a good supply of water in the dry season; in the wet season they are supplemented by a number of burns, which, though flowing now, have their mouths blocked up with bars of sand, and yield nothing except by percolation; the Lake rises at least four feet perpendicularly in the wet season, and has enough during the year from these perennial brooks to supply the Shiré's continual flow.

[It will be remembered that the beautiful river Shiré carries off the waters of Lake Nyassa and joins the Zambesi near Mount Morambala, about ninety miles from the sea. It is by this water-way that Livingstone always hoped to find an easy access to Central Africa. The only obstacles that exist are, first, the foolish policy of the Portuguese with regard to Customs' duties at the mouth of the Zambesi; and secondly, a succession of cataracts on the Shiré, which impede navigation for seventy miles. The first hindrance may give way under more liberal views than those which prevail at present at the Court of Lisbon, and then the remaining difficulty—accepted as a fact—will be solved by the establishment of a boat service both above and below the cataracts. Had Livingstone survived he would have been cheered by hearing that already several schemes are afoot to plant Missions in the vicinity of Lake Nyassa, and we may with confidence look to the revival of the very enterprise which he presently so bitterly deplores as a thing of the past, for Bishop Steere has fully determined to re-occupy the district in which fell his predecessor, Bishop Mackenzie, and others attached to the Universities Mission.]

In the course of this day's march we were pushed close to the Lake by Mount Gomé, and, being now within three miles of the end of the Lake, we could see the whole plainly. There we first saw the Shiré emerge, and there also we first gazed on the broad waters of Nyassa.

Many hopes have been disappointed here. Far down on the right bank of the Zambesi lies the dust of her whose death changed all my future prospects; and now, instead of a check being given to the slave-trade by lawful commerce on the Lake, slave-dhows prosper!

An Arab slave-party fled on hearing of us yesterday. It is impossible not to regret the loss of good Bishop Mackenzie, who sleeps far down the Shiré, and with him all hope of the Gospel being introduced into Central Africa. The silly abandonment of all the advantages of the Shiré route by the Bishop's successor I shall ever bitterly deplore, but all will come right some day, though I may not live to participate in the joy, or even see the commencement of better times.

In the evening we reached the village of Cherekalongwa on the brook Pamchololo, and were very jovially received by the headman with beer. He says that Mukaté,[19] Kabinga, and Mponda alone supply the slave-traders now by raids on the Manganja, but they go S.W. to the Maravi, who, impoverished by a Mazitu raid, sell each other as well.

14th, September, 1866.—At Cherekalongwa's (who has a skin disease, believed by him to have been derived from eating fresh-water turtles), we were requested to remain one day in order that he might see us. He had heard much about us; had been down the Shiré, and as far as Mosambique, but never had an Englishman in his town before. As the heat is great we were glad of the rest and beer, with which he very freely supplied us.

I saw the skin of a Phenembe, a species of lizard which devours chickens; here it is named Salka. It had been flayed by a cut up the back—body, 12 inches; across belly, 10 inches.

After nearly giving up the search for Dr. Roscher's point of reaching the Lake—because no one, either Arab or native, had the least idea of either Nusseewa or Makawa, the name given to the place—I discovered it in Lesséfa, the accentuated *é* being sounded as our *e* in *set*. This word would puzzle a German philologist, as being the origin of Nussewa, but the Waiyau pronounce it Loséwa, the Arabs Lusséwa, and Roscher's servant transformed the *L* and *é* into *N* and *ee*, hence Nusseewa. In confirmation of this rivulet Leséfa, which is opposite Kotakota, or, as the Arabs pronounce it, Nkotakota, the chief is Mangkaka (Makawa), or as there is a confusion of names as to chief it may be Mataka, whose town and district is called Moembé, the town Pamoembe = Mamemba.

I rest content with Kingomango so far verifying the place at which he arrived two months after we had discovered Lake Nyassa. He deserved all the credit due to finding the way thither, but he travelled as an Arab, and no one suspected him to be anything else. Our visits have been known far and wide, and great curiosity excited; but Dr. Roscher merits the praise only of preserving his *incognito* at a distance from Kilwa: his is almost the only case known of successfully assuming the Arab guise—Burckhardt is the exception. When Mr. Palgrave came to Muscat, or a town in Oman where our political agent Col. Desborough was stationed, he was introduced to that functionary by an interpreter as Hajee Ali, &c. Col. Desborough replied, "You are no Hajee Ali, nor anything else but Gifford Palgrave, with whom I was schoolfellow at the Charter House." Col. Desborough said he knew him at once, from a peculiar way of holding his head, and Palgrave begged him not to disclose his real character to his interpreter, on whom, and some others, he had been imposing. I was told this by Mr. Dawes, a Lieutenant in the Indian navy, who accompanied Colonel Pelly in his visit to the Nejed, Riad, &c, and took observations for him.

Tañgaré is the name of a rather handsome bean, which possesses intoxicating qualities. To extract these it is boiled, then peeled, and new water supplied: after a second and third boiling it is pounded, and the meal taken to the river and the water allowed to percolate through it several times. Twice cooking still leaves the intoxicating quality; but if eaten then it does not cause death: it is curious that the natives do not use it expressly to produce intoxication. When planted near a tree it grows all over it, and yields abundantly: the skin of the pod is velvety, like our broad beans.

Another bean, with a pretty white mark on it, grows freely, and is easily cooked, and good: it is here called *Gwingwiza*.

15th September, 1866.—We were now a short distance south of the Lake, and might have gone west to Mosauka's (called by some Pasauka's) to cross the Shiré there, but I thought that my visit to Mukaté's, a Waiyau chief still further south, might do good. He, Mponda, and Kabinga, are the only three chiefs who still carry on raids against the Manganja at the instigation of the coast Arabs, and they are now sending periodical marauding parties to the Maravi (here named Malola) to supply the Kilwa slave-traders. We marched three hours southwards, then up the hills of the range which flanks all the lower part of the Lake. The altitude of the town is about 800 feet above the Lake. The population near the chief is large, and all the heights as far as the eye can reach are crowned with villages. The second range lies a few miles off, and is covered with trees as well as the first, the nearest high mass is Mañgoché. The people live amidst plenty. All the chiefs visited by the Arabs have good substantial square houses built for their accommodation. Mukaté never saw a European before, and everything about us is an immense curiosity to him and to his people. We had long visits from him. He tries to extract a laugh out of every remark. He is darker than the generality of Waiyau, with a full beard trained on the chin, as all the people hereabouts have—Arab fashion. The courts of his women cover a large space, our house being on one side of them. I tried to go out that way, but wandered, so the ladies sent a servant to conduct me out in the direction I wished to go, and we found egress by passing through some huts with two doors in them.

16th September, 1866.—At Mukaté's. The Prayer Book does not give ignorant persons any idea of an unseen Being addressed, it looks more like reading or speaking to the book: kneeling and praying with eyes shut is better than, our usual way of holding Divine service.

We had a long discussion about the slave-trade. The Arabs have told the chief that our object in capturing slavers is to get them into our own possession, and make them of our own religion.

The evils which we have seen—the skulls, the ruined villages, the numbers who perish on the way to the coast and on the sea, the wholesale murders committed by the Waiyau to build up Arab villages elsewhere—these things Mukaté often tried to turn off with a laugh, but our remarks are safely lodged in many hearts. Next day, as we went along, our guide spontaneously delivered their substance to the different villages along our route. Before we reached him, a headman, in convoying me a mile or two, whispered to me, "Speak to Mukaté to give his forays up."

It is but little we can do, but we lodge a protest in the heart against a vile system, and time may ripen it. Their great argument is, "What could we do without Arab cloth?" My answer is, "Do what you did before the Arabs came into the country." At the present rate of destruction of population, the whole country will soon be a desert.

An earthquake happened here last year, that is about the end of it or beginning of this (the crater on the Grand. Comoro Island smoked for three months about that time); it shook all the houses and everything, but they observed no other effects.[20] No hot springs are known here.

17th September, 1866.—We marched down from Mukaté's and to about the middle of the Lakelet Pamalombé. Mukaté had no people with canoes near the usual crossing place, and he sent a messenger to see that we were fairly served. Here we got the Manganja headmen to confess that an earthquake had happened; all the others we have inquired of have denied it; why, I cannot conceive. The old men said that they had felt earthquakes twice, once near sunset and the next time at night—they shook everything, and were accompanied with noise, and all the fowls cackled; there was no effect on the Lake observed. They profess ignorance of any tradition of the water having stood higher. Their traditions say that they came originally from the west, or west north-west, which they call "Maravi;" and that their forefathers taught them to make nets and kill fish. They have no trace of any teaching by a higher instructor; no carvings or writings on the rocks; and they never heard of a book until we came among them. Their forefathers never told them that after or at death they went to God, but they had heard it said of such a one who died, "God took him."

18th September, 1866.—We embarked the whole party in eight canoes, and went up the Lake to the point of junction between it and the prolongation of Nyassa above it, called Massangano ("meetings"), which took us two hours. A fishing party there fled on seeing us, though we shouted that we were a travelling party (or "Olendo ").

Mukaté's people here left us, and I walked up to the village of the fugitives with one attendant only. Their suspicions were so thoroughly aroused that they would do nothing. The headman (Pima) was said to be absent; they could not lend us a hut, but desired us to go on to Mponda's. We put up a shed for ourselves, and next morning, though we pressed them for a guide, no one would come.

From Pima's village we had a fine view of Pamalombé and the range of hills on its western edge, the range which flanks the lower part of Nyassa,—on part of which Mukaté lives,—the gap of low land south of it behind which Shirwa Lake lies, and Chikala and Zomba nearly due south from us. People say hippopotami come from Lake Shirwa into Lake Nyassa. There is a great deal of vegetation in Pamalombé, gigantic rushes, duckweed, and great quantities of aquatic plants on the bottom; one slimy translucent plant is washed ashore in abundance. Fish become very fat on these plants; one called "kadiakola" I eat much of; it has a good mass of flesh on it.

It is probable that the people of Lake Tanganyika and Nyassa, and those on the Rivers Shiré and Zambesi, are all of one stock, for the dialects vary very little.[21] I took observations on this point. An Arab slave-party, hearing of us, decamped.

19th September, 1866.—When we had proceeded a mile this morning we came to 300 or 400 people making salt on a plain impregnated with it. They lixiviate the soil and boil the water, which has filtered through a bunch of grass in a hole in the bottom of a pot, till all is evaporated and a mass of salt left. We held along the plain till we came to Mponda's, a large village, with a stream running past. The plain at the village is very fertile, and has many large trees on it. The cattle of Mponda are like fatted Madagascar beasts, and the hump seems as if it would weigh 100 lbs.[22] The size of body is so enormous that their legs, as remarked by our men, seemed very small. Mponda is a blustering sort of person, but immensely interested in everything European. He says that he would like to go with me. "Would not care though he were away ten years." I say that he may die in the journey.—"He will die here as well as there, but he will see all the wonderful doings of our country." He knew me, having come to the boat, to take a look *incognito* when we were here formerly.

We found an Arab slave-party here, and went to look at the slaves; seeing this; Mponda was alarmed lest we should proceed to violence in his town, but I said to him that we went to look only. Eighty-five slaves were in a pen formed of dura stalks *(Holcus sorghum)*. The majority were boys of about eight or ten years of age; others were grown men and women. Nearly all were in the taming-stick; a few of the younger ones were in thongs, the thong passing round the neck of each. Several pots were on the fires cooking dura and beans. A crowd went with us, expecting a scene, but I sat down, and asked a few questions about the journey, in front. The slave-party consisted of five or six half-caste coast Arabs, who said that they came from Zanzibar; but the crowd made such a noise that we could not hear ourselves speak. I asked if they had any objections to my looking at the slaves, the owners pointed out the different slaves, and said that after feeding them, and accounting for the losses in the way to the coast, they made little by the trip. I suspect that the gain is made by those who ship them to the ports of Arabia, for at Zanzibar most of the younger slaves we saw went at about seven dollars a head. I said to them it was a bad business altogether. They presented fowls to me in the evening.

20th September, 1866.—The chief begged so hard that I would stay another day and give medicine to a sick child, that I consented. He promised plenty of food, and, as an earnest of his sincerity, sent an immense pot of beer in the evening. The child had been benefited by the medicine given yesterday. He offered more food than we chose to take.

The agricultural class does not seem to be a servile one: all cultivate, and the work is esteemed. The chief was out at his garden when we arrived, and no disgrace is attached to the field labourer. The slaves very likely do the chief part of the work, but all engage in it, and are proud of their skill. Here a great deal of grain is raised, though nearly all the people are Waiyau or Machinga. This is remarkable, as they have till lately been marauding and moving from place to place. The Manganja possessed the large breed of humped cattle which fell into the hands of the Waiyau, and knew how to milk them. Their present owners never milk them, and they have dwindled into a few instead of the thousands of former times.[23]

A lion killed a woman early yesterday morning, and ate most of her undisturbed.

It is getting very hot; the ground to the feet of the men "burns like fire" after noon, so we are now obliged to make short marches, and early in the morning chiefly.

Wikatani—Bishop Mackenzie's favourite boy—met a brother here, and he finds that he has an elder brother and a sister at Kabinga's. The father who sold him into slavery is dead. He wishes to stop with his relatives, and it will be well if he does. Though he has not much to say, what he does advance against the slave-trade will have its weight, and it will all be in the way of preparation for better times and more light.

The elder brother was sent for, but had not arrived when it was necessary for us to leave Mponda's on the Rivulet Ntemangokwé. I therefore gave Wikatani some cloth, a flint gun instead of the percussion one he carried, some flints, paper to write upon, and commended him to Mponda's care till his relatives arrived. He has lately shown a good deal of levity, and perhaps it is best that he should have a touch of what the world is in reality.

[In a letter written about this time Dr. Livingstone, in speaking of Wikatani, says, "He met with a brother, and found that he had two brothers and one or two sisters living down at the western shore of Lake Pamelombé under Kabinga. He thought that his relatives would not again sell him. I had asked him if he wished to remain, and he at once said yes, so I did not attempt to dissuade him: his excessive levity will perhaps be cooled by marriage. I think he may do good by telling some of what he has seen and heard. I asked him if he would obey an order from his chief to hunt the Manganja, and he said, 'No.' I hope he won't. In the event of any mission coming into the country of Mataka, he will go there. I gave him paper to write to you,[24] and, commending him to the chiefs, bade the poor boy farewell. I was sorry to part with him, but the Arabs tell the Waiyau chiefs that our object in liberating slaves is to make them our own and turn them to our religion. I had declared to them, through Wikatani as interpreter, that they never became our slaves, and were at liberty to go back to their relatives if they liked; and now it was impossible to object to Wikatani going without stultifying my own statements." It is only necessary to repeat that Wikatani and Chuma had been liberated from the slavers by Dr. Livingstone and Bishop Mackenzie in 1861; they were mere children when set free.

We must not forget to record the fact that when Mr. Young reached Maponda, two years afterwards, to ascertain whether the Doctor really had been murdered, as Musa declared, he was most hospitably received by the chief, who had by this time a great appreciation of everything English.]

The lines of tattoo of the different tribes serve for ornaments, and are resorted to most by the women; it is a sort of heraldry closely resembling the Highland tartans.

Manganja and Machinga women.

FOOTNOTES:

16. Coal was shown to a group of natives when first the *Pioneer* ascended the river Shiré. Members of numerous tribes were present, and all recognised it at once as Makala or coal.—ED.

17. Dr. Livingstone heard this subsequently when at Casembe's.

18. The greater part were driven down into the Manganja country by war and famine combined, and eventually filled the slave gangs of the Portuguese, whose agents went from Tette and Senna to procure them.—ED.

19. Pronounced Mkata by the Waiyau.—ED.

20. Earthquakes are by no means uncommon. A slight shock was felt in 1861 at Magomero; on asking the natives if they knew the cause of it, they replied that on one occasion, after a very severe earthquake which shook boulders off the mountains, all the wise men of the country assembled to talk about it and came to the following conclusion, that a star had fallen from heaven into the sea, and that the bubbling caused the whole earth to rock; they said the effect was the same as that caused by throwing, a red-hot stone into a pot of water.—ED.

21. The Waiyau language differs very much from the Nyassa, and is exceedingly difficult to master: it holds good from the coast to Nyassa, but to the west of the Lake the Nyassa tongue is spoken over a vast tract.—ED.

22. We shall see that more to the north the hump entirely disappears.

23. It is very singular to witness the disgust with which the idea of drinking milk is received by most of these tribes when we remember that the Caffre nations on the south, and again, tribes more to the north, subsist principally on it. A lad will undergo punishment rather than milk a goat. Eggs are likewise steadily eschewed.—ED.

24. To myself.—ED.

* * * * *

CHAPTER V.

Crosses Cape Maclear. The havildar demoralised. The discomfited chief. Beaches Marenga's town. The earth-sponge. Description of Marenga's town. Rumours of Mazitu. Musa and the Johanna men desert. Beaches Kimsusa's. His delight at seeing the Doctor once more. The fat ram. Kimsusa relates his experience of Livingstone's advice. Chuma finds relatives. Kimsusa solves the transport difficulty nobly. Another old fishing acquaintance. Description of the people and country on the west of the Lake. The Kanthundas. Kauma. Iron-smelting. An African Sir Colin Campbell. Milandos.

21st September, 1866.—We marched westwards, making across the base of Cape Maclear. Two men employed as guides and carriers, went along grumbling that their dignity was so outraged by working—"only fancy Waiyau carrying like slaves!!" They went but a short distance, and took advantage of my being in front to lay down the loads, one of which consisted of the havildar's bed and cooking things; here they opened the other bundle and paid themselves— the gallant havildar sitting and looking on. He has never been of the smallest use, and lately has pretended to mysterious pains in his feet; no swelling or other symptom accompanied this complaint. On coming to Pima's village he ate a whole fowl and some fish for supper, slept soundly till daybreak, then on awaking commenced a furious groaning—"feet were so bad." I told him that people usually moaned when insensible, but he had kept quiet till he awaked; he sulked at this, and remained all day, though I sent a man to carry his kit for him, and when he came up he had changed the seat of his complaint from his feet to any part of his abdomen. He gave off his gun-belt and pouch to the carrier. This was a blind to me, for I examined and found that he had already been stealing and selling his ammunition: this is all preparatory to returning to the coast with some slave-trader. Nothing can exceed the ease and grace with which sepoys can glide from a swagger into the most abject begging of food from the villagers. He has remained behind.

22nd September, 1866.—The hills we crossed were about 700 feet above Nyassa, generally covered with trees; no people were seen. We slept by the brook Sikoché. Rocks of hardened sandstone rested on mica schist, which had an efflorescence of alum on it, above this was dolomite; the hills often capped with it and oak-spar, giving a snowy appearance. We had a Waiyau party with us—six handsomely-attired women carried huge pots of beer for their husbands, who very liberally invited us to partake. After seven hours' hard travelling we came to the village, where we spend Sunday by the torrent Usangazi, and near a remarkable mountain, Namasi. The chief, a one-eyed man, was rather coy—coming *incognito* to visit us; and, as I suspected that he was present, I asked if the chief were an old woman, afraid to look at and welcome a stranger? All burst into a laugh, and looked at him, when he felt forced to join in it, and asked what sort of food we liked best. Chuma put this clear enough by saying, "He eats everything eaten by the Waiyau." This tribe, or rather the Machinga, now supersede the Manganja. We passed one village of the latter near this, a sad, tumble-down affair, while the Waiyau villages are very neat, with handsome straw or reed fences all around their huts.

24th September, 1866.—We went only 2-1/2 miles to the village of Marenga, a very large one, situated at the eastern edge of the bottom of the heel of the Lake. The chief is ill of a loathsome disease derived direct from the Arabs. Raised patches of scab of circular form disfigure the face and neck as well as other parts. His brother begged me to see him and administer some remedy for the same complaint. He is at a village a little way off, and though sent for, was too ill to come or to be carried. The tribe is of Babisa origin. Many of these people had gone to the coast as traders, and returning with arms and ammunition joined the Waiyau in their forays on the Manganja, and eventually set themselves up as an independent tribe. The women do not wear the lip-ring, though the majority of them are Waiyau. They cultivate largely, and have plenty to eat. They have cattle, but do not milk them.

The bogs, or earthen sponges,[25] of this country occupy a most important part in its physical geography, and probably explain the annual inundations of most of the rivers. Wherever a plain sloping towards a narrow opening in hills or higher ground exists, there we have the conditions requisite for the formation of an African sponge. The vegetation, not being of a heathy or peat-forming kind, falls down, rots, and then forms rich black loam. In many cases a mass of this loam, two or three feet thick, rests on a bed of pure river sand, which is revealed by crabs and other aquatic animals bringing it to the surface. At present, in the dry season, the black loam is cracked in all directions, and the cracks are often as much as three inches wide, and very deep. The whole surface has now fallen down, and rests on the sand, but when the rains come, the first supply is nearly all absorbed in the sand. The black loam forms soft slush, and floats on the sand. The narrow opening prevents it from moving off in a landslip, but an oozing spring rises at that spot. All the pools in the lower portion of this spring-course are filled by the first rains, which happen south of the equator when the sun goes vertically over any spot. The second, or greater rains, happen in his course north again, when all the bogs and river-courses being wet, the supply runs off, and forms the inundation: this was certainly the case as observed on the Zambesi and Shiré, and, taking the different times for the sun's passage north of the equator, it explains the inundation of the Nile.

25th September, 1866.—Marenga's town on the west shore of Lake Nyassa is very large, and his people collected in great numbers to gaze at the stranger. The chief's brother asked a few questions, and I took the occasion to be a good one for telling him something about the Bible and the future state. The men said that their fathers had never told them aught about the soul, but they thought that the whole man rotted and came to nothing. What I said was very nicely put by a volunteer spokesman, who seemed to have a gift that way, for all listened most attentively, and especially when told that our Father in heaven loved all, and heard prayers addressed to Him.

Marenga came dressed in a red-figured silk shawl, and attended by about ten court beauties, who spread a mat for him, then a cloth above, and sat down as if to support him. He asked me to examine his case inside a hut. He exhibited his loathsome skin disease, and being blacker than his wives, the blotches with which he was covered made him appear very ugly. He thought that the disease was in the country before Arabs came. Another new disease acquired from them was the small-pox.

26th September, 1866.—An Arab passed us yesterday, his slaves going by another route across the base of Cape Maclear. He told Musa that all the country in front was full of Mazitu; that forty-four Arabs and their followers had been killed by them at Kasungu, and he only escaped. Musa and all the Johanna men now declared that they would go no farther. Musa said, "No good country that; I want to go back to Johanna to see my father and mother and son." I took him to Marenga, and asked the chief about the Mazitu. He explained that the disturbance was caused by the Manganja finding that Jumbé brought Arabs and ammunition into the country every year, and they resented it in consequence; they would not allow more to come, because they were the sufferers, and their nation was getting destroyed.

I explained to Musa that we should avoid the Mazitu: Marenga added, "There are no Mazitu near where you are going;" but Musa's eyes *stood out* with terror, and he said, "I no can believe that man." But I inquired, "How can you believe the Arab so easily?" Musa answered, "I ask him to tell me true, and he say true, true," &c.

When we started, all the Johanna men walked off, leaving the goods on the ground. They have been such inveterate thieves that I am not sorry to get rid of them; for though my party is now inconveniently small, I could not trust them with flints in their guns, nor allow them to remain behind, for their object was invariably to plunder their loads.

[Here then we have Livingstone's account of the origin of that well-told story, which at first seemed too true. How Mr. Edward Young, R.N., declared it to be false, and subsequently proved it untrue, is already well known. This officer's quick voyage to Lake Nyassa reflected the greatest credit on him, and all hearts were filled with joy when he returned and reported the tale of Livingstone's murder to be merely an invention of Musa and his comrades.]

I ought to mention that the stealing by the Johanna men was not the effect of hunger; it attained its height when we had plenty.

If one remained behind, we knew his object in delaying was stealing. He gave what he filched to the others, and Musa shared the dainties they bought with the stolen property. When spoken to he would say, "I every day tell Johanna men no steal Doctor's things." As he came away and left them in the march, I insisted out his bringing up all his men; this he did not relish, and the amount stolen was not small. One stole fifteen pounds of fine powder, another seven, another left six table-cloths out of about twenty-four; another called out to a man to bring a fish, and he would buy it with beads, the beads being stolen, and Musa knew it all and connived at it; but it was terror that drove him away at last.

With our goods in canoes we went round the bottom of the heel of Nyassa, slept among reeds, and next morning (27th) landed at Msangwa, which is nearly opposite Kimsusa's, or Katosa's, as the Makololo called him. A man had been taken off by a crocodile last night; he had been drinking beer, and went down to the water to cool himself, where he lay down, and the brute seized him. The water was very muddy, being stirred up by an east wind, which lashed the waves into our canoes, and wetted our things. The loud wail of the women is very painful to hear; it sounds so dolefully.

28th, September, 1866.—We reached Kinisusa's, below Mount Mulundini, of Kirk's range.[26] The chief was absent, but he was sent for immediately: his town has much increased since I saw it last.

29th September, 1866.—Another Arab passed last night, with the tale that his slaves had all been taken from him by the Mazitu. It is more respectable to be robbed by them than by the Manganja, who are much despised and counted nobodies. I propose to go west of this among the Maravi until quite away beyond the disturbances, whether of Mazitu or Manganja.

30th September, 1866.—We enjoy our Sunday here. We have abundance of food from Kimsusa's wife. The chief wished me to go alone and enjoy his drinking bout, and then we could return to this place together; but this was not to my taste.

1st October, 1866.—Kimsusa, or Mehusa, came this morning, and seemed very glad again to see his old friend. He sent off at once to bring an enormous ram, which had either killed or seriously injured a man. The animal came tied to a pole to keep him off the man who held it, while a lot more carried him. He was prodigiously fat;[27] this is a true African way of showing love—plenty of fat and beer. Accordingly the chief brought a huge basket of "pombe," the native beer, and another of "nsima," or porridge, and a pot of cooked meat; to these were added a large basket of maize. So much food had been brought to us, that we had at last to explain that we could not carry it.

[The Doctor states a fact in the next few lines which shows that the Africans readily profit by advice which appeals to their common sense, and we make this observation in full knowledge of similar instances.]

Kimsusa says that they felt earthquakes at the place Mponda now occupies, but none where he is now. He confirms the tradition that the Manganja came from the west or W.N.W. He speaks more rationally about the Deity than some have done, and adds, that it was by following the advice which I gave him the last time I saw him, and not selling his people, that his village is now three times its former size. He has another village besides, and he was desirous that I should see that too; that was the reason he invited me to come, but the people would come and visit me.

2nd October, 1866.—Kimsusa made his appearance early with a huge basket of beer, 18 inches high and 15 inches in diameter. He served it out for a time, taking deep draughts himself, becoming extremely loquacious in consequence. He took us to a dense thicket behind his town, among numbers of lofty trees, many of which I have seen nowhere else; that under which we sat bears a fruit in clusters, which is eatable, and called "*Mbedwa.*" A space had been cleared, and we were taken to this shady spot as the one in which business of importance and secrecy is transacted. Another enormous basket of beer was brought here by his wives, but there was little need for it, for Kimsusa talked incessantly, and no business was done.

3rd October, 1866.—The chief came early, and sober. I rallied him on his previous loquacity, and said one ought to find time in the morning if business was to be done: he took it in good part, and one of his wives joined in bantering him. She is *the* wife and the mother of the sons in whom he delights, and who will succeed him. I proposed to him to send men with me to the Babisa country, and I would pay them there, where they could buy ivory for him with the pay, and, bringing it back, he would be able to purchase clothing without selling his people. He says that his people would not bring the pay or anything else back. When he sends to purchase ivory he gives the price to Arabs or Babisa, and they buy for him and conduct his business honestly; but his people, the Manganja, cannot be trusted: this shows a remarkable state of distrust, and, from previous information, it is probably true.

A party of the Arab Khambuiri's people went up lately to the Maravi country above this, and immediately west of Kirk's range, to purchase slaves: but they were attacked by the Maravi, and dispersed with slaughter: this makes Kimsusa's people afraid to venture there. They had some quarrel with the Maravi also of their own, and no intercourse now took place. A path further south was followed by Mponda lately, and great damage done, so it would not be wise to go on his footsteps. Kimsusa said he would give me carriers to go up to the Maravi, but he wished to be prepaid: to this I agreed, but even then he could not prevail on anyone to go. He then sent for an old Mobisa man, who has a village under him, and acknowledges Kimsusa's power. He says that he fears that, should he force his Manganja to go, they would leave us on the road, or run away on the first appearance of danger; but this Mobisa man would be going to his own country, and would stick by us. Meanwhile the chief overstocks us with beer and other food.

4th October, 1866.—The Mobisa man sent for came, but was so ignorant of his own country, not knowing the names of the chief Babisa town or any of the rivers, that I declined his guidance. He would only have been a clog on us; and anything about the places in front of us we could ascertain at the villages where we touch by inquiry as well as he could.

A woman turned up here, and persuaded Chuma that she was his aunt. He wanted to give her at once a fathom of calico and beads, and wished me to cut his pay down for the purpose. I persuaded him to be content with a few beads for her. He gave her his spoon and some other valuables, fully persuaded that she was a relative, though he was interrogated first as to his father's name, and tribe, &c., before she declared herself.

It shows a most forgiving disposition on the part of these boys to make presents to those who, if genuine relations, actually sold them. But those who have been caught young, know nothing of the evils of slavery, and do not believe in its ills. Chuma, for instance, believes now that he was caught and sold by the Manganja, and not by his own Waiyau, though it was just in the opposite way that he became a slave, and he asserted and believes that no Waiyau ever sold his own child. When reminded that Wikatani was sold by his own father, he denied it; then that the father of Chimwala, another boy, sold him, his mother, and sister, he replied, "These are Machinga." This is another tribe of Waiyau; but this showed that he was determined to justify his countrymen at any rate. I mention this matter, because though the Oxford and Cambridge Mission have an advantage in the instruction of boys taken quite young from slavers, yet these same boys forget the evils to which they were exposed and from which they were rescued, and it is even likely that they will, like Chuma, deny that any benefit was conferred upon them by their deliverance. This was not stated broadly by Chuma, but his tone led one to believe that he was quite ready to return to the former state.

5th October, 1866.—The chief came early with an immense basket of beer, as usual. We were ready to start: he did not relish this; but I told him it was clear that his people set very light by his authority. He declared that he would force them or go himself, with his wives as carriers. This dawdling and guzzling had a bad effect on my remaining people. Simon, a Nassick lad, for instance, overheard two words which he understood; these were "Mazitu" and "lipululu," or desert; and from these he conjured up a picture of Mazitu rushing out upon us from the jungle, and killing all without giving us time to say a word! To this he added scraps of distorted information: Khambuiri was a very bad chief in front, &c., all showing egregious cowardice; yet he came to give me advice. On asking what he knew (as he could not speak the language), he replied that he heard the above two words, and that Chuma could not translate them, but he had caught them, and came to warn me.

The chief asked me to stay over to-day, and he would go with his wives to-morrow; I was his friend, and he would not see me in difficulties without doing his utmost. He says that there is no danger of our not finding people for carrying loads. It is probable that Khambuiri's people went as marauders, and were beaten off in consequence.

6th October, 1866.—We marched about seven miles to the north to a village opposite the pass Tapiri, and on a rivulet, Godedza. It was very hot. Kimsusa behaves like a king: his strapping wives came to carry loads, and shame his people. Many of the young men turned out and took the loads, but it was evident that they feared retaliation if they ventured up the pass. One wife carried beer, another meal; and as soon as we arrived, cooking commenced: porridge and roasted goat's flesh made a decent meal. A preparation of meal called "Toku" is very refreshing and brings out all the sugary matter in the grain: he gave me some in the way, and, seeing I liked it, a calabash full was prepared for me in the evening. Kimsusa delights in showing me to his people as his friend. If I could have used his pombe, or beer, it would have put some fat on my bones, but it requires a strong digestion; many of the chiefs and their wives live on it almost entirely. A little flesh is necessary to relieve the acidity it causes; and they keep all flesh very carefully, no matter how high it may become: drying it on a stage over a fire prevents entire putridity.

7th October, 1866.—I heard hooping-cough[28] in the village. We found our visitors so disagreeable that I was glad to march; they were Waiyau, and very impudent, demanding gun or game medicine to enable them to shoot well: they came into the hut uninvited, and would take no denial. It is probable that the Arabs drive a trade in gun medicine: it is inserted in cuts made above the thumb, and on the forearm. Their superciliousness shows that they feel themselves to be the dominant race. The Manganja trust to their old bows and arrows; they are much more civil than Ajawa or Waiyau.

[The difference between these two great races is here well worthy of the further notice which Livingstone no doubt would have given it. As a rule, the Manganja are extremely clever in all the savage arts and manufactures. Their looms turn out a strong serviceable cotton cloth; their iron weapons and implements show a taste for design which is not reached by the neighbouring tribes, and in all matters that relate to husbandry they excel: but in dash and courage they are deficient. The Waiyau, on the contrary, have round apple-shaped heads, as distinguished from the long well-shaped heads of the poor Manganja; they are jocular and merry, given to travelling, and bold in war—these are qualities which serve them well as they are driven from pillar to post through slave wars and internal dissension, but they have not the brains of the Manganja, nor the talent to make their mark in any direction where brains are wanted.]

A Manganja man, who formerly presented us with the whole haul of his net, came and gave me four fowls: some really delight in showing kindness. When we came near the bottom of the pass Tapiri, Kimsusa's men became loud against his venturing further; he listened, then burst away from them: he listened again, then did the same; and as he had now got men for us, I thought it better to let him go.

In three hours and a quarter we had made a clear ascent of 2200 feet above the Lake. The first persons we met were two men and a boy, who were out hunting with a dog and basket-trap. This is laid down in the run of some small animal; the dog chases it, and it goes into the basket which is made of split bamboo, and has prongs looking inwards, which prevent its egress: mouse traps are made in the same fashion. I suspected that the younger of the men had other game in view, and meant, if fit opportunity offered, to insert an arrow in a Waiyau, who was taking away his wife as a slave. He told me before we had gained the top of the ascent that some Waiyau came to a village, separated from his by a small valley, picked a quarrel with the inhabitants, and then went and took the wife and child of a poorer countryman to pay these pretended offences.

8th October, 1866.—At the first village we found that the people up here and those down below were mutually afraid of each other. Kimsusa came to the bottom of the range, his last act being the offer of a pot of beer, and a calabash of Toku, which latter was accepted. I paid his wives for carrying our things: they had done well, and after we gained the village where we slept, sang and clapped their hands vigorously till one o'clock in the morning, when I advised them to go to sleep. The men he at last provided were very faithful and easily satisfied. Here we found the headman, Kawa, of Mpalapala, quite as hospitable. In addition to providing a supper, it is the custom to give breakfast before starting. Resting on the 8th to make up for the loss of rest on Sunday; we marched on Tuesday (the 9th), but were soon brought to a stand by Gombwa, whose village, Tamiala, stands on another ridge.

Gombwa, a laughing, good-natured man, said that he had sent for all his people to see me; and I ought to sleep, to enable them to look on one the like of whom had never come their way before. Intending to go on, I explained some of my objects in coming through the country, advising the people to refrain from selling each other, as it ends in war and depopulation. He was cunning, and said, "Well, you must sleep here, and all my people will come and hear those words of peace." I explained that I had employed carriers, who expected to be paid though I had gone but a small part of a day; he replied, "But they will go home and come again to-morrow, and it will count but one day." I was thus constrained to remain.

9th October, 1866.—Both barometer and boiling-point showed an altitude of upwards of 4000 feet above the sea. This is the hottest month, but the air is delightfully clear, and delicious. The country is very fine, lying in long slopes, with mountains rising all around, from 2000 to 3000 feet above this upland. They are mostly jagged and rough (not rounded like those near to Mataka's): the long slopes are nearly denuded of trees, and the patches of cultivation are so large and often squarish in form, that but little imagination is requisite to transform the whole into the cultivated fields of England; but no hedgerows exist. The trees are in clumps on the tops of the ridges, or at the villages, or at the places of sepulture. Just now the young leaves are out, but are not yet green. In some lights they look brown, but with transmitted light, or when one is near them, crimson prevails. A yellowish-green is met sometimes in the young leaves, and brown, pink, and orange-red. The soil is rich, but the grass is only excessively rank in spots; in general it is short. A kind of trenching of the ground is resorted to; they hoe deep, and draw it well to themselves: this exposes the other earth to the hoe. The soil is burned too: the grass and weeds are placed in flat heaps, and soil placed over them: the burning is slow, and most of the products of combustion are retained to fatten the field; in this way the people raise large crops. Men and women and children engage in field labour, but at present many of the men are engaged in spinning buazé[29] and cotton. The former is made into a coarse sacking-looking stuff, immensely strong, which seems to be worn by the women alone; the men are clad in uncomfortable goatskins. No wild animals seem to be in the country, and indeed the population is so large they would have very unsettled times of it. At every turning we meet people, or see their villages; all armed with bows and arrows. The bows are unusually long: I measured one made of bamboo, and found that along the bowstring it measured six feet four inches. Many carry large knives of fine iron; and indeed the metal is abundant. Young men and women wear the hair long, a mass of small ringlets comes down and rests on the shoulders, giving them the appearance of the ancient Egyptians. One side is often cultivated, and the mass hangs jauntily on that side; some few have a solid cap of it. Not many women wear the lip-ring: the example of the Waiyau has prevailed so far; but some of the young women have raised lines crossing each other on the arms, which must have cost great pain: they have also small cuts, covering in some cases the whole body. The Maravi or Manganja here may be said to be in their primitive state. We find them very liberal with their food: we give a cloth to the headman of the village where we pass the night, and he gives a goat, or at least cooked fowls and porridge, at night and morning.

Tattoo on Women.

We were invited by Gombwa in the afternoon to speak the same words to his people that we used to himself in the morning. He nudged a boy to respond, which is considered polite, though he did it only with a rough hem! at the end of each sentence. As for our general discourse we mention our relationship to our Father: His love to all His children—the guilt of selling any of His children—the consequence; *e.g.* it begets war, for they don't like to sell their own, and steal from other villagers, who retaliate. Arabs and Waiyau invited into the country by their selling, foster feuds, and war and depopulation ensue. We mention the Bible—future state—prayer: advise union, that they should unite as one family to expel enemies, who came first as slave-traders, and ended by leaving the country a wilderness. In reference to union, we showed that they ought to have seen justice done to the man who lost his wife and child at their very doors; but this want of cohesion is the bane of the Manganja. If the evil does not affect themselves they don't care whom it injures; and Gombwa confirmed this, by saying that when he routed Khambuiri's people, the villagers west of him fled instead of coming to his aid.

We hear that many of the Manganja up here are fugitives from Nyassa.

10th October, 1866.—Kawa and his people were with us early this morning, and we started from Tamiala with them. The weather is lovely, and the scenery, though at present tinged with yellow from the grass, might be called glorious. The bright sun and delicious air are quite exhilarating. We passed a fine flowing rivulet, called Levizé, going into the Lake, and many smaller runnels of delicious cold water. On resting by a dark sepulchral grove, a tree attracted the attention, as nowhere else seen: it is called Bokonto, and said to bear eatable fruit. Many fine flowers were just bursting into full blossom. After about four hours' march we put up at Chitimba, the village of Kañgomba, and were introduced by Kawa, who came all the way for the purpose.

11th October, 1866.—A very cold morning, with a great bank of black clouds in the east, whence the wind came. Therm. 59°; in hut 69°. The huts are built very well. The roof, with the lower part plastered, is formed so as not to admit a ray of light, and the only visible mode of ingress for it is by the door. This case shows that winter is cold: on proposing to start, breakfast was not ready: then a plan was formed to keep me another day at a village close by, belonging to one Kulu, a man of Kauma, to whom we go next. It was effectual, and here we are detained another day. A curiously cut-out stool is in my hut, made by the Mkwisa, who are south-west of this: it is of one block, but hollowed out, and all the spaces indicated are hollow too: about 2-1/2 feet long by 1-1/2 foot high.

Curiously cut-out stool of one block of wood.

12th October, 1866.—We march westerly, with a good deal of southing. Kulu gave us a goat, and cooked liberally for us all. He set off with us as if to go to Kauma's in our company, but after we had gone a couple of miles he slipped behind, and ran away. Some are naturally mean, and some naturally noble: the mean cannot help showing their nature, nor can the noble; but the noble-hearted must enjoy life most. Kulu got a cloth, and he gave us at least its value; but he thought he had got more than he gave, and so by running away that he had done us nicely, without troubling himself to go and introduce us to Kauma. I usually request a headman of a village to go with us. They give a good report of us, if for no other reason than for their own credit, because no one likes to be thought giving his countenance to people other than respectable, and it costs little.

We came close to the foot of several squarish mountains, having perpendicular sides. One, called "Ulazo pa Malungo," is used by the people, whose villages cluster round its base as a storehouse for grain. Large granaries stand on its top, containing food to be used in case of war. A large cow is kept up there, which is supposed capable of knowing and letting the owners know when war is coming.[30] There is a path up, but it was not visible to us. The people are all Kanthunda, or climbers, not Maravi. Kimsusa said that he was the only Maravi chief, but this I took to be an ebullition of beer bragging: the natives up here, however, confirm this, and assert that they are not Maravi, who are known by having markings down the side of the face.

We spent the night at a Kanthunda village on the western side of a mountain called Phunzé (the *h* being an aspirate only). Many villages arc planted round its base, but in front, that is, westwards, we have plains, and there the villages are as numerous: mostly they are within half a mile of each other, and few are a mile from other hamlets. Each village has a clump of trees around it: this is partly for shade and partly for privacy from motives of decency. The heat of the sun causes the effluvia to exhale quickly, so they are seldom offensive. The rest of the country, where not cultivated, is covered with grass, the seed-stalks about knee deep. It is gently undulating, lying in low waves, stretching N.E. and S.W. The space between each wave is usually occupied by a boggy spot or watercourse, which in some cases is filled with pools with trickling rills between. All the people are engaged at present in making mounds six or eight feet square, and from two to three feet high. The sods in places not before hoed are separated from the soil beneath and collected into flattened heaps, the grass undermost; when dried, fire is applied and slow combustion goes on, most of the products of the burning being retained in the ground, much of the soil is incinerated. The final preparation is effected by the men digging up the subsoil round the mound, passing each hoeful into the left hand, where it pulverizes, and is then thrown on to the heap. It is thus virgin soil on the top of the ashes and burned ground of the original heap, very clear of weeds. At present many mounds have beans and maize about four inches high. Holes, a foot in diameter and a few inches deep, are made irregularly over the surface of the mound, and about eight or ten grains put into each: these are watered by hand and calabash, and kept growing till the rains set in, when a very early crop is secured.

13th October, 1866.—After leaving Phunzé, we crossed the Leviñgé, a rivulet which flows northwards, and then into Lake Nyassa; the lines of gentle undulation tend in that direction. Some hills appear on the plains, but after the mountains which we have left behind they are mere mounds. We are over 3000 feet above the sea, and the air is delicious; but we often pass spots covered with a plant which grows in marshy places, and its heavy smell always puts me in mind that at other seasons this may not be so pleasant a residence. The fact of even maize being planted on mounds where the ground is naturally quite dry, tells a tale of abundant humidity of climate.

Kauma, a fine tall man, with a bald head and pleasant manners, told us that some of his people had lately returned from the Chibisa or Babisa country, whither they had gone to buy ivory, and they would give me information about the path. He took a fancy to one of the boys' blankets; offering a native cloth, much larger, in exchange, and even a sheep to boot; but the owner being unwilling to part with his covering, Kauma told me that he had not sent for his Babisa travellers on account of my boy refusing to deal with him. A little childish this, but otherwise he was very hospitable; he gave me a fine goat, which, unfortunately, my people left behind.

The chief said that no Arabs ever came his way, nor Portuguese native traders. When advising them to avoid the first attempts to begin the slave-trade, as it would inevitably lead to war and depopulation, Kauma replied that the chiefs had resolved to unite against the Waiyau of Mpondé should he come again on a foray up to the highlands; but they are like a rope of sand, there is no cohesion among them, and each village is nearly independent of every other: they mutually distrust each other.

14th October, 1866.—Spent Sunday here. Kauma says that his people are partly Kanthunda and partly Chipéta. The first are the mountaineers, the second dwellers on the plains. The Chipéta have many lines of marking: they are all only divisions of the great Manganja tribe, and their dialects differ very slightly from that spoken by the same people on the Shiré. The population is very great and very ceremonious. When we meet anyone he turns aside and sits down: we clap the hand on the chest and say, "Re peta—re peta," that is, "we pass," or "let us pass:" this is responded to at once by a clapping of the hands together. When a person is called at a distance he gives two loud claps of assent; or if he rises from near a superior he does, the same thing, which is a sort of leave-taking.

We have to ask who are the principal chiefs in the direction which we wish to take, and decide accordingly. Zomba was pointed out as a chief on a range of hills on our west: beyond him lies Undi m'senga. I had to take this route, as my people have a very vivid idea of the danger of going northwards towards the Mazitu. We made more southing than we wished. One day beyond Zomba and W.S.W. is the part called Chindando, where the Portuguese formerly went for gold. They don't seem to have felt it worth while to come here, as neither ivory nor gold could be obtained if they did. The country is too full of people to allow any wild animals elbow-room: even the smaller animals are hunted down by means of nets and dogs.

We rested at Pachoma; the headman offering a goat and beer, but I declined, and went on to Molomba. Here Kauma's carriers turned because a woman had died that morning as we left the village. They asserted that had she died before we started not a man would have left: this shows a reverence for death, for the woman was no relative of any of them. The headman of Molomba was very poor but very liberal, cooking for us and presenting a goat: another headman from a neighbouring village, a laughing, good-natured old man, named Chikala, brought beer and a fowl in the morning. I asked him to go on with us to Mironga, it being important, as above-mentioned, to have the like of his kind in our company, and he consented. We saw Mount Ngala in the distance, like a large sugar-loaf shot up in the air: in our former route to Kasungu we passed north of it.

16th October, 1866.—Crossed the rivulet Chikuyo going N. for the Lake, and Mironga being but one-and-a-half hour off, we went on to Chipanga: this is the proper name of what on the Zambesi is corrupted into Shupanga. The headman, a miserable hemp-consuming[31] leper, fled from us. We were offered a miserable hut, which we refused, Chikala meanwhile went through the whole village seeking a better, which we ultimately found: it was not in this chief to be generous, though Chikala did what he could in trying to indoctrinate him: when I gave him a present he immediately proposed to *sell* a goat! We get on pretty well however.

Zomha is in a range of hills to our west, called Zala nyama. The Portuguese, in going to Casembe, went still further west than this.

Passing on we came to a smithy, and watched the founder at work drawing off slag from the bottom of his furnace. He broke through the hardened slag by striking it with an iron instrument inserted in the end of a pole, when the material flowed out of the small hole left for the purpose in the bottom of the furnace. The ore (probably the black oxide) was like sand, and was put in at the top of the furnace, mixed with charcoal. Only one bellows was at work, formed out of a goatskin, and the blast was very poor. Many of these furnaces, or their remains, are met with on knolls; those at work have a peculiarly tall hut built over them.

On the eastern edge of a valley lying north and south, with the Diampwé stream flowing along it, and the Dzala nyama range on the western side, are two villages screened by fine specimens of the *Ficus Indica*. One of these is owned by the headman Theresa, and there we spent the night. We made very short marches, for the sun is very powerful, and the soil baked hard, is sore on the feet: no want of water, however, is felt, for we come to supplies every mile or two.

The people look very poor, having few or no beads; the ornaments being lines and cuttings on the skin. They trust more to buazé than cotton. I noticed but two cotton patches. The women are decidedly plain; but monopolize all the buazé cloth. Theresa was excessively liberal, and having informed us that Zomba lived some distance up the range and was not the principal man in these parts, we, to avoid climbing the hills, turned away to the north, in the direction of the paramount chief, Chisumpi, whom we found to be only traditionally great.

20th October, 1866.—In passing along we came to a village embowered in fine trees; the headman is Kaveta, a really fine specimen of the Kanthunda, tall, well-made, with a fine forehead and Assyrian nose. He proposed to us to remain over night with him, and I unluckily declined.

Convoying us out a mile, we parted with this gentleman, and then came to a smith's village, where the same invitation was given and refused. A sort of infatuation drove us on, and after a long hot march we found the great Chisumpi, the facsimile in black of Sir Colin Campbell; his nose, mouth, and the numerous wrinkles on his face were identical with those of the great General, but here all resemblance ceased. Two men had preceded us to give information, and when I followed I saw that his village was one of squalid misery, the only fine things about being the lofty trees in which it lay. Chisumpi begged me to sleep at a village about half a mile behind: his son was browbeating him on some domestic affair, and the older man implored me to go. Next morning he came early to that village, and arranged for our departure, offering nothing, and apparently not wishing to see us at all. I suspect that though paramount chief, he is weak-minded, and has lost thereby all his influence, but in the people's eyes he is still a great one.

Several of my men exhibiting symptoms of distress, I inquired for a village in which we could rest Saturday and Sunday, and at a distance from Chisumpi. A headman volunteered to lead us to one west of this. In passing the sepulchral grove of Chisumpi our guide remarked, "Chisumpi's forefathers sleep there." This was the first time I have heard the word "sleep" applied to death in these parts. The trees in these groves, and around many of the villages, are very large, and show what the country would become if depopulated.

We crossed the Diampwé or Adiampwé, from five to fifteen yards wide, and well supplied with water even now. It rises near the Ndomo mountains, and flows northwards into the Lintipé and Lake. We found Chitokola's village, called Paritala, a pleasant one on the east side of the Adiampwé Valley. Many elephants and other animals feed in the valley, and we saw the Bechuana Hopo[32] again after many years.

The Ambarré, otherwise Nyumbo plant, has a pea-shaped, or rather papilionaceous flower, with a fine scent. It seems to grow quite wild; its flowers are yellow.

Chaola is the poison used by the Maravi for their arrows, it is said to cause mortification.

One of the wonders usually told of us in this upland region is that we sleep without fire. The boys' blankets suffice for warmth during the night, when the thermometer sinks to 64°-60°, but no one else has covering sufficient; some huts in process of building here show that a thick coating of plaster is put on outside the roof before the grass thatch is applied; not a chink is left for the admission of air.

Ohitikola was absent from Paritala when we arrived on some *milando* or other. These *milandos* are the business of their lives. They are like petty lawsuits; if one trespasses on his neighbour's rights in any way it is a *milando*, and the headmen of all the villages about are called on to settle it. Women are a fruitful source of *milando*. A few ears of Indian corn had been taken by a person, and Chitikola had been called a full day's journey off to settle this *milando*. He administered *Muavé*[33] and the person vomited, therefore innocence was clearly established! He came in the evening of the 21st footsore and tired, and at once gave us some beer. This perpetual reference to food and drink is natural, inasmuch as it is the most important point in our intercourse. While the chief was absent we got nothing; the queen even begged a little meat for her child, who was recovering from an attack of small-pox. There being no shops we had to sit still without food. I took observations for longitude, and whiled away the time by calculating the lunars. Next day the chief gave us a goat cooked whole and plenty of porridge: I noticed that he too had the Assyrian type of face.

FOOTNOTES:

25. Dr. Livingstone's description of the "Sponge" will stand the reader in good stead when he comes to the constant mention of these obstructions in the later travels towards the north.—ED.

26. So named when Dr. Livingstone, Dr. Kirk, and Mr. Charles Livingstone, discovered Lake Nyassa together.

27. The sheep are of the black-haired variety: their tails grow to an enormous size. A rain which came from Nunkajowa, a Waiyau chief, on a former occasion, was found to have a tail weighing 11 lbs.; but for the journey, and two or three days short commons, an extra 2 or 3 lbs. of fat «would have been on it.—ED.

28. This complaint has not been reported as an African disease before; it probably clings to the higher levels.—ED.

29. A fine fibre derived from the shoots of a shrub (*Securidaca Longipedunculata*).

30. Several superstitions of this nature seem to point to a remnant of the old heathen ritual, and the worship of gods in mountain groves.

31. Hemp = bangé is smoked throughout Central Africa, and if used in excess produces partial imbecility.—ED.

32. The Hopo is a funnel-shaped fence which encloses a considerable tract of country: a "drive" is organised, and animals of all descriptions are urged on till they become jammed together in the neck of the hopo, where they are speared to death or else destroyed in a number of pitfalls placed there for the purpose.

33. The ordeal poison.

* * * * *

CHAPTER VI.

Progress northwards. An African forest. Destruction by Mazitu. Native salutations. A disagreeable chief. On the watershed between the Lake and the Loangwa River. Extensive iron-workings. An old Nimrod. The Bua Eiver. Lovely scenery. Difficulties of transport. Chilobé. An African Pythoness. Enlists two Waiyou bearers. Ill. The Chitella bean. Rains set in. Arrives at the Loangwa.

We started with Chitikola as our guide on the 22nd of October, and he led us away westwards across the Lilongwé River, then turned north till we came to a village called Mashumba, the headman of which was the only chief who begged anything except medicine, and he got less than we were in the habit of giving in consequence: we give a cloth usually, and clothing being very scarce this is considered munificent.[34]

We had the Zalanyama range on our left, and our course was generally north, but we had to go in the direction of the villages which were on friendly terms with our guides, and sometimes we went but a little way, as they studied to make the days as short as possible. The headman of the last village, Chitoku, was with us, and he took us to a village of smiths, four furnaces and one smithy being at work. We crossed the Chiniambo, a strong river coming from Zalanyama and flowing into the Mirongwé, which again goes into Lintipé. The country near the hills becomes covered with forest, the trees are chiefly Masuko Mochenga (the gum-copal tree), the bark-cloth tree and rhododendrons. The heath known at the Cape as *Rhinoster bosch* occurs frequently, and occasionally we have thorny acacias. The grass is short, but there is plenty of it.

24th October, 1866.—Our guide, Mpanda, led us through the forest by what he meant to be a short cut to Chimuna's. We came on a herd of about fifteen elephants, and many trees laid down by these animals: they seem to relish the roots of some kinds, and spend a good deal of time digging them up; they chew woody roots and branches as thick as the handle of a spade. Many buffaloes feed here, and we viewed a herd of elands; they kept out of bow-shot only: a herd of the baama or hartebeest stood at 200 paces, and one was shot.

While all were rejoicing over the meat we got news, from the inhabitants of a large village in full flight, that the Mazitu were out on a foray. While roasting and eating meat I went forward with Mpanda to get men from Chimuna to carry the rest, but was soon recalled. Another crowd were also in full retreat; the people were running straight to the Zalanyama range regardless of their feet, making a path for themselves through the forest; they had escaped from the Mazitu that morning; "they saw them!" Mpanda's people wished to leave and go to look after their own village, but we persuaded them, on pain of a *milando*, to take us to the nearest village, that was at the bottom of Zalanyama proper, and we took the spoor of the fugitives. The hard grass with stalks nearly as thick as quills must have hurt their feet sorely, but what of that in comparison with dear life! We meant to take our stand on the hill and defend our property in case of the Mazitu coming near; and we should, in the event of being successful, be a defence to the fugitives who crowded up its rocky sides, but next morning we heard that the enemy had gone to the south. Had we gone forward, as we intended, to search for men to carry the meat we should have met the marauders, for the men of the second party of villagers had remained behind guarding their village till the Mazitu arrived, and they told us what a near escape I had had from walking into their power.

25th October, 1866.—Came along northwards to Chimuna's town, a large one of Chipéta with many villages around. Our path led through the forest, and as we emerged into the open strath in which the villages lie, we saw the large anthills, each the size of the end of a one-storied cottage, covered with men on guard watching for the Mazitu.

A long line of villagers were just arriving from the south, and we could see at some low hills in that direction the smoke arising from the burning settlements. None but men were present, the women and the chief were at the mountain called Pambé; all were fully armed with their long bows, some flat in the bow, others round, and it was common to have the quiver on the back, and a bunch of feathers stuck in the hair like those in our Lancers' shakos. But they remained not to fight, but to watch their homes and stores of grain from robbers amongst their own people in case no Mazitu came! They gave a good hut, and sent off at once to let the chief at Pambé know of our arrival. We heard the cocks crowing up there in the mountain as we passed in the morning. Chimuna came in the evening, and begged me to remain a day in his village, Pamaloa, as he was the greatest chief the Chipéta had. I told him all wished the same thing, and if I listened to each chief we should never get on, and the rains were near, but we had to stay over with him.

26th October, 1866.—All the people came down to-day from Pambé, and crowded to see the strangers. They know very little beyond their own affairs, though these require a good deal of knowledge, and we should be sorely put about if, without their skill, we had to maintain an existence here. Their furnaces are rather bottle shaped, and about seven feet high by three broad. One toothless patriarch had heard of books and umbrellas, but had never seen either. The oldest inhabitant had never travelled far from the spot in which he was born, yet he has a good knowledge of soils and agriculture, hut-building, basket-making, pottery, and the manufacture of bark-cloth and skins for clothing, as also making of nets, traps, and cordage.

Chimuna had a most ungainly countenance, yet did well enough: he was very thankful for a blister on his loins to ease rheumatic pains, and presented a huge basket of porridge before starting, with a fowl, and asked me to fire a gun that the Mazitu might hear and know that armed men were here. They all say that these marauders flee from fire-arms, so I think that they are not Zulus at all, though adopting some of their ways.

In going on to Mapuio's we passed several large villages, each surrounded by the usual euphorbia hedge, and having large trees for shade. We are on & level, or rather gently amdulating country, rather bare of trees. At the junctions of these earthen waves we have always an oozing bog, this often occurs in the slope down the trough of this terrestrial sea; bushes are common, and of the kind which were cut down as trees. Yellow haematite is very abundant, but the other rocks scarcely appear in the distance; we have mountains both on the east and west.

On arriving at Mapuio's village, he was, as often happens, invisible, but he sent us a calabash of fresh-made beer, which is very refreshing, gave us a hut, and promised to cook for us in the evening. We have to employ five or six carriers, and they rule the length of the day's march. Those from Chimuna's village growled at the cubit of calico with which we paid them, but a few beads pleased them perfectly, and we parted good friends. It is not likely I shall ever see them again, but I always like to please them, because it is right to consider their desires. Is that not what is meant in "Blessed is he that considereth the poor"? There is a great deal of good in these poor people. In cases of *milando* they rely on the most distant relations and connections to plead their cause, and seldom are they disappointed, though time at certain seasons, as for instance at present, is felt by all to be precious. Every man appears with hoe or axe on shoulder, and the people often only sit down as we pass and gaze at us till we are out of sight.

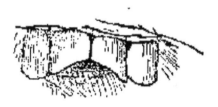

Women's Teeth hollowed.

Many of the men have large slits in the lobe of the ear, and they have their distinctive tribal tattoo. The women indulge in this painful luxury more than the men, probably because they have very few ornaments. The two central front teeth are hollowed at the cutting edge. Many have quite the Grecian facial angle. Mapuio has thin legs and quite a European face. Delicate features and limbs are common, and the spur-heel is as scarce as among Europeans; small feet and hands are the rule.

Clapping the hands in various ways is the polite way of saying "Allow me," "I beg pardon," "Permit me to pass," "Thanks," it is resorted to in respectful introduction and leave-taking, and also is equivalent to "Hear hear." When inferiors are called they respond by two brisk claps of the hands, meaning "I am coming." They are very punctilious amongst each other. A large ivory bracelet marks the headman of a village; there is nothing else to show differences of rank.

28th October, 1866.—We spent Sunday at Mapuio's and had a long talk with him; his country is in a poor state from the continual incursions of the Mazitu, who are wholly unchecked.

29th October, 1866.—We marched westwards to Makosa's village, and could not go further, as the next stage is long and through an ill-peopled country. The morning was lovely, the whole country bathed in bright sunlight, and not a breath of air disturbed the smoke as it slowly curled up from the heaps of burning weeds, which the native agriculturist wisely destroys. The people generally were busy hoeing in the cool of the day. One old man in a village where we rested had trained the little hair he had left into a tail, which, well plastered with fat, he had bent on itself and laid flat on his crown; another was carefully paring a stick for stirring the porridge, and others were enjoying the cool shade of the wild fig-trees which are always planted at villages. It is a sacred tree all over Africa and India, and the tender roots which drop down towards the ground are used as medicine—a universal remedy. Can it be a tradition of its being like the tree of life, which Archbishop Whately conjectures may have been used in Paradise to render man immortal? One kind of fig-tree is often seen hacked all over to get the sap, which is used as bird-lime; bark-cloth is made of it too. I like to see the men weaving or spinning, or reclining under these glorious canopies, as much as I love to see our more civilized people lolling on their sofas or ottomans.

The first rain—a thunder shower—fell in the afternoon, air in shade before it 92°; wet bulb 74°. At noon the soil in the sun was 140°, perhaps more, but I was afraid of bursting the thermometer, as it was graduated only a few degrees above that. This rain happened at the same time that the sun was directly overhead on his way south; it was but a quarter of an inch, but its effect was to deprive us of all chance of getting the five carriers we needed, all were off to their gardens to commit the precious seed to the soil. We got three, but no one else would come, so we have to remain here over to-day (30th October).

30th October, 1866.—The black traders come from Tette to this country to buy slaves, and as a consequence here we come to bugs again, which we left when we passed the Arab slave-traders' beat.

31st October, 1866.—We proceed westwards, and a little south through a country covered with forest trees, thickly planted, but small, generally of bark-cloth and gum-copal trees, masukos, rhododendrons, and a few acacias. At one place we saw ten wild hogs in a group, but no other animal, though marks of elephants, buffaloes, and other animals having been about in the wet season were very abundant. The first few miles were rather more scant of water than usual, but we came to the Leué, a fine little stream with plenty of water sand from 20 to 30 yards wide; it is said by the people to flow away westwards into the Loangwa.

1st November 1866.—In the evening we made the Chigumokiré, a nice rivulet, where we slept, and the next morning we proceeded to Kangené, whose village is situated on a mass of mountains, and to reach which we made more southing than we wished. Our appearance on the ascent of the hill caused alarm, and we were desired to wait till our spokesman had explained the unusual phenomenon of a white man.

This kept us waiting in the hot sun among heated rocks, and the chief, being a great ugly public-house-keeper looking person, excused his incivility by saying that his brother had been killed by the Mazitu, and he was afraid that we were of the same tribe. On asking if Mazitu wore clothes like us he told some untruths, and, what has been an unusual thing, began to beg powder and other things. I told him how other chiefs had treated us, which made him ashamed. He represented the country in front to the N.W. to be quite impassable from want of food: the Mazitu had stripped it of all provisions, and the people were living on what wild fruits they could pick up.

2nd November, 1866.—Kangené is very disagreeable naturally, and as we have to employ five men as carriers, we are in his power.

We can scarcely enter into the feelings of those who are harried by marauders. Like Scotland in the twelfth and thirteenth centuries harassed by Highland Celts on one side and by English Marchmen on the other, and thus kept in the rearward of civilisation, these people have rest neither for many days nor for few. When they fill their garners they can seldom reckon on eating the grain, for the Mazitu come when the harvest is over and catch as many able-bodied young persons as they can to carry away the corn. Thus it was in Scotland so far as security for life and property was concerned; but the Scotch were apt pupils of more fortunate nations. To change of country they were as indifferent as the Romans of the olden times; they were always welcome in France, either as pilgrims, scholars, merchants, or soldiers; but the African is different. If let alone the African's mode of life is rather enjoyable; he loves agriculture, and land is to be had anywhere. He knows nothing of other countries, but he has imbibed the idea of property in man. This Kangené told me that he would like to give me a slave to look after my goats: I believe he would rather give a slave than a goat!

We were detained by the illness of Simon for four days. When he recovered we proposed to the headman to start with five of his men, and he agreed to let us have them; but having called them together such an enormous demand was made for wages, and in advance, that on the 7th of November we took seven loads forward through a level uninhabited country generally covered with small trees, slept there, and on the morning of the 8th, after leaving two men at our depôt, came back, and took the remaining five loads.

Kangené was disagreeable to the last. He asked where we had gone, and, having described the turning point as near the hill Chimbimbé, he complimented us on going so far, and then sent an offer of three men; but I preferred not to have those who would have been spies unless he could give five and take on all the loads. He said that he would find the number, and after detaining us some hours brought two, one of whom, primed with beer, babbled out that he was afraid of being killed by us in front. I asked whom we had killed behind, and moved off. The headman is very childish, does women's work—cooking and pounding; and in all cases of that kind the people take after their leader. The chiefs have scarcely any power unless they are men of energy; they have to court the people rather than be courted. We came much further back on our way from Mapuio's than we liked; in fact, our course is like that of a vessel baffled with foul winds: this is mainly owing to being obliged to avoid places stripped of provisions or suffering this spoliation. The people, too, can give no information about others at a distance from their own abodes. Even the smiths, who are a most plodding set of workers, are as ignorant as the others: they supply the surrounding villages with hoes and knives, and, combining agriculture with handicraft, pass through life. An intelligent smith came as our guide from Chimbimbé Hill on the 7th, and did not know a range of mountains about twenty miles off: "it was too far off for him to know the name."

9th November, 1866.—The country over which we actually travel is level and elevated, but there are mountains all about, which when put on the map make it appear to be a mountainous region. We are on the watershed, apparently between the Loangwa of Zumbo on the west, and the Lake on the east. The Leué or Leuia is said by the people to flow into the Loangwa. The Chigumokiré coming from the north in front, eastward of Irongwé (the same mountains on which Kangené skulks out of sight of Mazitu), flows into the Leué, and north of that we have the Mando, a little stream, flowing into the Bua. The rivulets on the west flow in deep defiles, and the elevation on which we travel makes it certain that no water can come from the lower lands on the west. It seems that the Portuguese in travelling to Casembe did not inquire of the people where the streams they crossed went, for they are often wrongly put, and indicate the direction only in which they appeared to be flowing at their crossing places. The natives have a good idea generally of the rivers into which the streams flow, though they are very deficient in information as to the condition of the people that live on their banks. Some of the Portuguese questions must have been asked through slaves, who would show no hesitation in answering. Maxinga, or Machinga, means "mountains" only; once or twice it is put down Saxa de Maxinga, or Machinga, or Mcanga, which translated from the native tongue means "rocks of mountains, or mountains of rocks."

10th November, 1866.—We found the people on the Mando to be Chawa or Ajawa, but not of the Waiyau race: they are Manganja, and this is a village of smiths. We got five men readily to go back and bring up our loads; and the sound of the hammer is constant, showing a great deal of industry. They combine agriculture, and hunting with nets, with their handicraft.

A herd of buffaloes came near the village, and I went and shot one, thus procuring a supply of meat for the whole party and villagers too. The hammer which we hear from dawn till sunset is a large stone, bound with the strong inner bark of a tree, and loops left which form handles. Two pieces of bark form the tongs, and a big stone sunk into the ground the anvil. They make several hoes in a day, and the metal is very good; it is all from yellow haematite, which abounds all over this part of the country; the bellows consist of two goatskins with sticks at the open ends, which are opened and shut at every blast.

Forging Hoes.

13th November, 1866.—A lion came last night and gave a growl or two on finding he could not get our meat: a man had lent us a hunting net to protect it and us from intruders of this sort. The people kept up a shouting for hours afterwards, in order to keep him away by the human voice.

We might have gone on, but I had a galled heel from new shoes. Wild figs are rather nice when quite ripe.

14th November, 1866.—We marched northwards round the end of Chisia Hill, and remained for the night at a blacksmith's, or rather founder's village; the two occupations of founder and smith are always united, and boys taught to be smiths in Europe or India would find themselves useless if unable to smelt the ore. A good portion of the trees of the country have been cut down for charcoal, and those which now spring up are small; certain fruit trees alone are left. The long slopes on the undulating country, clothed with fresh foliage, look very beautiful. The young trees alternate with patches of yellow grass not yet burned; the hills are covered with a thick mantle of small green trees with, as usual, large ones at intervals. The people at Kalumbi, on the Mando (where we spent four days), had once a stockade of wild fig *(Ficus Indica)* and euphorbia round their village, which has a running rill on each side of it; but the trees which enabled them to withstand a siege by Mazitu fell before elephants and buffaloes during a temporary absence of the villagers; the remains of the stockade are all around it yet. Lions sometimes enter huts by breaking through the roof: elephants certainly do, for we saw a roof destroyed by one; the only chance for the inmates is to drive a spear into the belly of the beast while so engaged.

A man came and reported the Mazitu to be at Chanyandula's village, where we are going. The headman advised remaining at his village till we saw whether they came this way or went by another path. The women were sent away, but the men went on with their employments; two proceeded with the building of a furnace on an anthill, where they are almost always placed, and they keep a look-out while working. We have the protection of an all-embracing Providence, and trust that He, whose care of His people exceeds all that our utmost self-love can attain, will shield us and make our way prosperous.

16th November, 1866.—An elephant came near enough last night to scream at us, but passed on, warned, perhaps, by the shouting of the villagers not to meddle with man. No Mazitu having come, we marched on and crossed the Bua, eight yards wide and knee deep. It rises in the northern hills a little beyond Kanyindula's village, winds round his mountains, and away to the east. The scenery among the mountains is very lovely: they are covered with a close mantle of green, with here and there red and light-coloured patches, showing where grass has been burned off recently and the red clay soil is exposed; the lighter portions are unburned grass or rocks. Large trees are here more numerous, and give an agreeable change of contour to the valleys and ridges of the hills; the boughs of many still retain a tinge of red from young leaves. We came to the Bua again before reaching Kanyenjé, as Kanyindula's place is called. The iron trade must have been carried on for an immense time in the country, for one cannot go a quarter of a mile without meeting pieces of slag and broken pots, calcined pipes, and fragments of the furnaces, which are converted by the fire into brick. It is curious that the large stone sledge-hammers now in use are not called by the name stone-hammers, but by a distinct word, "kama:" nyundo is one made of iron.

When we arrived at Kanyenjé, Kanyindula was out collecting charcoal. He sent a party of men to ask if we should remain next day: an old, unintellectual-looking man was among the number sent, who had twenty-seven rings of elephant's skin on his arm, all killed by himself by the spear alone: he had given up fighting elephants since the Mazitu came, whom we heard had passed away to the south-east of this place, taking all the crops of last year, and the chief alone has food. He gave us some, which was very acceptable, as we got none at the two villages south of this. Kanyindula came himself in the evening, an active, stern-looking man, but we got on very well with him.

The people say that they were taught to smelt iron by Chisumpi, which is the name of Mulungu (God), and that they came from Lake Nyassa originally; if so, they are greatly inferior to the Manganja on the Lake in pottery, for the fragments, as well as modern whole vessels, are very coarse; the ornamentation is omitted or merely dots. They never heard of aërolites, but know hail.

I notice here that the tree Mfu, or Mö, having sweet-scented leaves, yields an edible plum in clusters. Bua-bwa is another edible fruit-tree with palmated leaves.

Mbéu is a climbing, arboraceous plant, and yields a very pleasant fruit, which tastes like gooseberries: its seeds are very minute.

18th and 19th November, 1866.—Rain fell heavily yesterday afternoon, and was very threatening to-day; we remain to sew a calico tent.

20th November, 1866.—Kanyindula came with three carriers this morning instead of five, and joined them in demanding prepayment: it was natural for him to side with them, as they have more power than he has, in fact, the chiefs in these parts all court their people, and he could feel more interest in them than in an entire stranger whom he might never see again: however, we came on without his people, leaving two to guard the loads.

About four miles up the valley we came to a village named Kanyenjeré Mponda, at the fountain-eye of the Bua, and thence sent men back for the loads, while we had the shelter of good huts during a heavy thunder-shower, and made us willing to remain all night. The valley is lovely in the extreme. The mountains on each side are gently rounded, and, as usual, covered over with tree foliage, except where the red soil is exposed by recent grass-burnings. Quartz rocks jut out, and much drift of that material has been carried down by the gullies into the bottom. These gullies being in compact clay, the water has but little power of erosion, so they are worn deep but narrow. Some fragments of titaniferous iron ore, with haematite changed by heat, and magnetic, lay in the gully, which had worn itself a channel on the north side of the village. The Bua, like most African streams whose sources I have seen, rises in an oozing boggy spot. Another stream, the Tembwé, rises near the same spot, and flows N.W. into, the Loangwa. We saw Shuaré palms in its bed.

21st November, 1866.—We left Bua fountain, lat. 13° 40' south, and made a short march to Mokatoba, a stockaded village, where the people refused to admit us till the headman, came. They have a little food here, and sold us some. We have been on rather short commons for some time, and this made our detention agreeable. We rose a little in altitude after leaving this morning, then, though in the same valley, made a little descent towards the N.N.W. High winds came driving over the eastern range, which is called Mchinjé, and bring large masses of clouds, which are the rain-givers. They seem to come from the south-east. The scenery of the valley is lovely and rich in the extreme. All the foliage is fresh washed and clean; young herbage is bursting through the ground; the air is deliciously cool, and the birds are singing joyfully: one, called Mzié, is a good songster, with a loud melodious voice. Large game abounds, but we do not meet with it.

We are making our way slowly to the north, where food is said to be abundant. I divided about 50 lbs. of powder among the people of my following to shoot with, and buy goats or other food as we could. This reduces our extra loads to three—four just now, Simon being sick again. He rubbed goat's-fat on a blistered surface, and caused an eruption of pimples.

Mem.—The people assent by lifting up the head instead of nodding it down as we do; deaf mutes are said to do the same.

22nd November, 1866.—Leaving Mokatoba village, and proceeding down the valley, which on the north is shut up apparently by a mountain called Kokwé, we crossed the Kasamba, about two miles from Mokatoba, and yet found it, though so near its source, four yards wide, and knee deep. Its source is about a mile above Mokatoba, in the same valley, with the Bua and Tembwé. We were told that elephants were near, and we saw where they had been an hour before; but after seeking about could not find them. An old man, in the deep defile between Kokwé and Yasika Mountains, pointed to the latter, and said, "Elephants! why, there they are. Elephants, or tusks, walking on foot are never absent;" but though we were eager for flesh, we could not give him credit, and went down the defile which gives rise to the Sandili River: where we crossed it in the defile, it was a mere rill, having large trees along its banks, yet it is said to go to the Loangwa of Zumbo, N.W. or N.N.W. We were now in fact upon the slope which inclines to that river, and made a rapid descent in altitude. We reached Silubi's village, on the base of a rocky detached hill. No food to be had; all taken by Mazitu, so Silubi gave me some Masuko fruit instead. They find that they can keep the Mazitu off by going up a rocky eminence, and hurling stones and arrows down on the invaders: they can defend themselves also by stockades, and these are becoming very general.

On leaving Silubi's village, we went to a range of hills, and after passing through found that we had a comparatively level country on the north: it would be called a well-wooded country if we looked at it only from a distance. It is formed into long ridges, all green and wooded; but clumps of large trees, where villages have been, or are still situated, show that the sylvan foliage around and over the whole country is that of mere hop-poles. The whole of this upland region might be called woody, if we bear in mind that where the population is dense, and has been long undisturbed, the trees are cut down to the size of low bush. Large districts are kept to about the size of hop-poles, growing on pollards three or four feet from the ground, by charcoal burners, who, in all instances, are smiths too.

On reaching Zeoré's village, on the Lokuzhwa, we found it stockaded, and stagnant pools round three sides of it. The Mazitu had come, pillaged all the surrounding villages, looked at this, and then went away; so the people had food to sell. They here call themselves Echéwa, and have a different marking from the Atumboka. The men have the hair dressed as if a number of the hairs of elephants' tails were stuck around the head: the women wear a small lip-ring, and a straw or piece of stick in the lower lip, which dangles down about level with the lower edge of the chin: their clothing in front is very scanty. The men know nothing of distant places, the Manganja being a very stay-at-home people. The stockades are crowded with huts, and the children have but small room to play in the narrow spaces between.

25th November, 1866.—Sunday at Zeoré's. The villagers thought we prayed for rain, which was much needed. The cracks in the soil have not yet come together by the «welling of soil produced by moisture. I disabused their minds about rain-making prayers, and found the headman intelligent.

I did not intend to notice the Lokuzhwa, it is such a contemptible little rill, and not at present running; but in going to our next point, Mpandé's village, we go along its valley, and cross it several times, as it makes for the Loangwa in the north. The valley is of rich dark red loam, and so many lilies of the Amaryllis kind have established themselves as completely to mask the colour of the soil. They form a covering of pure white where the land has been cleared by the hoe. As we go along this valley to the Loangwa, we descend in altitude. It is said to rise at "Nombé rumé," as we formerly heard.

27th November, 1866.—Zeoré's people would not carry without prepayment, so we left our extra loads as usual and went on, sending men back for them: these, however, did not come till 27th, and then two of my men got fever. I groan in spirit, and do not know how to make our gear into nine loads only. It is the knowledge that we shall be detained, some two or three months during the heavy rains that makes me cleave to it as means of support.

Advantage has been taken by the people, of spots where the Lokuzhwa goes round three parts of a circle, to erect their stockaded villages. This is the case here, and the water, being stagnant, engenders disease. The country abounds in a fine light blue flowering perennial pea, which the people make use of as a relish. At present the blossoms only are collected and boiled. On inquiring the name, *chilóbé*, the men asked me if we had none in our country. On replying in the negative, they looked with pity on us: "What a wretched, country not to have chilóbé." It is on the highlands above; we never saw it elsewhere! Another species of pea *(Chilobé Weza)*, with reddish flowers, is eaten in the same way; but it has spread but little in comparison. It is worth remarking that porridge of maize or sorghum is never offered without some pulse, beans, or bean leaves, or flowers, they seem to feel the need of it, or of pulse, which is richer in flesh-formers than the porridge.

Last night a loud clapping of hands by the men was followed by several half-suppressed screams by a woman. They were quite *eldritch*, as if she could not get them out. Then succeeded a lot of utterances as if she were in ecstasy, to which a man responded, "Moio, moio." The utterances, so far as I could catch, were in five-syllable snatches—abrupt and laboured. I wonder if this "bubbling or boiling over" has been preserved as the form in which the true prophets of old gave forth their "burdens"? One sentence, frequently repeated towards the close of the effusion, was "*linyama uta*," "flesh of the bow," showing that the Pythoness loved venison killed by the bow. The people applauded, and attended, hoping, I suppose, that rain would follow her efforts. Next day she was duly honoured by drumming and dancing.[35]

Prevalent beliefs seem to be persistent in certain tribes. That strange idea of property in man that permits him to be sold to another is among the Arabs, Manganja, Makoa, Waiyau, but not among Kaffirs or Zulus, and Bechuanas. If we exclude the Arabs, two families of Africans alone are slavers on the east side of the Continent.

30th November, 1866.—We march to Chilunda's or Embora's, still on the Lokuzhwa, now a sand-stream about twenty yards wide, with pools in its bed; its course is pretty much north or N.N.W. We are now near the Loangwa country, covered with a dense dwarf forest, and the people collected in stockades. This village is on a tongue of land (between Lokuzhwa and another sluggish rivulet), chosen for its strength. It is close to a hill named Chipemba, and there are ranges of hills both east and west in the distance. Embora came to visit us soon after we arrived—a tall man with a Yankee face. He was very much tickled when asked if he were a Motumboka. After indulging in laughter at the idea of being one of such a small tribe of Manganja, he said proudly, "That he belonged to the Echéwa, who inhabited all the country to which I was going." They are generally smiths; a mass of iron had just been brought in to him from some outlying furnaces. It is made into hoes, which are sold for native cloths down the Loangwa.

3rd December, 1866.—March through a hilly country covered with dwarf forest to Kandé's village, still on the Lokuzhwa. We made some westing. The village was surrounded by a dense hedge of bamboo and a species of bushy fig that loves edges of water-bearing streams: it is not found where the moisture is not perennial. Kandé is a fine tall smith; I asked him if he knew his antecedents; he said he had been bought by Babisa at Chipéta, and left at Chilunda's, and therefore belonged to no one. Two Waiyau now volunteered to go on with us, and as they declared their masters were killed by the Mazitu, and Kandé seemed to confirm them, we let them join. In general, runaway slaves are bad characters, but these two seem good men, and we want them to fill up our complement: another volunteer we employ as goatherd.

A continuous tap-tapping in the villages shows that bark cloth is being made. The bark, on being removed from the-tree, is steeped in water, or in a black muddy hole, till the outer of the two inner barks can be separated, then commences the tapping with a mallet to separate and soften the fibres. The head of this is often of ebony, with the face cut into small furrows, which, without breaking, separate and soften the fibres.

Mallet for Separating Fibres of Bark.

4th December, 1866.—Marched westwards, over a hilly, dwarf forest-covered country: as we advanced, trees increased in size, but no people inhabited it; we spent a miserable night at Katétté, wetted by a heavy thunder-shower, which lasted a good while. Morning *(5th December)* muggy, clouded all over, and rolling thunder in distance. Went three hours with, for a wonder, no water, but made westing chiefly, and got on to the Lokuzhwa again: all the people are collected on it.

6th December, 1866.—Too ill to march.

7th December, 1866.—Went on, and passed Mesumbé's village, also protected by bamboos, and came to the hill Mparawé, with a village perched on its northern base and well up its sides. The Babisa have begun to imitate the Mazitu by attacking and plundering Manganja villages. Muasi's brother was so attacked, and now is here and eager to attack in return. In various villages we have observed miniature huts, about two feet high, very neatly thatched and plastered, here we noticed them in dozens. On inquiring, we were told that when a child or relative dies one is made, and when any pleasant food is cooked or beer brewed, a little is placed in the tiny hut for the departed soul, which is believed to enjoy it.

The Lokuzhwa is here some fifty yards wide, and running. Numerous large pitholes in the fine-grained schist in its bed show that much water has flowed in it.

8th December, 1866.—A kind of bean called "chitetta" is eaten here, it is an old acquaintance in the Bechuana country, where it is called "mositsané," and is a mere plant; here it becomes a tree, from fifteen to twenty feet high. The root is used for tanning; the bean is pounded, and then put into a sieve of bark cloth to extract, by repeated washings, the excessively astringent matter it contains. Where the people have plenty of water, as here, it is used copiously in various processes, among Bechuanas it is scarce, and its many uses unknown: the pod becomes from fifteen to eighteen inches long, and an inch in diameter.

9th December, 1866.—A poor child, whose mother had died, was unprovided for; no one not a relative will nurse another's child. It called out piteously for its mother by name, and the women (like the servants in the case of the poet Cowper when a child), said, "She is coming." I gave it a piece of bread, but it was too far gone, and is dead to-day.

An alarm of Mazitu sent all the villagers up the sides of Mparawé this morning. The affair was a chase of a hyaena, but everything is Mazitu! The Babisa came here, but were surrounded and nearly all cut off. Muasi was so eager to be off with a party to return the attack on the Mazitu, that, when deputed by the headman to give us a guide, he got the man to turn at the first village, so we had to go on without guides, and made about due north.

11th December, 1866.—We are now detained in the forest, at a place called Chondé Forest, by set-in rains. It rains every day, and generally in the afternoon; but the country is not wetted till the "set-in" rains commence; the cracks in the soil then fill up and everything rushes up with astonishing rapidity; the grass is quite crisp and soft. After the fine-grained schist, we came on granite with large flakes of talc in it. This forest is of good-sized trees, many of them mopané. The birds now make much melody and noise—all intent on building.

12th December, 1866.—Across an undulating forest country north we got a man to show us the way, if a pathless forest can so be called. We used a game-path as long as it ran north, but left it when it deviated, and rested under a baobab-tree with a marabou's nest—a bundle of sticks on a branch; the young ones uttered a hard chuck, chuck, when the old ones flew over them. A sun-bird, with bright scarlet throat and breast, had its nest on another branch, it was formed like the weaver's nest, but without a tube. I observed the dam picking out insects from the bark and leaves of the baobab, keeping on the wing the while: it would thus appear to be insectivorous as well as a honey-bibber. Much spoor of elands, zebras, gnus, kamas, pallahs, buffaloes, reed-bucks, with tsetse, their parasites.

13th December, 1866.—Reached the Tokosusi, which is said to rise at Nombé Rumé, about twenty yards wide and knee deep, swollen by the rains: it had left a cake of black tenacious mud on its banks. Here I got a pallah antelope, and a very strange flower called "katendé," which was a whorl of seventy-two flowers sprung from a flat, round root; but it cannot be described. Our guide would have crossed the Tokosusi, which was running north-west to join the Loangwa, and then gone to that river; but always when we have any difficulty the "lazies" exhibit themselves. We had no grain; and three remained behind spending four hours at what we did in an hour and a quarter. Our guide became tired and turned, not before securing another; but he would not go over the Loangwa; no one likes to go out of his own country: he would go westwards to Maranda's, and nowhere else. A "set-in" rain came on after dark, and we went on through slush, the trees sending down heavier drops than the showers as we neared the Loangwa; we forded several deep gullies, all flowing north or north-west into it. The paths were running with water, and when we emerged from the large Mopané Forest, we came on the plain of excessively adhesive mud, on which Maranda's stronghold stands on the left bank of Loangwa, here a good-sized river. The people were all afraid of us, and we were mortified to find that food is scarce. The Mazitu have been here three times, and the fear they have inspired, though they were successfully repelled, has prevented agricultural operations from being carried on.

Mem.—A flake of reed is often used in surgical operations among the natives, as being sharper than their knives.

FOOTNOTES:

34. A cloth means two yards of unbleached calico.

35. Chuma remembers part of the words of her song to be as follows:—
    Kowé! kowé! n'andambwi,
    M'vula léru, korolé ko okwé,
    Waie, ona, kordi, mvula!

    He cannot translate it as it is pure Manganja, but with the exception of the first line—which relates to a little song-bird with a beautiful note, it is a mere reiteration "rain will surely come to-day."—ED.

* * * * *

CHAPTER VII.

Crosses the Loangwa. Distressing march. The king-hunter. Great hunger. Christmas feast necessarily postponed. Loss of goats. Honey-hunters. A meal at last. The Babisa. The Mazitu again. Chitembo's. End of 1866. The new year. The northern brim of the great Loangwa Valley. Accident to chronometers. Meal gives out. Escape from a Cobra capella. Pushes for the Chambezé. Death of Chitané. Great pinch for food. Disastrous loss of medicine chest. Bead currency. Babisa. The Chambezé. Beaches Chitapangwa's town. Meets Arab traders from Zanzibar. Sends off letters. Chitapangwa and his people. Complications.

16th December, 1866.—We could get no food at any price on 15th, so we crossed the Loangwa, and judged it to be from seventy to a hundred yards wide: it is deep at present, and it must always be so, for some Atumboka submitted to the Mazitu, and ferried them over and back again. The river is said to rise in the north; it has alluvial banks with large forest trees along them, bottom sandy, and great sandbanks are in it like the Zambesi. No guide would come, so we went on without one. The "lazies" of the party seized the opportunity of remaining behind—wandering, as they said, though all the cross paths were marked.[36] This evening we secured the latitude 12° 40' 48" S., which would make our crossing place about 12° 45' S. Clouds prevented observations, as they usually do in the rainy season.

17 December, 1866.—We went on through a bushy country without paths, and struck the Pamazi, a river of sixty yards wide, in steep banks and in flood, and held on as well as we could through a very difficult country, the river forcing us north-west: I heard hippopotami in it. Game is abundant but wild; we shot two poku antelopes[37] here, called "tsébulas," which drew a hunter to us, who consented for meat and pay to show us a ford. He said that the Pamazi rises in a range of mountains we can now see (in general we could see no high ground during our marches for the last fortnight), we forded it, thigh deep on one side and breast deep on the other. We made only about three miles of northing, and found the people on the left bank uncivil: they would not lend a hut, so we soon put up a tent of waterproof cloth and branches.

18th December, 1866.—As the men grumbled at their feet being pierced by thorns in the trackless portions we had passed I was anxious to get a guide, but the only one we could secure would go to Molenga's only; so I submitted, though this led us east instead of north. When we arrived we were asked what we wanted, seeing we brought neither slaves nor ivory: I replied it was much against our will that we came; but the guide had declared that this was the only way to Casembe's, our next stage. To get rid of us they gave a guide, and we set forward northwards. The Mopané Forest is perfectly level, and after rains the water stands in pools; but during most of the year it is dry. The trees here were very large, and planted some twenty or thirty yards apart: as there are no branches on their lower parts animals see very far. I shot a gnu, but wandered in coming back to the party, and did not find them till it was getting dark. Many parts of the plain are thrown up into heaps, of about the size of one's cap (probably by crabs), which now, being hard, are difficult to walk over; under the trees it is perfectly smooth. The Mopané-tree furnishes the iron wood of the Portuguese Pao Ferro: it is pretty to travel in and look at the bright sunshine of early morning; but the leaves hang perpendicularly as the sun rises high, and afford little or no shade through the day,[38] so as the land is clayey, it becomes hard-baked thereby.

We observed that the people had placed corn-granaries at different parts of this forest, and had been careful to leave no track to them—a provision in case of further visits of Mazitu. King-hunters[39] abound, and make the air resound with their stridulous notes, which commence with a sharp, shrill cheep, and then follows a succession of notes, which resembles a pea in a whistle. Another bird is particularly conspicuous at present by its chattering activity, its nest consists of a bundle of fine seed-stalks of grass hung at the end of a branch, the free ends being left untrimmed, and no attempt at concealment made. Many other birds are now active, and so many new notes are heard, that it is probable this is a richer ornithological region than the Zambesi. Guinea-fowl and francolins are in abundance, and so indeed are all the other kinds of game, as zebras, pallahs, gnus.

19th December, 1866.—I got a fine male kudu. We have no grain, and live on meat alone, but I am better off than the men, inasmuch as I get a little goat's-milk besides. The kudu stood five feet six inches high; horns, three feet on the straight.

20th December, 1866.—Reached Casembe,[40] a miserable hamlet of a few huts. The people here are very suspicious, and will do nothing but with a haggle for prepayment; we could get no grain, nor even native herbs, though we rested a day to try.

After a short march we came to the Nyamazi, another considerable rivulet coming from the north to fall into the Loangwa. It has the same character, of steep alluvial banks, as Pamazi, and about the same width, but much shallower; loin deep, though somewhat swollen; from fifty to sixty yards wide. We came to some low hills, of coarse sandstone, and on crossing these we could see, by looking back, that for many days we had been travelling over a perfectly level valley, clothed with a mantle of forest. The barometers had shown no difference of level from about 1800 feet above the sea. We began our descent into this great valley when we left the source of the Bua; and now these low hills, called Ngalé or Ngaloa, though only 100 feet or so above the level we had left, showed that we had come to the shore of an ancient lake, which probably was let off when the rent of Kebra-basa on the Zambesi was made, for we found immense banks of well-rounded shingle above—or, rather, they may be called mounds of shingle—all of hard silicious schist with a few pieces of fossil-wood among them. The gullies reveal a stratum of this well-rounded shingle, lying on a soft greenish sandstone, which again lies on the coarse sandstone first observed. This formation is identical with that observed formerly below the Victoria Falls. We have the mountains still on our north and north-west (the so-called mountains of Bisa, or Babisa), and from them the Nyamazi flows, while Pamazi comes round the end, or what appears to be the end, of the higher portion. *(22nd December, 1866.)* Shot a bush-buck; and slept on the left bank of Nyamazi.

23rd December, 1866.—Hunger sent us on; for a meat diet is far from satisfying: we all felt very weak on it, and soon tired on a march, but to-day we hurried on to Kavimba, who successfully beat off the Mazitu. It is very hot, and between three and four hours is a good day's march. On sitting down to rest before entering the village we were observed, and all the force of the village issued to kill us as Mazitu, but when we stood up the mistake was readily perceived, and the arrows were placed again in their quivers. In the hut four Mazitu shields show that they did not get it all their own way; they are miserable imitations of Zulu shields, made of eland and water-buck's hides, and ill sewn.

A very small return present was made by Kavimba, and nothing could be bought except at exorbitant prices. We remained all day on the 24th haggling and trying to get some grain. He took a fancy to a shirt, and left it to his wife to bargain for. She got the length of cursing and swearing, and we bore it, but could get only a small price for it. We resolved to hold our Christmas some other day, and in a better place. The women seem ill-regulated here— Kavimba's brother had words with his spouse, and at the end of every burst of vociferation on both sides called out, "Bring the Muavi! bring the Muavi!" or ordeal.

Christmas-day, 1866.—No one being willing to guide us to Moerwa's, I hinted to Kavimba that should we see a rhinoceros I would kill it. He came himself, and led us on where he expected to find these animals, but we saw only their footsteps. We lost our four goats somewhere—stolen or strayed in the pathless forest, we do not know which, but the loss I felt very keenly, for whatever kind of food we had, a little milk made all right, and I felt strong and well, but coarse food hard of digestion without it was very trying. We spent the 26th in searching for them, but all in vain. Kavimba had a boy carrying two huge elephant spears, with these he attacks that large animal single-handed. We parted from him, as I thought, good friends, but a man who volunteered to act as guide saw him in the forest afterwards, and was counselled by him to leave us as we should not pay him. This hovering near us after we parted makes me suspect Kavimba of taking the goats, but I am not certain. The loss affected me more than I could have imagined. A little indigestible porridge, of scarcely any taste, is now my fare, and it makes me dream of better.

27th December, 1866.—Our guide asked for his cloth to wear on the way, as it was wet and raining, and his bark cloth was a miserable covering. I consented, and he bolted on the first opportunity; the forest being so dense he was soon out of reach of pursuit: he had been advised to this by Kavimba, and nothing else need have been expected. We then followed the track of a travelling party of Babisa, but the grass springs up over the paths, and it was soon lost: the rain had fallen early in these parts, and the grass was all in seed. In the afternoon we came to the hills in the north where Nyamazi rises, and went up the bed of a rivulet for some time, and then ascended out of the valley. At the bottom of the ascent and in the rivulet the shingle stratum was sometimes fifty feet thick, then as we ascended we met mica schist tilted on edge, then grey gneiss, and last an igneous trap among quartz rocks, with a great deal of bright mica and talc in them. On resting near the top of the first ascent two honey hunters came to us. They were using the honey-guide as an aid, the bird came to us as they arrived, waited quietly during the half-hour they smoked and chatted, and then went on with them.[41]

The tsetse flies, which were very numerous at the bottom, came up the ascent with us, but as we increased our altitude by another thousand feet they gradually dropped off and left us: only one remained in the evening, and he seemed out of spirits. Near sunset we encamped by water on the cool height, and made our shelters with boughs of leafy trees; mine was rendered perfect by Dr. Stenhouse's invaluable patent cloth, which is very superior to mackintosh: indeed the india-rubber cloth is not to be named in the same day with it.

28th December, 1866.—Three men, going to hunt bees, came to us as we were starting and assured us that Moerwa's was near. The first party had told us the same thing, and so often have we gone long distances as "*pafupi*" (near), when in reality they were "*patari*" (far), that we begin to think *pafupi* means "I wish you to go there," and *patari* the reverse. In this case *near* meant an hour and three-quarters from our sleeping-place to Moerwa's!

When we look back from the height to which we have ascended we see a great plain clothed with dark green forest except at the line of yellowish grass, where probably the Loangwa flows. On the east and south-east this plain is bounded at the extreme range of our vision by a wall of dim blue mountains forty or fifty miles off. The Loangwa is said to rise in the Chibalé country due north of this Malambwé (in which district Moerwa's village is situated), and to flow S.E., then round to where we found it.

Moerwa came to visit me in my hut, a rather stupid man, though he has a well-shaped and well-developed forehead, and tried the usual little arts of getting us to buy all we need here though the prices are exorbitant. "No people in front, great hunger there." "We must buy food here and carry it to support us." On asking the names of the next headman he would not inform me, till I told him to try and speak like a man; he then told us that the first Lobemba chief was Motuna, and the next Chafunga. We have nothing, as we saw no animals in our way hither, and hunger is ill to bear. By giving Moerwa a good large cloth he was induced to cook a mess of maëre or millet and elephant's stomach; it was so good to get a full meal that I could have given him another cloth, and the more so as it was accompanied by a message that he would cook more next day and in larger quantity. On inquiring next evening he said "the man had told lies," he had cooked nothing more: he was prone to lie himself, and was a rather bad specimen of a chief.

The Babisa have round bullet heads, snub noses, often high cheek-bones, an upward slant of the eyes, and look as if they had a lot of Bushman blood in them, and a good many would pass for Bushmen or Hottentots. Both Babisa and Waiyau may have a mixture of the race, which would account for their roving habits. The women have the fashion of exposing the upper part of the buttocks by letting a very stiff cloth fall down behind. Their teeth are filed to points, they wear no lip-ring, and the hair is parted so as to lie in a net at the back part of the head. The mode of salutation among the men is to lie down nearly on the back, clapping the hands, and making a rather inelegant half-kissing sound with the lips.

29th December, 1866.—We remain a day at Malambwé, but get nothing save a little maëre,[42] which grates in the teeth and in the stomach. To prevent the Mazitu starving them they cultivate small round patches placed at wide intervals in the forest, with which the country is covered. The spot, some ten yards or a little more in diameter, is manured with ashes and planted with this millet and pumpkins, in order that should Mazitu come they may be unable to carry off the pumpkins, or gather the millet, the seed of which is very small. They have no more valour than the other Africans, but more craft, and are much given to falsehood. They will not answer common questions except by misstatements, but this may arise in our case from our being in disfavour, because we will not sell all our goods to them for ivory.

30th December, 1866.—Marched for Chitemba's, because it is said he has not fled from the Mazitu, and therefore has food to spare. While resting, Moerwa, with all his force of men, women, and dogs, came up, on his way to hunt elephants. The men were furnished with big spears, and their dogs are used to engage the animal's attention while they spear it; the women cook the meat and make huts, and a smith goes with them to mend any spear that may be broken.

We pass over level plateaux on which the roads are wisely placed, and do not feel that we are travelling in a mountainous region. It is all covered with dense forest, which in many cases is pollarded, from being cut for bark cloth or for hunting purposes. Masuko fruit abounds. From the cisalpinae and gum-copal trees bark cloth is made.

We now come to large masses of haematite, which is often ferruginous: there is conglomerate too, many quartz pebbles being intermixed. It seems as if when the lakes existed in the lower lands, the higher levels gave forth great quantities of water from chalybeate fountains, which deposited this iron ore. Grey granite or quartz with talc in it or gneiss lie under the haematite.

The forest resounds with singing birds, intent on nidification. Francolins abound, but are wild. "Whip-poor-wills," and another bird, which has a more laboured treble note and voice—"Oh, oh, oh!" Gay flowers blush unseen, but the people have a good idea of what is eatable and what not. I looked at a woman's basket of leaves which she had collected for supper, and it contained eight or ten kinds, with mushrooms and orchidaceous flowers. We have a succession of showers to-day, from N.E. and E.N.E. We are uncertain when we shall come to a village, as the Babisa will not tell us where they are situated. In the evening we encamped beside a little rill, and made our shelters, but we had so little to eat that

I dreamed the night long of dinners I had eaten, and might have been eating.

I shall make this beautiful land better known, which is an essential part of the process by which it will become the "pleasant haunts of men." It is impossible to describe its rich luxuriance, but most of it is running to waste through the slave-trade and internal wars.

31st December, 1866.—When we started this morning after rain, all the trees and grass dripping, a lion roared, but we did not see him. A woman had come a long way and built a neat miniature hut in the burnt-out ruins of her mother's house: the food-offering she placed in it, and the act of filial piety, no doubt comforted this poor mourner's heart!

We arrived at Chitembo's village and found it deserted. The Babisa dismantle their huts and carry off the thatch to their gardens, where they live till harvest is over. This fallowing of the framework destroys many insects, but we observed that wherever Babisa and Arab slavers go they leave the breed of the domestic bug: it would be well if that were all the ill they did! Chitembo was working in his garden when we arrived, but soon came, and gave us the choice of all the standing huts: he is an old man, much more frank and truthful than our last headman, and says that Chitapanga is paramount chief of all the Abemba.

Three or four women whom we saw performing a rain dance at Moerwa's were here doing the same; their faces smeared with meal, and axes in their hands, imitating as well as they could the male voice. I got some maëre or millet here and a fowl.

We now end 1866. It has not been so fruitful or useful as I intended. Will try to do better in 1867, and be better—more gentle and loving; and may the Almighty, to whom I commit my way, bring my desires to pass, and prosper me! Let all the sins of '66 be blotted out for Jesus' sake.

* * * * *

1st January, 1867.—May He who was full of grace and truth impress His character on mine. Grace—eagerness to show favour; truth—truthfulness, sincerity, honour—for His mercy's sake.

We remain to-day at Mbulukuta-Chitembo's district, by the boys' desire, because it is New Year's day, and also because we can get some food.

2nd and 3rd January, 1867.—Remain on account of a threatened *set-in* rain. Bought a senzé *(Aulocaudatus Swindernianus)*, a rat-looking animal; but I was glad to get anything in the shape of meat.

4th January, 1867.—It is a *set-in* rain. The boiling-point thermometer shows an altitude of 3565 feet above the sea. Barometer, 3983 feet ditto. We get a little maëre here, and prefer it to being drenched and our goods spoiled. We have neither sugar nor salt, so there are no soluble goods; but cloth and gunpowder get damaged easily. It is hard fare and scanty; I feel always hungry, and am constantly dreaming of better food when I should be sleeping. Savoury viands of former times come vividly up before the imagination, even in my waking hours; this is rather odd as I am not a dreamer; indeed I scarcely ever dream but when I am going to be ill or actually so.[43]

We are on the northern brim (or north-western rather) of the great Loangwa Valley we lately crossed: the rain coming from the east strikes it, and is deposited both above and below, while much of the valley itself is not yet well wetted. Here all the grasses have run up to seed, and yet they are not more than two feet or so in the seed-stalks. The pasturage is very fine. The people employ these continuous or *set-in* rains for hunting the elephant, which gets bogged, and sinks in from fifteen to eighteen inches in soft mud, then even he, the strong one, feels it difficult to escape.[44]

5th January, 1867.—Still storm-stayed. We shall be off as soon as we get a fair day and these heavy rains cease.

6th January, 1867.—After service two men came and said that they were going to Lobemba, and would guide us to Motuna's village; another came a day or two ago, but he had such a villainous look we all shrank from him. These men's faces pleased us, but they did not turn out all we expected, for they guided us away westwards without a path: it was a drizzling rain, and this made us averse to striking off in the forest without them. No inhabitants now except at wide intervals, and no animals either. In the afternoon we came to a deep ravine full of gigantic timber trees and bamboos, with the Mavoché River at the bottom. The dampness had caused the growth of lichens all over the trees, and the steep descent was so slippery that two boys fell, and he who carried the chronometers, twice: this was a misfortune, as it altered the rates, as was seen by the first comparison of them together in the evening. No food at Motuna's village, yet the headman tried to extort two fathoms of calico on the ground that he was owner of the country: we offered to go out of his village and make our own sheds on "God's land," that is, where it is uncultivated, rather than have any words about it: he then begged us to stay. A very high mountain called Chikokwé appeared W.S.W. from this village; the people who live on it are called Matumba; this part is named Lokumbi, but whatever the name, all the people are Babisa, the dependants of the Babemba, reduced by their own slaving habits to a miserable jungly state. They feed much on wild fruits, roots, and leaves; and yet are generally plump. They use a wooden hoe for sowing their maëre, it is a sort of V-shaped implement, made from a branch with another springing out of it, about an inch in diameter at the sharp point, and with it they claw the soil after scattering the seed; about a dozen young men were so employed in the usual small patches as we passed in the morning.

The country now exhibits the extreme of leafiness and the undulations are masses of green leaves; as far as the eye can reach with distinctness it rests on a mantle of that hue, and beyond the scene becomes dark blue. Near at hand many gay flowers peep out. Here and there the scarlet martagón (*Lilium chalcedonicum*), bright blue or yellow gingers; red, orange, yellow, and pure white orchids; pale lobelias, &c.; but they do not mar the general greenness. As we ascended higher on the plateau, grasses, which have pink and reddish brown seed-vessels imparted distinct shades of their colours to the lawns, and were grateful to the eye. We turned aside early in our march to avoid being wetted by rains, and took shelter in some old Babisa sheds; these, when the party is a slaving one, are built so as to form a circle, with but one opening: a ridge pole, or rather a succession of ridge poles, form one long shed all round, with no partitions in the roof-shaped hut.

On the *9th of January* we ascended a hardened sandstone range. Two men who accompanied our guide called out every now and then to attract the attention of the honey-guide, but none appeared. A water-buck had been killed and eaten at one spot, the ground showing marks of a severe struggle, but no game was to be seen. Buffaloes and elephants come here at certain seasons; at present they have migrated elsewhere. The valleys are very beautiful: the oozes are covered with a species of short wiry grass, which gives the valleys the appearance of well-kept gentlemen's parks; but they are full of water to overflowing—immense sponges in fact;—and one has to watch carefully in crossing them to avoid plunging into deep water-holes, made by the feet of elephants or buffaloes. In the ooze generally the water comes half-way up the shoe, and we go plash, plash, plash, in the lawn-like glade. There are no people here now in these lovely wild valleys; but to-day we came to mounds made of old for planting grain, and slag from iron furnaces. The guide was rather offended because he did not get meat and meal, though he is accustomed to leaves at home, and we had none to give except by wanting ourselves: he found a mess without much labour in the forest. My stock of meal came to an end to-day, but Simon gave me some of his. It is not the unpleasantness of eating unpalatable food that teases one, but we are never satisfied; I could brace myself to dispose of a very unsavoury mess, and think no more about it; but this maëre engenders a craving which plagues day and night incessantly.

10th January, 1867.—We crossed the Muasi, flowing strongly to the east to the Loangwa River.

In the afternoon an excessively heavy thunderstorm wetted us all to the skin before any shelter could be made. Two of our men wandered, and other two remained behind lost, as our track was washed out by the rains. The country is a succession of enormous waves, all covered with jungle, and no traces of paths; we were in a hollow, and our firing was not heard till this morning, when we ascended a height and were answered. I am thankful that up one was lost, for a man might wander a long time before reaching a village. Simon gave me a little more of his meal this morning, and went without himself: I took my belt up three holes to relieve hunger. We got some wretched wild fruit like that called "jambos" in India, and at midday reached the village of Chafunga. Famine here too, but some men had killed an elephant and came to sell the dried meat: it was high, and so were their prices; but we are obliged to give our best from this craving hunger.

12th January, 1867.—Sitting down this morning near a tree my head was just one yard off a good-sized cobra, coiled up in the sprouts at its root, but it was benumbed with cold: a very pretty little puff-adder lay in the path, also benumbed; it is seldom that any harm is done by these reptiles here, although it is different in India. We bought up all the food we could get; but it did not suffice for the marches we expect to make to get to the Chambezé, where food is said to be abundant, we were therefore again obliged to travel on Sunday. We had prayers before starting; but I always feel that I am not doing right, it lessens the sense of obligation in the minds of my companions; but I have no choice. We went along a rivulet till it ended in a small lake, Mapampa or Chimbwé, about five miles long, and one and a half broad. It had hippopotami, and the poku fed on its banks.

15th January, 1867.—We had to cross the Chimbwé at its eastern end, where it is fully a mile wide. The guide refused to show another and narrower ford up the stream, which emptied into it from the east; and I, being the first to cross, neglected to give orders about the poor little dog, Chitané. The water was waist deep, the bottom soft peaty stuff with deep holes in it, and the northern side infested by leeches. The boys were—like myself—all too much engaged with preserving their balance to think of the spirited little beast, and he must have swam till he sunk. He was so useful in keeping all the country curs off our huts; none dare to approach and steal, and he never stole himself. He shared the staring of the people with his master, then in the march he took charge of the whole party, running to the front, and again to the rear, to see that all was right. He was becoming yellowish-red in colour; and, poor thing, perished in what the boys all call Chitané's water.

16th January, 1867.—March through the mountains, which are of beautiful white and pink dolomite, scantily covered with upland trees and vegetation. The rain, as usual, made us halt early, and wild fruits helped to induce us to stay.

In one place we lighted on a party of people living on Masuko fruit, and making mats of the Shuaré[45] palm petioles. We have hard lines ourselves; nothing but a little maëre porridge and dampers. We roast a little grain, and boil it, to make believe it is coffee. The guide, a maundering fellow, turned because he was not fed better than at home, and because he knew that but for his obstinacy we should not have lost the dog. It is needless to repeat that it is all forest on the northern slopes of the mountains—open glade and miles of forest; ground at present all sloppy; oozes full and overflowing—

feet constantly wet. Rivulets rush strongly with *clear* water, though they are in flood: we can guess which are perennial and which mere torrents that dry up; they flow northwards and westwards to the Chambezé.

17th January, 1867.—Detained in an old Babisa slaving encampment by set-in rain till noon, then set off in the midst of it. Came to hills of dolomite, but all the rocks were covered with white lichens (ash-coloured). The path took us thence along a ridge, which separates the Lotiri, running westwards, and the Lobo, going northwards, and we came at length to the Lobo, travelling along its banks till we reached the village called Lisunga, which was about five yards broad, and very deep, in flood, with clear water, as indeed are all the rivulets now; they can only be crossed by felling a tree on the bant and letting it fall across. They do not abrade their banks— vegetation protects them. I observed that the brown ibis, a noisy bird, took care to restrain his loud, harsh voice when driven from the tree in which his nest was placed, and when about a quarter of a mile off, then commenced his loud "Ha-ha-ha!"

18th January, 1867.—The headman of Lisunga, Chaokila, took our present, and gave nothing in return. A deputy from Chitapangwa came afterwards and demanded a larger present, as he was the greater man, and said that if we gave him two fathoms of calico, he would order all the people to bring plenty of food, not here only, but all the way to the paramount chief of Lobemba, Chitapangwa. I proposed that he should begin by ordering Chaokila to give us some in return for our present. This led, as Chaokila told us, to the cloth being delivered to the deputy, and we saw that all the starvelings south of the Chambezé were poor dependants on the Babemba, or rather their slaves, who cultivate little, and then only in the rounded patches above mentioned, so as to prevent their conquerors from taking away more than a small share. The subjects are Babisa—a miserable lying lot of serfs. This tribe is engaged in the slave-trade, and the evil effects are seen in their depopulated country and utter distrust of every one.

19th January, 1867.—Raining most of the day. Worked out the longitude of the mountain-station said to be Mpini, but it will be better to name it Chitané's, as I could not get the name from our maundering guide; he probably did not know it. Lat, 11° 9' 2" S.; long. 32° 1' 30" E.

Altitude above sea (barometer)   5353 feet;
Altitude above sea (boiling-point) 5385 feet.

———

Diff. 32.[46]

Nothing but famine and famine prices, the people living on mushrooms and leaves. Of mushrooms we observed that they choose five or six kinds, and rejected ten sorts. One species becomes as large as the crown of a man's hat; it is pure white, with a blush of brown in the middle of the crown, and is very good roasted; it is named "Motenta;" another, Mofeta; 3rd, Boséfwé; 4th, Nakabausa; 5th, Chisimbé, lobulated, green outside, and pink and fleshy inside; as a relish to others: some experience must have been requisite to enable them to distinguish the good from the noxious, of which they reject ten sorts.

We get some elephants' meat from the people, but high is no name for its condition. It is very bitter, but we used it as a relish to the maëre porridge: none of the animal is wasted; skin and all is cut up and sold, not one of us would touch it with the hand if we had aught else, for the gravy in which we dip our porridge is like an aqueous solution of aloes, but it prevents the heartburn, which maëre causes when taken alone. I take mushrooms boiled instead; but the meat is never refused when we can purchase it, as it seems to ease the feeling of fatigue which jungle-fruit and fare engenders. The appetite in this country is always very keen, and makes hunger worse to bear: the want of salt, probably, makes the gnawing sensation worse.

* * * * *

[We now come to a disaster which cannot be exaggerated in importance when we witness its after effects month by month on Dr. Livingstone. There can be little doubt that the severity of his subsequent illnesses mainly turned upon it, and it is hardly too much to believe that his constitution from this time was steadily sapped by the effects of fever-poison which he was powerless to counteract, owing to the want of quinine. In his allusion to Bishop Mackenzie's death, we have only a further confirmation of the one rule in all such cases which must be followed, or the traveller in Africa goes—not with his life in his hand, but in some luckless box, put in the charge of careless servants. Bishop Mackenzie had all his drugs destroyed by the upsetting of a canoe, in which was his case of medicines, and in a moment everything was soaked and spoilt.

It cannot be too strongly urged on explorers that they should divide their more important medicines in such a way that a *total loss* shall become well-nigh impossible. Three or four tin canisters containing some calomel, Dover's powder, colocynth, and, above all, a supply of quinine, can be distributed in different packages, and then, if a mishap occurs similar to that which Livingstone relates, the disaster is not beyond remedy.]

* * * * *

20th January, 1867.—A guide refused, so we marched without one. The two Waiyau, who joined us at Kandé's village, now deserted. They had been very faithful all the way, and took our part in every case. Knowing the language well, they were extremely useful, and no one thought that they would desert, for they were free men—their masters had been killed by the Mazitu—and this circumstance, and their uniform good conduct, made us trust them more than we should have done any others who had been slaves. But they left us in the forest, and heavy rain came on, which obliterated every vestige of their footsteps. To make the loss the more galling, they took what we could least spare—the medicine-box, which they would only throw away as soon as they came to examine their booty. One of these deserters exchanged his load that morning with a boy called Baraka, who had charge of the medicine-box, because he was so careful. This was done, because with the medicine-chest were packed five large cloths and all Baraka's clothing and beads, of which he was very careful. The Waiyau also offered to carry this burden a stage to help Baraka, while he gave his own load, in which there was no cloth, in exchange. The forest was so dense and high, there was no chance of getting a glimpse of the fugitives, who took all the dishes, a large box of powder, the flour we had purchased dearly to help us as far as the Chambezé, the tools, two guns, and a cartridge-pouch; but the medicine-chest was the sorest loss of all! I felt as if I had now received the sentence of death, like poor Bishop Mackenzie.

All the other goods I had divided in case of loss or desertion, but had never dreamed of losing the precious quinine and other remedies; other losses and annoyances I felt as just parts of that undercurrent of vexations which is not wanting in even the smoothest life, and certainly not worthy of being moaned over in the experience of an explorer anxious to benefit a country and people—but this loss I feel most keenly. Everything of this kind happens by the permission of One who watches over us with most tender care; and this may turn out for the best by taking away a source of suspicion among more superstitious, charm-dreading people further north. I meant it as a source of benefit to my party and to the heathen.

We returned to Lisunga, and got two men off to go back to Chafunga's village, and intercept the deserters if they went there; but it is likely that, having our supply of flour, they will give our route a wide berth and escape altogether. It is difficult to say from the heart, "Thy will be done;" but I shall try. These Waiyau had few advantages: sold into slavery in early life, they were in the worst possible school for learning to be honest and honourable, they behaved well for a long time; but, having had hard and scanty fare in Lobisa, wet and misery in passing through dripping forests, hungry nights and fatiguing days, their patience must have been worn out, and they had no sentiments of honour, or at least none so strong as we ought to have; they gave way to the temptation which their good conduct had led us to put in their way. Some we have come across in this journey seemed born essentially mean and base—a great misfortune to them and all who have to deal with them, but they cannot be so blamable as those who have no natural tendency to meanness, and whose education has taught them to abhor it. True; yet this loss of the medicine-box gnaws at the heart terribly.

21st and 22nd January, 1867.—Remained at Lisunga—raining nearly all day; and we bought all the maëre the chief would sell. We were now forced to go on and made for the next village to buy food. Want of food and rain are our chief difficulties now, more rain falls here on this northern slope of the upland than elsewhere; clouds come up from the north and pour down their treasures in heavy thunder-showers, which deluge the whole country south of the edge of the plateau: the rain-clouds come from the west chiefly.

23rd January, 1867.—A march of five and three-quarter hours brought us yesterday to a village, Chibanda's stockade, where "no food" was the case, as usual. We crossed a good-sized rivulet, the Mapampa (probably ten yards wide), dashing along to the east; all the rest of the way was in dark forest. I sent off the boys to the village of Muasi to buy food, if successful, to-morrow we march for the Chambezé, on the other side of which all the reports agree in the statement that there plenty of food is to be had. We all feel weak and easily tired, and an incessant hunger teases us, so it is no wonder if so large a space of this paper is occupied by stomach affairs. It has not been merely want of nice dishes, but real biting hunger and faintness.

24th January, 1867.—Four hours through unbroken, dark forest brought us to the Movushi, which here is a sluggish stream, winding through and filling a marshy valley a mile wide. It comes from south-east, and falls into the Chambezé, about 2' north of our encampment. The village of Moaba is on the east side of the marshy valley of the Movuhi, and very difficult to be approached, as the water is chin-deep in several spots. I decided to make sheds on the west side, and send over for food, which, thanks to the Providence which watches over us, we found at last in a good supply of maëre and some ground-nuts; but through, all this upland region the trees yielding bark-cloth, or *nyanda*, are so abundant, that the people are all well-clothed with it, and care but little for our cloth. Red and pink beads are in fashion, and fortunately we have red.

* * * * *

[We may here add a few particulars concerning beads, which form such an important item of currency all through Africa. With a few exceptions they are all manufactured in Venice. The greatest care must be exercised, or the traveller—ignorant of the prevailing fashion in the country he is about to explore—finds himself with an accumulation of beads of no more value than tokens would be if tendered in this country for coin of the realm.

Thanks to the kindness of Messrs. Levin & Co., the bead merchants, of Bevis Marks, E.C., we have been able to get some idea of the more valuable beads, through a selection made by Susi and Chuma in their warehouse. The Waiyou prefer exceedingly small beads, the size of mustard-seed, and of various colours, but they must be opaque: amongst them dull white chalk varieties, called "Catchokolo," are valuable, besides black and pink, named, respectively, "Bububu" and "Sekundereché" = the "dregs of pombe." One red bead, of various sizes, which has a white centre, is always valuable in every part of Africa. It is called "Sami-sami" by the Suahélé, "Chitakaraka" by the Waiyou, "Mangazi," = "blood," by the Nyassa, and was found popular even amongst the Manyuema, under the name of "Maso-kantussi", "bird's eyes." Whilst speaking of this distant tribe, it is interesting to observe that one peculiar long bead, recognised as common in the Manyuema land, is only sent to the West Coast of Africa, and *never* to the East. On Chuma pointing to it as a sort found at the extreme limit explored by Livingstone, it was at once seen that he must have touched that part of Africa which begins to be within the reach of the traders in the Portuguese settlements. "Machua Kanga" = "guinea fowl's eyes," is another popular variety; and the "Moiompio" = "new heart," a large pale blue bead, is a favourite amongst the Wabisa; but by far the most valuable of all is a small white oblong bead, which, when strung, looks like the joints of the cane root, from which it takes its name, "Salani" = cane. Susi says that 1 lb. weight of these beads would buy a tusk of ivory, at the south end of Tanganyika, so big that a strong man could not carry it more than two hours.]

* * * * *

25th January, 1867.—Remain and get our maëre ground into flour. Moaba has cattle, sheep, and goats. The other side of the Chambezé has everything in still greater abundance; so we may recover our lost flesh. There are buffaloes in this quarter, but we have not got a glimpse of any. If game was to be had, I should have hunted; but the hopo way of hunting prevails, and we pass miles of hedges by which many animals must have perished. In passing-through the forests it is surprising to see none but old footsteps of the game; but the hopo destruction accounts for its absence. When the hedges are burned, then the manured space is planted with pumpkins and calabashes.

I observed at Chibanda's a few green mushrooms, which, on being peeled, showed a pink, fleshy inside; they are called "chisimba;" and only one or two are put into the mortar, in which the women pound the other kinds, to give relish, it was said, to the mass: I could not ascertain what properties chisimba had when taken alone; but mushroom diet, in our experience, is good only for producing dreams of the roast beef of bygone days. The saliva runs from the mouth in these dreams, and the pillow is wet with it in the mornings.

These Babisa are full of suspicion; everything has to be paid for accordingly in advance, and we found that giving a present to a chief is only putting it in his power to cheat us out of a supper. They give nothing to each other for nothing, and if this is enlargement of mind produced by commerce, commend me to the untrading African!

Fish now appear in the rivulets. Higher altitudes have only small things, not worth catching.

An owl makes the woods resound by night and early morning with his cries, which consist of a loud, double-initial note, and then a succession of lower descending notes. Another new bird, or at least new to me, makes the forests ring.

When the vultures see us making our sheds, they conclude that we have killed some animal; but after watching awhile, and seeing no meat, they depart. This is suggestive of what other things prove, that it is only by sight they are guided.[47]

With respect to the native head-dresses the colouring-matter, "nkola," which seems to be camwood, is placed as an ornament on the head, and some is put on the bark-cloth to give it a pleasant appearance. The tree, when cut, is burned to bring out the strong colour, and then, when it is developed, the wood is powdered.

The gum-copal trees now pour out gum where wounded, and I have seen masses of it fallen on the ground.

26th January, 1867.—Went northwards along the Movushi, near to its confluence with Chambezé, and then took lodging in a deserted temporary village. In the evening I shot a poku, or tsébula, full-grown male. It measured from snout to insertion of tail, 5 feet 3 inches; tail, 1 foot; height at withers, 3 feet; circumference of chest, 5 feet; face to insertion of horns, 9-1/2 inches; horns measured on curve, 16 inches. Twelve rings on horns, and one had a ridge behind, 1/2 inch broad, 1/2 inch high, and tapering up the horn; probably accidental. Colour: reddish-yellow, dark points in front of foot and on the ears, belly nearly white. The shell went through from behind the shoulder to the spleen, and burst on the other side, yet he ran 100 yards. I felt very thankful to the Giver of all good for this meat.

27th January, 1867.—A set-in rain all the morning, but having meat we were comfortable in the old huts. In changing my dress this morning I was frightened at my own emaciation.

28th January, 1867.—-We went five miles along the Movushi and the Chambezé to a crossing-place said to avoid three rivers on the other side, which require canoes just now, and have none. Our lat. 10° 34' S. The Chambezé was flooded with clear water, but the lines of bushy trees, which showed its real banks, were not more than forty yards apart, it showed its usual character of abundant animal life in its waters and on its banks, as it wended its way westwards. The canoe-man was excessively suspicious; when prepayment was acceded to, he asked a piece more, and although he was promised full payment as soon as we were all safely across he kept the last man on the south side as a hostage for this bit of calico: he then ran away. They must cheat each other sadly.

Went northwards, wading across two miles of flooded flats on to which the *Clarias Capensis*, a species of siluris, comes to forage out of the river. We had the Likindazi, a sedgy stream, with hippopotami, on our right. Slept in forest without seeing anyone. Then next day we met with a party who had come from their village to look for us. We were now in Lobemba, but these villagers had nothing but hopes of plenty at Chitapangwa's. This village had half a mile of ooze and sludgy marsh in front of it, and a stockade as usual. We observed that the people had great fear of animals at night, and shut the gates carefully, of even temporary villages. When at Molemba (Chitapangwa's village) afterwards, two men were killed by a lion, and great fear of crocodiles was expressed by our canoe-man at the Chambezé, when one washed in the margin of that river. There was evidence of abundance of game, elephants, and buffaloes, but we saw none.

29th January, 1867.—When near our next stage end we were shown where lightning had struck; it ran down a gum-copal tree without damaging it, then ten yards horizontally, and dividing there into two streams it went up an anthill; the withered grass showed its course very plainly, and next day (31st), on the banks of the

Mabula, we saw a dry tree which had been struck; large splinters had been riven off and thrown a distance of sixty yards in one direction and thirty yards in another: only a stump was left, and patches of withered grass where it had gone horizontally.

30th January, 1867.—Northwards through almost trackless dripping forests and across oozing bogs.

31st January, 1867.—Through forest, but gardens of larger size than in Lobisa now appear. A man offered a thick bar of copper for sale, a foot by three inches. The hard-leafed acacia and mohempi abound. The valleys, with the oozes, have a species of grass, having pink seed-stalks and yellow seeds: this is very pretty. At midday we came to the Lopiri, the rivulet which waters Chitapanga's stockade, and soon after found that his village has a triple stockade, the inner being defended also by a deep broad ditch and hedge of a solanaceous thorny shrub. It is about 200 yards broad and 500 long. The huts not planted very closely.

Chitapangwa receiving Dr. Livingstone.

The rivulets were all making for the Chambezé. They contain no fish, except very small ones—probably fry. On the other, or western side of the ridge, near which "Malemba" is situated, fish abound worth catching.

Chitapangwa

Chitapangwa, or Motoka, as he is also called, sent to inquire if we wanted an audience. "We must take something in our hands the first time we came before so great a man." Being tired from marching, I replied, "Not till the evening," and sent notice at 5 P.M. of my coming. We passed through the inner stockade, and then on to an enormous hut, where sat Chitapangwa, with three drummers and ten or more men, with two rattles in their hands. The drummers beat furiously, and the rattlers kept time to the drums, two of them advancing and receding in a stooping posture, with rattles near the ground, as if doing the chief obeisance, but still keeping time with the others. I declined to sit on the ground, and an enormous tusk was brought for me. The chief saluted courteously. He has a fat jolly face, and legs loaded with brass and copper leglets. I mentioned our losses by the desertion of the Waiyau, but his power is merely nominal, and he could do nothing. After talking awhile he came along with us to a group of cows, and pointed out one. "That is yours," said he. The tusk on which I sat was sent after me too as being mine, because I had sat upon it. He put on my cloth as token of acceptance, and sent two large baskets of sorghum to the hut afterwards, and then sent for one of the boys to pump him after dark.

Chitapangwa's Wives.

1st February, 1867.—We found a small party of black Arab slave-traders here from Bagamoio on the coast, and as the chief had behaved handsomely as I thought, I went this morning and gave him one of our best cloths; but when we were about to kill the cow, a man interfered and pointed out a smaller one. I asked if this was by the orders of the chief. The chief said that the man had lied, but I declined to take any cow at all if he did not give it willingly.

The slavers, the headman of whom was Magaru Mafupi, came and said that they were going off on the 2nd; (*2nd February, 1867*) but by payment I got them to remain a day, and was all day employed in writing despatches.

3rd February, 1867.—Magaru Mafupi left this morning with a packet of letters, for which he is to get Rs. 10 at Zanzibar.[48] They came by a much shorter route than we followed, in fact, nearly due west or south-west; but not a soul would tell us of this way of coming into the country when we were at Zanzibar. Bagamoio is only six hours north of Kurdary Harbour. It is possible that the people of Zanzibar did not know of it themselves, as this is the first time they have come so far. The route is full of villages and people who have plenty of goats, and very cheap. They number fifteen stations, or sultans, as they call the chiefs, and will be at Bagamoio in two months:—1. Chasa; 2. Lombé; 3. Ucheré; 4. Nyamiro; 5. Zonda; 6. Zambi; 7. Lioti; 8. Méreré; 9. Kirangabana; 10. Nkongozi; 11. Sombogo; 12. Suré; 13. Lomolasenga; 14. Kapass; 15, Chanzé. They are then in the country adjacent to Bagamoio. Some of these places are two or three days apart from each other.

They came to three large rivers: 1. Wembo; 2. Luaha; 3. Luvo; but I had not time to make further inquiries. They had one of Speke's companions to Tanganyika with them, named Janjé, or Janja, who could imitate a trumpet by blowing into the palm of his hand. I ordered another supply of cloth and beads, and I sent for a small quantity of coffee, sugar, candles, French preserved meats, a cheese in tin, six bottles of port-wine, quinine, calomel, and resin of jalap, to be sent to Ujiji.

I proposed to go a little way east with this route to buy goats, but Chitapangwa got very angry, saying, I came only to show my things, and would buy nothing: he then altered his tone, and requested me to take the cow first presented and eat it, and as we were all much in need I took it. We were to give only what we liked in addition; but this was a snare, and when I gave two more cloths he sent them back, and demanded a blanket. The boys alone have blankets; so I told him these were not slaves, and I could not take from them what I had once given. Though it is disagreeable to be thus victimized, it is the first time we have tasted fat for six weeks and more.

6th February, 1867.—Chitapangwa came with his wife to see the instruments which I explained to them as well as I could, and the books, as well as the Book of Books, and to my statements he made intelligent remarks. The boys are sorely afraid of him. When Abraham does not like to say what I state, he says to me "I don't know the proper word;" but when I speak without him, he soon finds them. He and Simon thought that talking in a cringing manner was the way to win him over, so I let them try it with a man he sent to communicate with us, and the result was this fellow wanted to open their bundles, pulled them about, and kept them awake most of the night. Abraham came at night: "Sir, what shall I do? they won't let me sleep." "You have had your own way," I replied, "and must abide by it." He brought them over to me in the morning, but I soon dismissed both him and them.

7th February, 1867.—I sent to the chief either to come to me or say Avhen I should come to him and talk; the answer I got was that he would come when shaved, but he afterwards sent a man to hear what I had to advance—this I declined, and when the rain ceased I went myself.

On coming into his hut I stated that I had given him four times the value of his cow, but if he thought otherwise, let us take the four cloths to his brother Moamba, and if he said that I had not given enough, I would buy a cow and send it back. This he did not relish at all. "Oh, great Englishman! why should we refer a dispute to an inferior. I am the great chief of all this country. Ingleze mokolu, you are sorry that you have to give so much for the ox you have eaten. You would not take a smaller, and therefore I gratified your heart by giving the larger; and why should not you gratify my heart by giving cloth sufficient to cover me, and please me?"

I said that my cloths would cover him, and his biggest wife too all over, he laughed at this, but still held out; and as we have meat, and he sent maize and calabashes, I went away. He turns round now, and puts the blame of greediness on me. I cannot enter into his ideas, or see his point of view; cannot, in fact, enter into his ignorance, his prejudices, or delusions, so it is impossible to pronounce a true judgment. One who has no humour cannot understand one who has: this is an equivalent case.

Rain and clouds so constantly, I could not get our latitude till last night, 10° 14' 6" S. On 8th got lunars. Long. 31° 46' 45" E. Altitude above sea, 4700 feet, by boiling-point and barometer.

8th February, 1867.—The chief demands one of my boxes and a blanket; I explain that one day's rain would spoil the contents, and the boys who have blankets, not being slaves, I cannot take from them what I have given. I am told that he declares that he will take us back to the Loangwa; make war and involve us in it, deprive us of food, &c.: this succeeds in terrifying the boys. He thinks that we have some self-interest to secure in passing through the country, and therefore he has a right to a share in the gain. When told it was for a public benefit, he pulled down the underlid of the right eye.[49] He believes we shall profit by our journey, though he knows not in what way.

It is possibly only a coincidence, but no sooner do we meet with one who accompanied Speke and Burton to Tanganyika, than the system of mulcting commences. I have no doubt but that Janjé told this man how his former employers paid down whatever was demanded of them.

10th February, 1867.—I had service in the open air, many looking on, and spoke afterwards to the chief, but he believes nothing save what Speke and Burton's man has told him. He gave us a present of corn and ground-nuts, and says he did not order the people not to sell grain to us. We must stop and eat green maize. He came after evening service, and I explained a little to him, and showed him woodcuts in the 'Bible Dictionary,' which he readily understood.

11th February, 1867.—The chief sent us a basket of hippopotamus flesh from the Chambezé, and a large one of green maize. He says the three cloths I offered are still mine: all he wants is a box and blanket; if not a blanket, a box must be given, a tin one. He keeps out of my way, by going to the gardens every morning. He is good-natured, and our intercourse is a laughing one; but the boys betray their terrors in their tone of voice, and render my words powerless.

The black and white, and the brownish-grey water wagtails are remarkably tame. They come about the huts and even into them, and no one ever disturbs them. They build their nests about the huts. In the Bechuana country, a fine is imposed on any man whose boys kill one, but why, no one can tell me. The boys with me aver that they are not killed, because the meat is not eaten! or because they are so tame!!

13th February, 1867.—I gave one of the boxes at last, Chitapangwa offering a heavy Arab wooden one to preserve our things, which I declined to take, as I parted with our own partly to lighten a load. Abraham unwittingly told me that he had not given me the chiefs statement in full when he pressed me to take his cow. It was, "Take and eat the one you like, and give me a blanket." Abraham said "He has no blanket." Then he said to me, "Take it and eat it, and give him any pretty thing you like." I was thus led to mistake the chief, and he, believing that he had said explicitly he wanted a blanket for it, naturally held out. It is difficult to get these lads to say what one wants uttered: either with enormous self-conceit, they give different, and, as they think, better statements, suppress them altogether, or return false answers: this is the great and crowning difficulty of my intercourse.

I got ready to go, but the chief was very angry, and came with all his force, exclaiming that I wanted to leave against his will and power, though he wished to adjust matters, and send me away nicely. He does not believe that we have no blankets. It is hard to be kept waiting here, but all may be for the best: it has always turned out so, and I trust in Him on whom I can cast all my cares. The Lord look on this and help me. Though I have these nine boys, I feel quite alone.

I gave the chief some seeds, peas, and beans, for which he seemed thankful, and returned little presents of food and beer frequently. The beer of maëre is stuffed full of the growing grain as it begins to sprout, it is as thick as porridge, very strong and bitter, and goes to the head, requiring a strong digestion to overcome it.

February, 1867.—I showed the chief one of the boys' blankets, which he is willing to part with for two of our cloths, each of which is larger than it, but he declines to receive it, because we have new ones. I invited him, since he disbelieved my assertions, to look in our bales, and if he saw none, to pay us a fine for the insult: he consented in a laughing way to give us an ox. All our personal intercourse has been of the good-natured sort. It is the communications to the boys, by three men who are our protectors, or rather spies, that is disagreeable; I won't let them bring those fellows near me.

10th February, 1867.—He came early in the morning, and I showed that I had no blanket, and he took the old one, and said that the affair was ended. A long misunderstanding would have been avoided, had Abraham told me fully what the chief said at first.

16th February, 1867.—The chief offered me a cow for à piece of red serge, and after a deal of talk and Chitapangwa swearing that no demand would be made after the bargain was concluded, I gave the serge, a cloth, and a few beads for a good fat cow. The serge was two fathoms, a portion of that which Miss Coutts gave me when leaving England in 1858.

The chief is not so bad, as the boys are so cowardly. They assume a chirping, piping tone of voice in speaking to him, and do not say what at last has to be said, because in their cringing souls they believe they know what should be said better than I do. It does not strike them in the least that I have grown grey amongst these people; and it is immense conceit in mere boys to equal themselves to me. The difficulty is greater, because when I do ask their opinions I only receive the reply, "It is as you please, sir." Very likely some men of character may arise and lead them; but such as I have would do little to civilise.

17th February, 1867.—Too ill with rheumatic-fever to have service; this is the first attack of it I ever had—and no medicine! but I trust in the Lord, who healeth His people.

18th February, 1867.—This cow we divided at once. The last one we cooked, and divided a full, hearty meal to all every evening.

The boom—booming of water dashing against or over the rocks is heard at a good distance from most of the burns in this upland region; hence it is never quite still.

The rocks here are argillaceous schist, red and white. *(Keel, Scottice.)*

19th February, 1867.—Chitapangwa begged me to stay another day, that one of the boys might mend his blanket; it has been worn every night since April, and I, being weak and giddy, consented. A glorious day of bright sunlight after a night's rain. We scarcely ever have a twenty-four hours without rain, and never half that period without thunder.

The camwood (?) is here called molombwa, and grows very abundantly. The people take the bark, boil, and grind it fine: it is then a splendid blood-red, and they use it extensively as an ornament, sprinkling it on the bark-cloth, or smearing it on the head. It is in large balls, and is now called mkola. The tree has pinnated, alternate lanceolate, leaves, and attains a height of 40 or 50 feet, with a diameter of 15 or 18 inches finely and closely veined above, more widely beneath.

I am informed by Abraham that the Nyumbo (Numbo or Mumbo) is easily propagated by cuttings, or by cuttings of the roots. A bunch of the stalks is preserved in the soil for planting next year, and small pieces are cut off, and take root easily; it has a pea-shaped flower, but we never saw the seed. It is very much better here than I have seen it elsewhere; and James says that in his country it is quite white and better still; what I have seen is of a greenish tinge after it is boiled.

[Amongst the articles brought to the coast the men took care not to lose a number of seeds which they found in Dr. Livingstone's boxes after his death. These have been placed in the hands of the authorities at Kew, and we may hope that in some instances they have maintained vitality.

It is a great pity that there is such a lack of enterprise in the various European settlements on the East Coast of Africa. Were it otherwise a large trade in valuable woods and other products would assuredly spring up. Ebony and lignum vitae abound; Dr. Livingstone used hardly any other fuel when he navigated the *Pioneer*, and no wood was found to make such "good steam." India-rubber may be had for the collecting, and we see that even the natives know some of the dye-woods, besides which the palm-oil tree is found, indigo is a weed everywhere, and coffee is indigenous.]

FOOTNOTES:

36. In coming to cross roads it is the custom of the leader to "mark" all side paths and wrong turnings by making a scratch across them with his spear, or by breaking a branch and laying it across: in this way those who follow are able to avoid straying off the proper road.—ED.

37. Heleotragus Vardonii.

38. The tamarind does the same thing in the heat of the day.

39. A species of kingfisher, which stands flapping its wings and attempting to sing in a ridiculous manner. It never was better described than by one observer who, after watching it through its performance, said it was "a toy-shoppy bird."—ED.

40. Not the great chief near Lake Moero of the same name.

41. This extraordinary bird flies from tree to tree in front of the hunter, chirrupping loudly, and will not be content till he arrives at the spot where the bees'-nest is; it then waits quietly till the honey is taken, and feeds on the broken morsels of comb which fall to its share.

42. Eleusine Coracana.

43. It may not be altogether without interest to state that Livingstone could fall asleep when he wished at the very shortest notice. A mat, and a shady tree under which to spread it, would at any time afford him a refreshing sleep, and this faculty no doubt contributed much to his great powers of endurance.—ED.

44. When the elephant becomes confused by the yelping pack of dogs with which he is surrounded, the hunter stealthily approaches behind, and with one blow of a sharp axe hamstrings the huge beast.—ED.

45. Raphia.

46. Top of mountain (barometer) 6338 feat.

47. The experience of all African sportsmen tends towards the same conclusion. Vultures probably have their beats high overhead in the sky, too far to be seen by the eye. From this altitude they can watch a vast tract of country, and whenever the disturbed movements of game are observed they draw together, and for the first time are seen wheeling, about at a great height over the spot. So soon as an animal is killed, every tree is filled with them, but the hunter has only to cover the meat with boughs or reeds and the vultures are entirely at a loss—hidden, from view it is hidden altogether: the idea that they are attracted by their keen sense of smell is altogether erroneous,—ED.

48. These letters reached England safely.

49. It seems almost too ridiculous to believe that we have here the exact equivalent of the schoolboy's demonstrative "Do you see any green in my eye?" nevertheless it looks wonderfully like it!—ED.

* * * * *

CHAPTER VIII.

Chitapangwa's parting oath. Course laid for Lake Tanganyika.
Moamba's village. Another watershed. The Babemba tribe.
Ill with fever. Threatening attitude of Chibué's people.
Continued illness. Reaches cliffs overhanging Lake Liemba.
Extreme beauty of the scene. Dangerous fit of insensibility.
Leaves the Lake. Pernambuco cotton. Rumours of war
between Arabs and Nsama. Reaches Chitimba's village.
Presents Sultan's letter to principal Arab Harnees. The war
in Itawa. Geography of the Arabs. Ivory traders and slave-
dealers. Appeal to the Koran. Gleans intelligence of the
Wasongo to the eastward, and their chief, Meréré. Harnees
sets out against Nsama. Tedious sojourn. Departure for
Ponda. Native cupping.

20th February, 1867.—I told the chief before starting that my
heart was sore, because he was not sending me away so cordially as
I liked. He at once ordered men to start with us, and gave me a brass
knife with ivory sheath, which he had long worn, as a memorial. He
explained that we ought to go north as, if we made easting, we
should ultimately be obliged to turn west, and all our cloth would
be expended ere we reached the Lake Tanganyika; he took a piece
of clay off the ground and rubbed it on his tongue as an oath that
what he said was true, and came along with us to see that all was
right; and so we parted.

We soon ascended the plateau, which encloses with its edge
the village and stream of Molemba. Wild pigs are abundant, and
there are marks of former cultivation. A short march brought us

to an ooze, surrounded by hedges, game-traps, and pitfalls, where, as we are stiff and weak, we spend the night. Rocks abound of the same dolomite kind as on the ridge further south, between the Loangwa and Chambezé, covered, like them, with lichens, orchids, euphorbias, and upland vegetation, hard-leaved acacias, rhododendrons, masukos. The gum-copal tree, when perforated by a grub, exudes from branches no thicker than one's arm, masses of soft, gluey-looking gum, brownish yellow, and light grey, as much as would fill a soup-plate. It seems to yield this gum only in the rainy season, and now all the trees are full of sap and gum.

21st February, 1867.—A night with loud and near thunder, and much heavy rain, which came through the boys' sheds. Roads all plashy or running with water, oozes full, and rivulets overflowing; rocks of dolomite jutting out here and there. I noticed growing here a spikenard-looking shrub, six feet high, and a foot in diameter. The path led us west against my will. I found one going north; but the boys pretended that they did not see my mark, and went west, evidently afraid of incurring Moamba's displeasure by passing him. I found them in an old hut, and made the best of it by saying nothing. They said that they had wandered; that was, they had never left the west-going path.

22nd February, 1867.—We came to a perennial rivulet running north, the Merungu. Here we met Moamba's people, but declined going to his village, as huts are disagreeable; they often have vermin, and one is exposed to the gaze of a crowd through a very small doorway. The people in their curiosity often make the place dark, and the impudent ones offer characteristic remarks, then raise a laugh, and run away.

We encamped on the Meningu's right bank in forest, sending word to Moamba that we meant to do so. He sent a deputation, first of all his young men, to bring us; then old men, and lastly he came himself with about sixty followers. I explained that I had become sick by living in a little hut at Molemba; that I was better in the open air; that huts contained vermin; and that I did not mean to remain any while here, but go on our way. He pressed us to come to his village, and gave us a goat and kid, with a huge calabashful of beer. I promised to go over and visit him next day; and went accordingly.

23rd February, 1867.—Moamba's village was a mile off, and on the left bank of the Merengé, a larger stream than the Merungu flowing north and having its banks and oozes covered with fine, tall, straight, evergreen trees. The village is surrounded with a stockade, and a dry ditch some fifteen or twenty feet wide, and as many deep. I had a long talk with Moamba, a big, stout, public-house-looking person, with a slight outward cast in his left eye, but intelligent and hearty. I presented him with a cloth; and he gave me as much maëre meal as a man could carry, with a large basket of ground-nuts. He wished us to come to the Merengé, if not into his village, that he might see and talk with me: I also showed him some pictures in Smith's 'Bible Dictionary,' which he readily understood, and I spoke to him about the Bible. He asked me "to come next day and tell him about prayer to God," this was a natural desire after being told that we prayed.

He was very anxious to know why we were going to Tanganyika; for what we came; what we should buy there; and if I had any relations there. He then showed me some fine large tusks, eight feet six in length. "What do you wish to buy, if not slaves or ivory?" I replied, that the only thing I had seen worth buying was a fine fat chief like him, as a specimen, and a woman feeding him, as he had, with beer. He was tickled at this; and said that when we reached our country, I must put fine clothes on him. This led us to speak of our climate, and the production of wool.

24th February, 1867.—I went over after service, but late, as the rain threatened to be heavy. A case was in process of hearing, and one old man spoke an hour on end, the chief listening all the while with the gravity of a judge. He then delivered his decision in about five minutes, the successful litigant going off lullilooing. Each person, before addressing him, turns his back to him and lies down on the ground, clapping the hands: this is the common mode of salutation. Another form here in Lobemba is to rattle the arrows or an arrow on the bow, which all carry. We had a little talk with the chief; but it was late before the cause was heard through. He asked us to come and spend one night near him on the Merenga, and then go on, so we came over in the morning to the vicinity of his village. A great deal of copper-wire is here made, the wire-drawers using for one part of the process a seven-inch cable. They make very fine wire, and it is used chiefly as leglets and anklets; the chief's wives being laden with them, and obliged to walk in a stately style from the weight: the copper comes from Katanga.

26th February, 1867.—The chief wishes to buy a cloth with two goats, but his men do not bring them up quickly. Simon, one of the boys, is ill of fever, and this induces me to remain, though moving from one place to another is the only remedy we have in our power.

With the chief's men we did not get on well, but with himself all was easy. His men demanded prepayment for canoes to cross the river Loömbé; but in the way that he put it, the request was not unreasonable, as he gave a man to smooth our way, and get canoes, or whatever else was needed, all the way to Chibué's. I gave a cloth when he put it thus, and he presented a goat, a spear ornamented with copper-wire, abundance of meal, and beer, and numbo; so we parted good friends, as his presents were worth the cloth.

Holding a north-westerly course we met with the Chikosho flowing west, and thence came to the Likombé by a high ridge called Losauswa, which runs a long way westward. It is probably a watershed between streams going to the Chambezé and those that go to the northern rivers.

We have the Locopa, Loömbé, Nikéléngé, then Lofubu or Lovu; the last goes north into Liembe, but accounts are very confused. The Chambezé rises in the Mambivé country, which is north-east of Moamba, but near to it.

The forest through which we passed was dense, but scrubby; trees unhealthy and no drainage except through oozes. On the keel which forms a clay soil the rain runs off, and the trees attain a large size. The roads are not soured by the slow process of the ooze drainage. At present all the slopes having loamy or sandy soil are oozes, and full to overflowing; a long time is required for them to discharge their contents. The country generally may be called one covered with forest.

6th March, 1867.—We came after a short march to a village on the Molilanga, flowing east into the Loömbé, here we meet with bananas for the first time, called, as in Lunda, nkondé. A few trophies from Mazitu are hung up: Chitapangwa had twenty-four skulls ornamenting his stockade. The Babemba are decidedly more warlike than any of the tribes south of them: their villages are stockaded, and have deep dry ditches round them, so it is likely that Mochimbé will be effectually checked, and forced to turn his energies to something else than to marauding.

Our man from Moamba here refused to go further, and we were put on the wrong track by the headman wading through three marshes, each at least half a mile broad. The people of the first village we came to shut their gates on us, then came running after us; but we declined to enter their village: it is a way of showing their independence. We made our sheds on a height in spite of their protests. They said that the gates were shut by the boys; but when I pointed out the boy who had done it, he said that he had been ordered to do it by the chief. If we had gone in now we should have been looked on as having come under considerable obligations.

8th March, 1867.—We went on to a village on the Loömbé, where the people showed an opposite disposition, for not a soul was in it—all were out at their farms. When the good wife of the place came she gave us all huts, which saved us from a pelting shower. The boys herding the goats did not stir as we passed down the sides of the lovely valley. The Loömbé looks a sluggish stream from a distance. The herdsman said we were welcome, and he would show the crossing next day, he also cooked some food for us.

Guided by our host, we went along the Loömbé westwards till we reached the bridge (rather a rickety affair), which, when the water is low may be used as a weir. The Loömbé main stream is 66 feet wide, 6 feet deep, with at least 200 feet of flood beyond it. The water was knee deep on the bridge, but clear; the flooded part beyond was waist deep and the water flowing fast.

All the people are now transplanting tobacco from the spaces under the eaves of the huts into the fields. It seems unable to bear the greater heat of summer: they plant also a kind of liranda, proper for the cold weather. We thought that we were conferring a boon in giving peas, but we found them generally propagated all over the country already, and in the cold time too. We went along the Diola River to an old hut and made a fire; thence across country to another river, called Loendawé, 6 feet wide, and 9 feet deep.

10th March, 1867.—I have been ill of fever ever since we left Moamba's; every step I take jars in the chest, and I am very weak; I can scarcely keep up the march, though formerly I was always first, and had to hold in my pace not to leave the people altogether. I have a constant singing in the ears, and can scarcely hear the loud tick of the chronometers. The appetite is good, but we have no proper food, chiefly maëre meal or beans, or mapemba or ground-nuts, rarely a fowl.

The country is full of hopo-hedges, but the animals are harassed, and we never see them.

11th March, 1867..—Detained by a set-in rain. Marks on masses of dolomite elicited the information that a party of Londa smiths came once to this smelting ground and erected their works here. We saw an old iron furnace, and masses of haematite, which seems to have been the ore universally used.

12th March, 1867.—Rain held us back for some time, but we soon reached Chibué, a stockaded village. Like them all, it is situated by a stream, with a dense clump of trees on the waterside of some species of mangrove. They attain large size, have soft wood, and succulent leaves; the roots intertwine in the mud, and one has to watch that he does not step where no roots exist, otherwise he sinks up to the thigh. In a village the people feel that we are on their property, and crowd upon us inconveniently; but outside, where we usually erect our sheds, no such feeling exists, we are each on a level, and they don't take liberties.

The Balungu are marked by three or four little knobs on the temples, and the lobes of the ears are distended by a piece of wood, which is ornamented with beads; bands of beads go across the forehead and hold up the hair.

Chibué's village is at the source of the Lokwéna, which goes N. and N.E.; a long range of low hills is on our N.E., which are the Mambwé, or part of them. The Chambezé rises in them, but further south. Here the Lokwéna, round whose source we came on starting this morning to avoid wet feet, and all others north and west of this, go to the Lofu or Lobu, and into Liemba Lake. Those from the hills on our right go east into the Loanzu and so into the Lake.

15th March, 1867.—We now are making for Kasonso, the chief of the Lake, and a very large country all around it, passing the Lochenjé, five yards wide, and knee deep, then to the Chañumba. All flow very rapidly just now and are flooded with clean water. Everyone carries an axe, as if constantly warring with the forest. My long-continued fever ill disposes me to enjoy the beautiful landscape. We are evidently on the ridge, but people have not a clear conception of where the rivers run.

19th March, 1867.—A party of young men came out of the village near which we had encamped to force us to pay something for not going into their village. "The son of a great chief ought to be acknowledged," &c. They had their bows and arrows with them, and all ready for action. I told them we had remained near them because they said we could not reach Kasonso that day. Their headman had given us nothing. After talking a while, and threatening to do a deal to-morrow, they left, and through an Almighty Providence nothing was attempted. We moved on N.W. in forest, with long green tree-covered slopes on our right, and came to a village of Kasonso in a very lovely valley. Great green valleys were now scooped out, and many, as the Kakanza, run into the Lovu.

20th March, 1867.—The same features of country prevailed, indeed it was impossible to count the streams flowing N.W. We found Kasonso situated at the confluence of two streams; he shook hands a long while, and seems a frank sort of man. A shower of rain set the driver ants on the move, and about two hours after we had turned in we were overwhelmed by them. They are called Kalandu or Nkalanda.

To describe this attack is utterly impossible. I wakened covered with them: my hair was full of them. One by one they cut into the flesh, and the more they are disturbed, the more vicious are their bites; they become quite insolent. I went outside the hut, but there they swarmed everywhere; they covered the legs, biting furiously; it is only when they are tired that they leave off.

One good trait of the Balungu up here is, they retire when they see food brought to anyone, neither Babisa nor Makoa had this sense of delicacy: the Babemba are equally polite.

We have descended considerably into the broad valley of the Lake, and it feels warmer than on the heights. Cloth here is more valuable, inasmuch as bark-cloth is scarce. The skins of goats and wild animals are used, and the kilt is very diminutive among the women.

22nd March, 1867.—Cross Loéla, thirty feet wide and one deep, and meet with tsetse fly, though we have seen none since we left Chitapangwa's. Kasonso gave us a grand reception, and we saw men present from Tanganyika; I saw cassava here, but not in plenty.

28th March, 1867.—Set-in rain and Chuma fell ill. There are cotton bushes of very large size here of the South American kind. After sleeping in various villages and crossing numerous streams, we came to Mombo's village, near the ridge overlooking the Lake.

31st March, and 1st April, 1867.—I was too ill to march through. I offered to go on the 1st, but Kasonso's son, who was with us, objected. We went up a low ridge of hills at its lowest part, and soon after passing the summit the blue water loomed through the trees. I was detained, but soon heard the boys firing their muskets on reaching the edge of the ridge, which allowed of an undisturbed view. This is the south-eastern end of Liemba, or, as it is sometimes called, Tanganyika.[50] We had to descend at least 2000 feet before we got to the level of the Lake. It seems about eighteen or twenty miles broad, and we could see about thirty miles up to the north. Four considerable rivers flow into the space before us. The nearly perpendicular ridge of about 2000 feet extends with breaks all around, and there, embosomed in tree-covered rocks, reposes the Lake peacefully in the huge cup-shaped cavity.

I never saw anything so still and peaceful as it lies all the morning. About noon a gentle breeze springs up, and causes the waves to assume a bluish tinge. Several rocky islands rise in the eastern end, which are inhabited by fishermen, who capture abundance of fine large fish, of which they enumerate about twenty-four species. In the north it seems to narrow into a gateway, but the people are miserably deficient in geographical knowledge, and can tell us nothing about it. They suspect us, and we cannot get information, or indeed much of anything else. I feel deeply thankful at having got so far. I am excessively weak—cannot walk without tottering, and have constant singing in the head, but the Highest will lead me further.

Lat. of the spot we touched at first, 2nd April, 1867. Lat. 8° 46' 54" S., long. 31° 57'; but I only worked out (and my head is out of order) one set of observations. Height above level of the sea over 2800 feet, by boiling-point thermometers and barometer. The people won't let me sound the Lake.

After being a fortnight at this Lake it still appears one of surpassing loveliness. Its peacefulness is remarkable, though at times it is said to be lashed up by storms. It lies in a deep basin whose sides are nearly perpendicular, but covered well with trees; the rocks which appear are bright red argillaceous schist; the trees at present all green: down some of these rocks come beautiful cascades, and buffaloes, elephants, and antelopes wander and graze on the more level spots, while lions roar by night. The level place below is not two miles from the perpendicular. The village (Pambété), at which we first touched the Lake, is surrounded by palm-oil trees—not the stunted ones of Lake Nyassa, but the real West Coast palm-oil tree,[51] requiring two men to carry a bunch of the ripe fruit. In the morning and evening huge crocodiles may be observed quietly making their way to their feeding grounds; hippopotami snort by night and at early morning.

After I had been a few days here I had a fit of insensibility, which shows the power of fever without medicine. I found myself floundering outside my hut and unable to get in; I tried to lift myself from my back by laying hold of two posts at the entrance, but when I got nearly upright I let them go, and fell back heavily on my head on a box. The boys had seen the wretched state I was in, and hung a blanket at the entrance of the hut, that no stranger might see my helplessness; some hours elapsed before I could recognize where I was.

As for these Balungu, as they are called, they have a fear of us, they do not understand our objects, and they keep aloof. They promise everything and do nothing; but for my excessive weakness we should go on, but we wait for a recovery of strength.

As people they are greatly reduced in numbers by the Mazitu, who carried off very large numbers of the women, boys, girls, and children. They train or like to see the young men arrayed as Mazitu, but it would be more profitable if they kept them to agriculture. They are all excessively polite. The clapping of hands on meeting is something excessive, and then the string of salutations that accompany it would please the most fastidious Frenchman. It implies real politeness, for in marching with them they always remove branches out of the path, and indicate stones or stumps in it carefully to a stranger, yet we cannot prevail on them to lend carriers to examine the Lake or to sell goats, of which, however, they have very few, and all on one island.

The Village on Lake Liemba—Tanganyika.

The Lake discharges its water north-westward or rather nor-north-westwards. We observe weeds going in that direction, and as the Lonzua, the Kowé, the Kapata, the Luazé, the Kalambwé, flow into it near the east end, and the Lovu or Lofubu, or Lofu, from the south-west near the end it must find an exit for so much water. All these rivers rise in or near the Mambwé country, in lat. 10° S., where, too, the Chambezé rises. Liemba is said to remain of about the same size as we go north-west, but this we shall see for ourselves.

Elephants come all about us. One was breaking trees close by. I fired into his ear without effect: I am too weak to hold the gun steadily.

30th April, 1867.—We begin our return march from Liemba. Slept at a village on the Lake, and went on next day to Pambété, where we first touched it. I notice that here the people pound tobacco-leaves in a mortar after they have undergone partial fermentation by lying in the sun, then they put the mass in the sun to dry for use.

The reason why no palm-oil trees grow further east than Pambété is said to be the stony soil there, and this seems a valid one, for it loves rich loamy meadows.

1st May, 1867.—We intended to go north-west to see whether this Lake narrows or not, for all assert that it maintains its breadth such as we see it beyond Pemba as far as they know it; but when about to start the headman and his wife came and protested so solemnly that by going N.W. we should walk into the hands of a party of Mazitu there, that we deferred our departure. It was not with a full persuasion of the truth of the statement that I consented, but we afterwards saw good evidence that it was true, and that we were saved from being plundered. These marauders have changed their tactics, for they demand so many people, and so many cloths, and then leave. They made it known that their next scene of mulcting would be Mombo's village, and there they took twelve people—four slaves, and many cloths, then went south to the hills they inhabit. A strict watch was kept on their movements by our headman and his men. They trust to fleeing into a thicket on the west of the village should the Mazitu come.

I have been informed on good authority that Kasonso was on his way to us when news arrived that his young son had died. He had sent on beer and provisions for us, but the Mazitu intervening they were consumed.

The Mazitu having left we departed and slept half-way up the ridge. I had another fit of insensibility last night: the muscles of the back lose all power,[52] and there is constant singing in the ears, and inability to do the simplest sum. Cross the Aeezé (which makes the waterfall) fifteen yards wide and knee deep. The streams like this are almost innumerable.

Mombo's village. It is distressingly difficult to elicit accurate information about the Lake and rivers, because the people do not think accurately. Mombo declared that two Arabs came when we were below, and inquired for us, but he denied our presence, thinking thereby to save us trouble and harm.

The cotton cultivated is of the Pernambuco species, and the bushes are seven or eight feet high. Much cloth was made in these parts before the Mazitu raids began, it was striped black and white, and many shawls are seen in the country yet. It is curious that this species of cotton should be found only in the middle of this country.

In going westwards on the upland the country is level and covered with scraggy forest as usual, long lines of low hills or rather ridges of denudation run. N. and S. on our east. This is called Moami country, full of elephants, but few are killed. They do much damage, eating the sorghum in the gardens unmolested.

11th May, 1867.—A short march to-day brought us to a village on the same Moami, and to avoid a Sunday in the forest we remained. The elephants had come into the village and gone all about it, and to prevent their opening the corn safes the people had bedaubed them with elephant's droppings. When a cow would not give milk, save to its calf, a like device was used at Kolobeng; the cow's droppings were smeared on the teats, and the calf was too much disgusted to suck: the cow then ran till she was distressed by the milk fever and was willing to be relieved by the herdsman.

12th and 13th May, 1867.—News that the Arabs had been fighting with Nsama came, but this made us rather anxious to get northward along Liemba, and we made for Mokambola's village near the edge of the precipice which overhangs the Lake. Many Shuaré Raphia palms grow in the river which flows past it.

As we began our descent we saw the Lofu coming from the west and entering Liemba. A projection of Liemba comes to meet it, and then it is said to go away to the north or north-west as far as my informants knew. Some pointed due north, others north-west, so probably its true course amounts to N.N.W. We came to a village about 2' W. of the confluence, whose headman was affable and generous. The village has a meadow some four miles wide on the land side, in which buffaloes disport themselves, but they are very wild, and hide in the gigantic grasses. Sorghum, ground-nuts, and voandzeia grow luxuriantly. The Lofu is a quarter of a mile wide, but higher up three hundred yards. The valley was always clouded over at night so I could not get an observation except early in the morning when the cold had dissipated the clouds.

We remained here because two were lame, and all tired by the descent of upwards of 2000 feet, and the headman sent for fish for us. He dissuaded us strongly from attempting to go down the Liemba, as the son of Nsania (Kapoma) was killing all who came that way in revenge for what the Arabs had done to his father's people, and he might take us for Arabs. A Suaheli Arab came in the evening and partly confirmed the statements of the headman of Karambo; I resolved therefore to go back to Chitimba's in the south, where the chief portion of the Arabs are assembled, and hear from them more certainly.

The last we heard of Liemba was that at a great way north-west, it is dammed up by rocks, and where it surmounts these there is a great waterfall. It does not, it is said, diminish in size so far, but by bearings protracted it is two miles wide.

18th May, 1867.—Return to Mokambola's village, and leave for Chitimba's. Baraka stopped behind at the village, and James ran away to him, leaving his bundle, containing three chronometers, in the path: I sent back for them, and James came up in the evening; he had no complaint, and no excuse to make. The two think it will be easy to return to their own country by begging, though they could not point it out to me when we were much nearer to where it is supposed to be.

19th May, 1867.—Where we were brought to a standstill was miserably cold (55°), so we had prayers and went on S. and S.W. to the village of Chisáka.

20th May, 1867.—Chitimba's village was near in the same direction; here we found a large party of Arabs, mostly black Suahelis. They occupied an important portion of the stockaded village, and when I came in, politely showed me to a shed where they are in the habit of meeting. After explaining whence I had come, I showed them the Sultan's letter. Harnees presented a goat, two fowls, and a quantity of flour. It was difficult to get to the bottom of the Nsama affair, but according to their version that chief sent an invitation to them, and when they arrived called for his people, who came in crowds—as he said to view the strangers. I suspect that the Arabs became afraid of the crowds and began to fire; several were killed on both sides, and Nsama fled, leaving his visitors in possession of the stockaded village and all it contained. Others say that there was a dispute about an elephant, and that Nsama's people were the aggressors. At any rate it is now all confusion; those who remain at Nsama's village help themselves to food in the surrounding villages and burn them, while Chitimba has sent for the party who are quartered here to come to him. An hour or two after we arrived a body of men came from Kasonso, with the intention of proceeding into the country of Nsama, and if possible catching Nsama, "he having broken public law by attacking people who brought merchandise into the country." This new expedition makes the Arabs resolve to go and do what they can to injure their enemy. It will just be a plundering foray—each catching what he can, whether animal or human, and retiring when it is no longer safe to plunder!

This throws the barrier of a broad country between me and Lake "Moero" in the west, but I trust in Providence a way will be opened. I think now of going southwards and then westwards, thus making a long détour round the disturbed district.

The name of the principal Arab is Hamees Wodim Tagh, the other is Syde bin Alie bin Mansure: they are connected with one of the most influential native mercantile houses in Zanzibar. Hamees has been particularly kind to me in presenting food, beads, cloth, and getting information. Thami bin Snaelim is the Arab to whom my goods are directed at Ujiji.

24th May, 1867.—At Chitimba's we are waiting to see what events turn up to throw light on our western route. Some of the Arabs and Kasonso's men went off to-day: they will bring information perhaps as to Nsama's haunts, and then we shall move south and thence west. Wrote to Sir Thomas Maclear, giving the position of Liemba and to Dr. Seward, in case other letters miscarry. The hot season is beginning now. This corresponds to July further south.

Three goats were killed by a leopard close to the village in open day.

28th May, 1867.—Information came that Nsama begged pardon of the. Arabs, and would pay all that they had lost. He did not know of his people stealing from them: we shall hear in a day or two whether the matter is to be patched up or not. While some believe his statements, others say, "Nsama's words of peace are simply to gain time to make another stockade:" in the mean time Kasonso's people will ravage all his country on this eastern side.

Hamees is very anxious that I should remain a few days longer, till Kasonso's son, Kampamba, comes with *certain* information, and then he will see to our passing safely to Chiwéré's village from Kasonso's. All have confidence in this last-named chief as an upright man.

1st June, 1867.—Another party of marauders went off this morning to plunder Nsama's country to the west of the confluence of the Lofu as a punishment for a breach of public law. The men employed are not very willing to go, but when they taste the pleasure of plunder they will relish it more!

The watershed begins to have a northern slope about Moamba's, lat. 10° 10' S., but the streams are very tortuous, and the people have very confused ideas as to where they run. The Lokhopa, for instance, was asserted by all the men at Moamba's to flow into Lokholu, and then into a river going to Liemba, but a young wife of Moamba, who seemed very intelligent, maintained that Lokhopa and Lokholu went to the Chambezé; I therefore put it down thus. The streams which feed the Chambezé and the Liemba overlap each other, and it would require a more extensive survey than I can give to disentangle them.

North of Moamba, on the Merengé, the slope begins to Liemba. The Lofu rises in Chibué's country, and with its tributaries we have long ridges of denudation, each some 500 or 600 feet high, and covered with green trees. The valleys of denudation enclosed by these hill ranges guide the streams towards Liemba or the four rivers which flow into it. The country gradually becomes lower, warmer, and tsetse and mosquitoes appear; so at last we come to the remarkable cup-shaped cavity in which Liemba reposes. Several streams fall down the nearly perpendicular cliffs, and form beautiful cascades. The lines of denudation are continued, one range rising behind another as far as the eye can reach to the north and east of Liemba, and probably the slope continues away down to Tanganyika. The watershed extends westwards to beyond Casembe, and the Luapula, or Chambezé, rises in the same parallels of latitude as does the Lofu and the Lonzna.

The Arabs inform me that between this and the sea, about 200 miles distant, lies the country of the Wasango—called: Usango—a fair people, like Portuguese, and very friendly to strangers. The Wasango possess plenty of cattle: their chief is called Meréré.[53] They count this twenty-five days, while the distance thence to the sea at Bagamoio is one month and twenty-five days—say 440 miles. Uchéré is very far off northwards, but a man told me that he went to a salt-manufactory in that direction in eight days from Kasonso's. Meréré goes frequently on marauding expeditions for cattle, and is instigated thereto by his mother.

What we understand by primeval forest is but seldom seen in the interior here, though the country cannot be described otherwise than as generally covered with interminable forests. Insects kill or dwarf some trees, and men maim others for the sake of the bark-cloth; elephants break down a great number, and it is only here and there that gigantic specimens are seen: they may be expected in shut-in valleys among mountains, but on the whole the trees are scraggy, and the varieties not great. The different sorts of birds which sing among the branches seem to me to exceed those of the Zambesi region, but I do not shoot them: the number of new notes I hear astonishes me.

The country in which we now are is called by the Arabs and natives Ulungu, that farther north-west is named Marunga. Hamees is on friendly terms with the Mazitu (Watuta) in the east, who do not plunder. The chief sent a man to Kasonso lately, and he having received a present went away highly pleased.

Hamees is certainly very anxious to secure my safety. Some men came from the N.E. to inquire about the disturbance here and they recommend that I should go with them, and then up the east side of the Lake to Ujiji; but that would ruin my plan of discovering Moero and afterwards following the watershed, so as to be certain that this is either the watershed of the Congo or Kile. He was not well pleased when I preferred to go south and then westwards, as it looks like rejecting his counsel; but he said if I waited till his people came, then we should be able to speak with more certainty.

On inquiring if any large mountains exist in this country, I was told that Moufipa, or Fipa, opposite the lower end of the Lake, is largest—one can see Tanganyika from it. It probably gives rise to the Nkalambwé River and the Luazé.

There is nothing interesting in a heathen town. All are busy in preparing food or clothing, mats or baskets, whilst the women are cleaning or grinding their corn, which involves much hard labour. They first dry this in the sun, then put it into a mortar, and afterwards with a flat basket clean off the husks and the dust, and grind it between two stones, the next thing is to bring wood and water to cook it. The chief here was aroused the other day, and threatened to burn his own house and all his property because the people stole from it, but he did not proceed so far: it was probably a way of letting the Arab dependants know that he was aroused.

Some of the people who went to fight attacked a large village, and killed several men; but in shooting in a bushy place they killed one of their own party and wounded another.

On inquiring of an Arab who had sailed on Tanganyika which way the water flowed, he replied to the south!

The wagtails build in the thatch of the huts; they are busy, and men and other animals are active in the same way.

I am rather perplexed how to proceed. Some Arabs seem determined to go westwards as soon as they can make it up with Nsama, whilst others distrust him. One man will send his people to pick up what ivory they can, but he himself will retire to the Usango country. Nsama is expected to-day or to-morrow. It would be such a saving of time and fatigue for us to go due west rather than south, and then west, but I feel great hesitation as to setting out on the circuitous route. Several Arabs came from the Liemba side yesterday; one had sailed on Tanganyika, and described the winds there as very baffling, but no one of them has a clear idea of the Lake. They described the lower part as a "sea," and thought it different from Tanganyika.

Close observation of the natives of Ulungu makes me believe them to be extremely polite. The mode of salutation among relatives is to place the hands round each other's chests kneeling, they then clap their hands close to the ground. Some more abject individuals kiss the soil before a chief; the generality kneel only, with the fore-arms close to the ground, and the head bowed down to them, saying, "O Ajadla chiusa, Mari a bwino." The Usanga say, "Ajé senga." The clapping of hands to superiors, and even equals, is in some villages a perpetually recurring sound. Aged persons are usually saluted: how this extreme deference to each other could have arisen, I cannot conceive; it does not seem to be fear of each other that elicits it. Even the chiefs inspire no fear, and those cruel old platitudes about governing savages by fear seem unknown, yet governed they certainly are, and upon the whole very well. The people were not very willing to go to punish Nsama's breach of public law, yet, on the decision of the chiefs, they went, and came back, one with a wooden stool, another with a mat, a third with a calabash of ground-nuts or some dried meat, a hoe, or a bow— poor, poor pay for a fortnight's hard work hunting fugitives and burning villages.

16th June, 1867.—News came to-day that an Arab party in the south-west, in Lunda, lost about forty people by the small-pox ("ndué"), and that the people there, having heard of the disturbance with Nsama, fled from the Arabs, and would sell neither ivory nor food: this looks like another obstacle to our progress thither.

17th-19th June, 1867.—Hamees went to meet the party from the south-west, probably to avoid bringing the small-pox here. They remain at about two hours' distance. Hamees reports that though the strangers had lost a great many people by small-pox, they had brought good news of certain Arabs still further west: one, Seide ben Umale, or Salem, lived at a village near Casembe, ten days distant, and another, Juma Merikano, or Katata Katanga, at another village further north, and Seide ben Habib was at Phueto, which is nearer Tanganyika. This party comprises the whole force of Hamees, and he now declares that he will go to Nsama and make the matter up, as he thinks that he is afraid to come here, and so he will make the first approach to friendship.

On pondering over the whole subject, I see that, tiresome as it is to wait, it is better to do so than go south and then west, for if I should go I shall miss seeing Moero, which is said to be three days from Nsama's present abode. His people go there for salt, and I could not come to it from the south without being known to them, and perhaps considered to be an Arab. Hamees remarked that it was the Arab way first to smooth the path before entering upon it; sending men and presents first, thereby ascertaining the disposition of the inhabitants. He advises patience, and is in hopes of making a peace with Nsama. That his hopes are not unreasonable, he mentioned that when the disturbance began, Nsama sent men with two tusks to the village whence he had just been expelled, offering thereby to make the matter up, but the Arabs, suspecting treachery, fired upon the carriers and killed them, then ten goats and one tusk were sent with the same object, and met with a repulse; Hamees thinks that had he been there himself the whole matter would have been settled amicably.

All complain of cold here. The situation is elevated, and we are behind a clump of trees on the rivulet Chiloa, which keeps the sun off us in the mornings. This cold induces the people to make big fires in their huts, and frequently their dwellings are burned. Minimum temperature is as low as 46°; sometimes 33°.

24th June, 1867.—The Arabs are all busy reading their Koran, or Kurán, and in praying for direction; to-morrow they will call a meeting to deliberate as to what steps they will take in the Nsama affair. Hamees, it seems, is highly thought of by that chief, who says, "Let him come, and all will be right." Hamees proposes to go with but a few people. These Zanzibar men are very different from the slavers of the Waiyau country.

25th June, 1867.—The people, though called, did not assemble, but they will come to-morrow.

Young wagtails nearly full-fledged took wing, leaving one in the nest; from not being molested by the people they took no precautions, and ran out of the nest on the approach of the old ones, making a loud chirping. The old ones tried to induce the last one to come out too, by flying to the nest, and then making a sally forth, turning round immediately to see if he followed: he took a few days longer.

It was decided at the meeting that Hamees, with a few people only, should go to Nsama on the first day after the appearance of the new moon (they are very particular on this point); the present month having been an unhappy one they will try the next.

28th June, 1867.—A wedding took place among the Arabs to-day. About a hundred blank cartridges were fired off, and a procession of males, dressed in their best, marched through the village. They sang with all their might, though with but little music in the strain. Women sprinkled grain on their heads as wishes for plenty.[54]

Nsama is said to be waiting for the Arabs in his new stockade. It is impossible to ascertain exactly who is to blame in this matter, for I hear one side only; but the fact of the chiefs in this part of the country turning out so readily to punish his breach of public law, and no remonstrance coming from him, makes me suspect that Nsama is the guilty party. If he had been innocent he certainly would have sent to ask the Bulungu, or Bäulungu, why they had attacked his people without cause.

[Here is an entry concerning the tribe living far to the East.]

The Wasongo seem much like Zulus; they go naked, and have prodigious numbers of cattle, which occupy the same huts with their owners. Oxen two shukahs each; plenty of milk. Meréré is very liberal with his cattle, and gives every one an ox: there is no rice, but maize and maëre. Hamees left the people to cultivate rice. Meréré had plenty of ivory when the Arabs came first, but now has none.

1st July, 1867.—New moon to-day. They are very particular as to the time of offering up prayers, and in making charms. One to-night was at 10 P.M. exactly.

A number of cabalistic figures were drawn by Halfani, and it is believed that by these Nsama's whereabouts may be ascertained; they are probably remains of the secret arts which prevailed among Arabs before Mahomet appeared. These Suaheli Arabs appear to have come down the coast before that Prophet was born.

3rd July, 1867.—Kasonso's people are expected. All the captives that were taken are to be returned, and a quantity of cloth given to Nsama in addition: so far all seems right. The new moon will appear to-night. The Arabs count from one appearance to the next, not, as we do, from its conjunction with the sun to the next.

4th July, 1867.—Katawanya came from near Liemba to join the peacemakers. He and his party arrived at Liemba after we did; he sent his people all round to seek ivory; they don't care for anything but ivory, and cannot understand why I don't do the same.

6th July, 1867.—An earthquake happened at 3.30 P.M., accompanied with a hollow rumbling sound; it made me feel as if afloat, but it lasted only a few seconds. The boys came running to ask me what it was. Nowhere could it be safer; the huts will not fall, and there are no high rocks near. Barometer 25.0. Temperature 68° 5'. Heavy cumuli hanging about; no rain afterwards.

7th July, 1867.—Hamees started this morning with about 300 followers dressed in all their finery, and he declares that his sole object is peace. Kasonso, Mombo, Chitimba send their people, and go themselves to lend all their influence in favour of peace. Syde stops here. Before starting Syde put some incense on hot coals, and all the leaders of the party joined in a short prayer; they seem earnest and sincere in their incantations, according to their knowledge and belief. I wished to go too, but Hamees objected, as not being quite sure whether Nsama would be friendly, and he would not like anything to befall me when with him.

8th July, 1867.—Kasonso found an excuse for not going himself. Two men, Arabs it was said, came to Chibué's and were there killed, and Kasonso must go to see about it. The people who go carry food with them, evidently not intending to live by plunder this time.

While the peacemakers are gone I am employing time in reading Smith's 'Bible Dictionary,' and calculating different positions which have stood over in travelling. I don't succeed well in the Bäulungu dialect.

The owners of huts lent to strangers have a great deal of toil in consequence; they have to clean them after the visitors have withdrawn; then, in addition to this, to clean themselves, all soiled by the dust left by the lodgers; their bodies and clothes have to be cleansed afterwards—they add food too in all cases of acquaintanceship, and then we have to remember the labour of preparing that food. My remaining here enables me to observe that both men and women are in almost constant employment. The men are making mats, or weaving, or spinning; no one could witness their assiduity in their little affairs and conclude that they were a lazy people. The only idle time I observe here is in the mornings about seven o'clock, when all come and sit to catch the first rays of the sun as he comes over our clump of trees, but even that time is often taken as an opportunity for stringing beads.

I hear that some of Nsama's people crossed the Lovu at Karambo to plunder, in retaliation for what they have suffered, and the people there were afraid to fish, lest they should be caught by them at a distance from their stockades.

The Bäulungu men are in general tall and well formed, they use bows over six feet in length, and but little bent. The facial angle is as good in most cases as in Europeans, and they have certainly as little of the "lark-heel" as whites. One or two of the under front teeth are generally knocked out in women, and also in men.

14th July, 1867.—Syde added to his other presents some more beads: all have been very kind, which I attribute in a great measure to Seyed Majid's letter. Hamees crossed the Lovu to-day at a fordable spot. The people on the other side refused to go with a message to Nsama, so Hamees had to go and compel them by destroying their stockade. A second village acted in the same way, though told that it was only peace that was sought of Nsama: this stockade suffered the same fate, and then the people went to Nsama, and he showed no reluctance to have intercourse. He gave abundance of food, pombe, and bananas; the country being extremely fertile. Nsama also came and ratified the peace by drinking blood with several of the underlings of Hamees. He is said to be an enormously bloated old man, who cannot move unless carried, and women are constantly in attendance pouring pombe into him. He gave Hamees ten tusks, and promised him twenty more, and also to endeavour to make his people return what goods they plundered from the Arabs, and he is to send his people over here to call us after the new moon appears.

It is tiresome beyond measure to wait so long, but I hope to see Moero for this exercise of patience, and I could not have visited it had Hamees not succeeded in making peace.

17th July, 1867.—A lion roared very angrily at the village last night, he was probably following the buffaloes that sometimes come here to drink at night: they are all very shy, and so is all the game, from fear of arrows.

A curious disease has attacked my left eyelid and surrounding parts: a slight degree of itchiness is followed by great swelling of the part. It must be a sort of lichen; exposure to the sun seems to cure it, and this leads me to take long walks therein. This is about 30° 19' E. long.; lat. 8° 57' 55" S.

24th July, 1867.—A fire broke out at 4 A.M., and there being no wind the straw roofs were cleared off in front of it on our side of the village. The granaries were easily unroofed, as the roof is not attached to the walls, and the Arabs tried to clear a space on their side, but were unable, and then moved all their ivory and goods outside the stockade; their side of the village was all consumed, and three goats perished in the flames.

Chitimba has left us from a fear of his life, he says; it is probable that he means this flight to be used as an excuse to Nsama after we are gone. "And I, too, was obliged to flee from my village to save my life! What could I do?" This is to be his argument, I suspect.

A good many slaves came from the two villages that were destroyed: on inquiry I was told that these would be returned when Nsama gave the ivory promised.

When Nsama was told that an Englishman wished to go past him to Moero, he replied, "Bring him, and I shall send men to take him thither."

Hamees is building a "tembé," or house, with a flat roof, and walls plastered over with mud, to keep his ivory from fire while he is absent. We expect that Nsama will send for us a few days after the 2nd August, when the new moon appears; if they do not come soon Hamees will send men to Nsama without waiting for his messengers.

28th July, 1867.—Prayers, with the Litany.[55] Slavery is a great evil wherever I have seen it. A poor old woman and child are among the captives, the boy about three years old seems a mother's pet. His feet are sore from walking in the sun. He was offered for two fathoms, and his mother for one fathom; he understood it all, and cried bitterly, clinging to his mother. She had, of course, no power to help him; they were separated at Karungu afterwards.

[The above is an episode of every-day occurrence in the wake of the slave-dealer. "Two fathoms," mentioned as the price of the boy's life—the more valuable of the two, means four yards of unbleached calico, which is a universal article of barter throughout the greater part of Africa: the mother was bought for two yards. The reader must not think that there are no lower prices; in the famines which succeed the slave-dealer's raids, boys and girls are at times to be purchased by the dealer for a few handfuls of maize.]

29th July, 1867.—Went 2 1/2 hours west to village of Ponda, where a head Arab, called by the natives Tipo Tipo, lives; his name is Hamid bin Mahamed bin Juma Borajib. He presented a goat, a piece of white calico, and four big bunches of beads, also a bag of Holcus sorghum, and apologised because it was so little. He had lost much by Nsama; and received two arrow wounds there; they had only twenty guns at the time, but some were in the stockade, and though the people of Nsama were very numerous they beat them off, and they fled carrying the bloated carcase of Nsama with them. Some reported that boxes were found in the village, which belonged to parties who had perished before, but Syde assured me that this was a mistake.

Moero is three days distant, and as Nsama's people go thither to collect salt on its banks, it would have been impossible for me to visit it from the south without being seen, and probably suffering loss.

The people seem to have no family names. A man takes the name of his mother, or should his father die he may assume that. Marriage is forbidden to the first, second, and third degrees: they call first and second cousins brothers and sisters.

A woman, after cupping her child's temples for sore eyes, threw the blood over the roof of her hut as a charm.

[In the above process a goat's horn is used with a small hole in the pointed end. The base is applied to the part from which the blood is to be withdrawn, and the operator, with a small piece of chewed india-rubber in his mouth, exhausts the air, and at the proper moment plasters the small hole up with his tongue. When the cupping-horn is removed, some cuts are made with a small knife, and it is again applied. As a rough appliance, it is a very good one, and in great repute everywhere.]

FOOTNOTES:

50. It subsequently proved to be the southern extremity of this great Lake.
51. Elais, sp.(?).
52. This is a common symptom—men will suddenly lose all power in the lower extremities, and remain helpless where they fall.—ED.
53. The men heard in 1873 that he had been killed.
54. This comes near to the custom of throwing rice after the bride and bridegroom in England.—ED.
55. In his Journal the Doctor writes "S," and occasionally "Service," whenever a Sunday entry occurs. We may add that at all times during his travels the Services of the Church of England were resorted to by him.—ED.

* * * * *

CHAPTER IX.

Peace negotiations with Nsama. Geographical gleanings. Curious spider. Reach the River Lofu. Arrives at Nsama's. Hamees marries the daughter of Nsama. Flight of the bride. Conflagration in Arab quarters. Anxious to visit Lake Moero. Arab burial. Serious illness. Continues journey. Slave-traders on the march. Reaches Moero. Description of the Lake. Information concerning the Chambezé and Luapula. Hears of Lake Bemba. Visits spot of Dr. Lacerda's death. Casembe apprised of Livingstone's approach. Meets Mohamad Bogharib. Lakelet Mofwé. Arrives at Casembe's town.

1st August, 1867.—Hamees sends off men to trade at Chiweré's. *Zikwé* is the name for locust here. Nsigé or Zigé and Pansi the Suaheli names.

A perforated stone had been placed on one of the poles which form the gateway into this stockade, it is oblong, seven or eight inches long by four broad, and bevelled off on one side and the diameter of the hole in the middle is about an inch and a half: it shows evidence of the boring process in rings. It is of hard porphyry and of a pinkish hue, and resembles somewhat a weight for a digging stick I saw in 1841 in the hands of a Bushwoman: I saw one at a gateway near Kasonso's. The people know nothing of its use except as a charm to keep away evil from the village.

2nd August, 1867.—Chronometer A. stopped to-day without any apparent cause except the earthquake.

It is probably malaria which causes that constant singing in the ears ever since my illness at Lake Liemba.

3rd August, 1867.—We expect a message from Nsama every day, the new moon having appeared on the first of this month, and he was to send after its appearance.

5th August, 1867.—Men came yesterday with the message that Hamees must wait a little longer, as Nsama had not yet got all the ivory and the goods which were stolen: they remained over yesterday. The headman, Katala, says that Lunda is eight days from Nsama or Moero, and in going we cross a large river called Movue, which flows into Luapula; another river called Mokobwa comes from the south-east into Moero. Itawa is the name of Nsama's country and people.

A day distant from Nsama's place there is a hot fountain called "Paka pezhia," and around it the earth shakes at times: it is possible that the earthquake we felt here may be connected with this same centre of motion.

6th August, 1867.—The weather is becoming milder. An increase of cold was caused by the wind coming from the south. We have good accounts of the Wasongo from all the Arabs, their houses built for cattle are flat-roofed and enormously large; one, they say, is a quarter of a mile long. Meréré the chief has his dwelling-house within it: milk, butter, cheese, are in enormous quantities; the tribe, too, is very large. I fear that they may be spoiled by the Arab underlings.

7th August, 1867.—Some of my people went down to Karambo and were detained by the chief, who said "I won't let you English go away and leave me in trouble with these Arabs."

A slave had been given in charge to a man here and escaped, the Arabs hereupon went to Karambo and demanded payment from the chief there; he offered clothing, but they refused it, and would have a man; he then offered a man, but this man having two children they demanded all three. They bully as much as they please by their fire-arms. After being spoken to by my people the Arabs came away. The chief begged that I would come and visit him once more, for only one day, but it is impossible, for we expect to move directly. I sent the information to Hamees, who replied that they had got a clue to the man who was wiling away their slaves from them. My people saw others of the low squad which always accompanies the better-informed Arabs bullying the people of another village, and taking fowls and food without payment. Slavery makes a bad neighbourhood!

Hamees is on friendly terms with a tribe of Mazitu who say that they have given up killing people. They lifted a great many cattle, but have very few now; some of them came with him to show the way to Kasonso's.

Slaves are sold here in the same open way that the business is carried on in Zanzibar slave-market. A man goes about calling out the price he wants for the slave, who walks behind him; if a woman, she is taken into a hut to be examined in a state of nudity.

Some of the Arabs believe that meteoric stones are thrown at Satan for his wickedness. They believe that cannon were taken up Kilimanjaro by the first Arabs who came into the country, and there they lie. They deny that Van der Decken did more than go round a portion of the base of the mountain; he could not get on the mass of the mountain: all his donkeys and some of his men died by the cold. Hamees seems to be Cooley's great geographical oracle!

The information one can cull from the Arabs respecting the country on the north-west is very indefinite. They magnify the difficulties in the way by tales of the cannibal tribes, where anyone dying is bought and no one ever buried, but this does not agree with the fact, which also is asserted, that the cannibals have plenty of sheep and goats. The Rua is about ten days west of Tanganyika, and five days beyond it a lake or river ten miles broad is reached; it is said to be called Logarawá. All the water flows northwards, but no reliance can be placed on the statements. Kiombo is said to be chief of Rua country.

Another man asserts that Tanganyika flows northwards and forms a large water beyond Uganda, but no dependence can be placed on the statements of these half Arabs; they pay no attention to anything but ivory and food.

25th August, 1867.—Nsama requested the Arabs to give back his son who was captured; some difficulty was made about this by his captor, but Hamees succeeded in getting him and about nine others, and they are sent off to-day. We wait only for the people, who are scattered about the country. Hamees presented cakes, flour, a fowl and leg of goat, with a piece of eland meat: this animal goes by the same name here as at Kolobeng—"Pofu."[56]

A fig-tree here has large knobs on the bark, like some species of acacia; and another looks like the Malolo of the Zambesi magnified. A yellow wood gives an odour like incense when burned.

A large spider makes a nest inside the huts. It consists of a piece of pure white paper, an inch and a half broad, stuck flat on the wall; under this some forty or fifty eggs are placed, and then a quarter of an inch of thinner paper is put round it, apparently to fasten the first firmly. When making the paper the spider moves itself over the surface in wavy lines; she then sits on it with her eight legs spread over all for three weeks continuously, catching and eating any insects, as cockroaches, that come near her nest. After three weeks she leaves it to hunt for food, but always returns at night: the natives do not molest it.

A small ant masters the common fly by seizing a wing or leg, and holding on till the fly is tired out; at first the fly can move about on the wing without inconvenience, but it is at last obliged to succumb to an enemy very much smaller than itself.

A species of Touraco, new to me, has a broad yellow mask on the upper part of the bill and forehead; the topknot is purple, the wings the same as in other species, but the red is roseate. The yellow of the mask plates is conspicuous at a distance.

A large callosity forms on the shoulders of the regular Unyamwesi porters, from the heavy weights laid on them. I have noticed them an inch and a half thick along the top of the shoulders. An old man was pointed out to me who had once carried five frasilahs (= 175 lbs.) of ivory from his own country to the coast.

30th August, 1867.—We marched to-day from Chitimba's village after three months and ten days' delay. On reaching Ponda, 2-1/2 hours distant, we found Tipo Tipo, or Hamidi bin Mohamad, gone on, and so we followed him. Passed a fine stream flowing S.W. to the Lofu. Tipo Tipo gave me a fine fat goat.

31st August, 1867.—Pass along a fine undulating district, with much country covered with forest, but many open glades, and fine large trees along the water-courses. We were on the northern slope of the watershed, and could see far. Crossed two fine rivulets. The oozes still full and flowing.

1st September, 1867.—We had to march in the afternoon on account of a dry patch existing in the direct way. We slept without water, though by diverging a few miles to the north we should have crossed many streams, but this is the best path for the whole year.

Baraka went back to Tipo Tipo's village, thus putting his intention of begging among the Arab slaves into operation. He has only one complaint, and that is dislike to work. He tried perseveringly to get others to run away with him; lost the medicine-box, six table-cloths, and all our tools by giving his load off to a country lad while he went to collect mushrooms: he will probably return to Zanzibar, and be a slave to the Arab slaves after being a perpetual nuisance to us for upwards of a year.

2nd September, 1867.—When we reached the ford of the Lofu, we found that we were at least a thousand feet below Chitimba's. The last six hours of our march were without water, but when near to Chungu's village at the ford we came to fine flowing rivulets, some ten feet or so broad. Here we could see westwards and northwards the long lines of hills of denudation in Nsama's country, which till lately was densely peopled. Nsama is of the Babemba family. Kasonso, Chitimba, Kiwé, Urongwé, are equals and of one family, Urungai. Chungu is a pleasant person, and liberal according to his means. Large game is very abundant through all this country.

The Lofu at the ford was 296 feet, the water flowing briskly over hardened sandstone flag, and from thigh to waist deep; elsewhere it is a little narrower, but not passable except by canoes.

4th and 5th September, 1867.—Went seven hours west of the Lofu to a village called Hara, one of those burned by Hamees because the people would not take a peaceful message to Nsama. This country is called Itawa, and Hara is one of the districts. We waited at Hara to see if Nsama wished us any nearer to himself. He is very much afraid of the Arabs, and well he may be, for he was until lately supposed to be invincible. He fell before twenty muskets, and this has caused a panic throughout the country. The land is full of food, though the people have nearly all fled. The ground-nuts are growing again for want of reapers; and 300 people living at free-quarters make no impression on the food.

9th September, 1867.—Went three hours west of Hara, and came to Nsama's new stockade, built close by the old one burned by Tipo Tipo, as Hamidi bin Mohamed was named by Nsama.[57] I sent a message to Nsama, and received an invitation to come and visit him, but bring no guns. A large crowd of his people went with us, and before we came to the inner stockade they felt my clothes to see that no fire-arms were concealed about my person. When we reached Nsama, we found a very old man, with a good head and face and a large abdomen, showing that he was addicted to pombe: his people have to carry him. I gave him a cloth, and asked for guides to Moero, which he readily granted, and asked leave to feel my clothes and hair. I advised him to try and live at peace, but his people were all so much beyond the control of himself and headmen, that at last, after scolding them, he told me that he would send for me by night, and then we could converse, but this seems to have gone out of his head. He sent me a goat, flour, and pombe, and next day we returned to Hara.

Nsama's people have generally small, well-chiseled features, and many are really handsome, and have nothing of the West Coast Negro about them, but they file their teeth to sharp points, and greatly disfigure their mouths. The only difference between them and Europeans is the colour. Many of the men have very finely-formed heads, and so have the women; and the fashion of wearing the hair sets off their foreheads to advantage. The forehead is shaved off to the crown, the space narrowing as it goes up; then the back hair, is arranged into knobs of about ten rows.

10th September, 1867.—Some people of Ujiji have come to Nsama's to buy ivory with beads, but, finding that the Arabs have forestalled them in the market, they intend to return in their dhow, or rather canoe, which is manned by about fifty hands. My goods are reported safe, and the meat of the buffaloes which died in the way is there, and sun-dried. I sent a box, containing papers, books, and some clothes, to Ujiji.

14th September, 1867.—I remained at Hara, for I was ill, and Hamees had no confidence in Nsama, because he promised his daughter to wife by way of cementing the peace, but had not given her. Nsama also told Hamees to stay at Hara, and he would send him ivory for sale, but none came, nor do people come here to sell provisions, as they do elsewhere; so Hamees will return to Chitimba's, to guard his people and property there, and send on Syde Hamidi and his servants to Lopéré, Kabuiré, and Moero, to buy ivory. He advised me to go with them, as he has no confidence in Nsama; and Hamidi thought that this was the plan to be preferred: it would be slower, as they would purchase ivory on the road, but safer to pass his country altogether than trust myself in his power.

The entire population of the country has received a shock from the conquest of Nsama, and their views of the comparative values of bows and arrows and guns have undergone a great change. Nsama was the Napoleon of these countries; no one could stand before him, hence the defeat of the invincible Nsama has caused a great panic. The Arabs say that they lost about fifty men in all: Nsama must have lost at least an equal number. The people seem intelligent, and will no doubt act on the experience so dearly bought.

The Arrival of Hamees' Bride

In the midst of the doubts of Hamees a daughter of Nsama came this afternoon to be a wife and cementer of the peace! She came riding "pickaback" on a man's shoulders; a nice, modest, good-looking young woman, her hair rubbed all over with *nkola*, a red pigment, made from the camwood, and much used as an ornament. She was accompanied by about a dozen young and old female attendants, each carrying a small basket with some provisions, as cassava, ground-nuts, &c. The Arabs were all dressed in their finery, and the slaves, in fantastic dresses, flourished swords, fired guns, and yelled. When she was brought to Hamees' hut she descended, and with her maids went into the hut. She and her attendants had all small, neat features. I had been sitting with Hamees, and now rose up and went away; as I passed him, he spoke thus to himself: "Hamees Wadim Tagh! see to what you have brought yourself!!"

15th September, 1867.—A guide had come from Nsama to take us to the countries beyond his territory. Hamees set off this morning with his new wife to his father-in-law, but was soon met by two messengers, who said that he was not to come yet. We now sent for all the people who were out to go west or north-west without reference to Nsama.

16th-18th September, 1867.—Hamidi went to Nsama to try and get guides, but he would not let him come into his stockade unless he came up to it without either gun or sword. Hamidi would not go in on these conditions, but Nsama promised guides, and they came after a visit by Hamees to Nsama, which he paid without telling any of us: he is evidently ashamed of his father-in-law.

Those Arabs who despair of ivory invest their remaining beads and cloth in slaves.

20th September, 1867.—I had resolved to go to Nsama's, and thence to Moero to-day, but Hamees sent to say that men had come, and we were all to go with them on the 22nd. Nsama was so vacillating that I had no doubt but this was best.

Hamees' wife, seeing the preparations that were made for starting, thought that her father was to be attacked, so she, her attendants, and the guides decamped by night. Hamees went again to Nsama and got other guides to enable us to go off at once.

22nd September, 1867.—We went north for a couple of hours, then descended into the same valley as that in which I found Nsama. This valley is on the slope of the watershed, and lies east and west: a ridge of dark-red sandstone, covered with trees, forms its side on the south. Other ridges like this make the slope have the form of a stair with huge steps: the descent is gradually lost as we insensibly climb up the next ridge. The first plain between the steps is at times swampy, and the paths are covered with the impressions of human feet, which, being hardened by the sun, make walking on their uneven surface very difficult. Mosquitoes again; we had lost them during our long stay on the higher lands behind us.

23rd September, 1867.—A fire had broken out the night after we left Hara, and the wind being strong, it got the upper hand, and swept away at once the whole of the temporary village of dry straw huts: Hamees lost all his beads, guns, powder, and cloth, except one bale. The news came this morning, and prayers were at once offered for him with incense; some goods will also be sent, as a little incense was. The prayer-book was held in the smoke of the incense while the responses were made. These Arabs seem to be very religious in their way: the prayers were chiefly to Harasji, some relative of Mohamad.

24th September, 1867.—Roused at 3 A.M. to be told that the next stage had no water, and we should be oppressed with the midday heat if we went now. We were to go at 2 P.M. Hamidi's wife being ill yesterday put a stop to our march on that afternoon. After the first hour we descended from the ridge to which we had ascended, we had then a wall of tree-covered rocks on our left of more than a thousand feet in altitude; after flanking it for a while we went up, and then along it northwards till it vanished in forest. Slept without a fresh supply of water.

25th September, 1867.—Off at 5.30 A.M., through the same well-grown forest we have passed and came to a village stockade, where the gates were shut, and the men all outside, in fear of the Arabs; we then descended from the ridge on which it stood, about a thousand feet, into an immense plain, with a large river in the distance, some ten miles off.

26th September, 1867.—Two and a half hours brought us to the large river we saw yesterday; it is more than a mile wide and full of papyrus and other aquatic plants and very difficult to ford, as the papyrus roots are hard to the bare feet, and we often plunged into holes up to the waist. A loose mass floated in the middle of our path; one could sometimes get on along this while it bent and heaved under the weight, but through it he would plunge and find great difficulty to get out: the water under this was very cold from evaporation; it took an hour and a half to cross it. It is called Chiséra, and winds away to the west to fall into the Kalongosi and Moero. Many animals, as elephants, tahetsis, zebras, and buffaloes, graze on the long sloping banks of about a quarter of a mile down, while the ranges of hills we crossed as mere ridges now appear behind us in the south.

27th September, 1867.—The people are numerous and friendly. One elephant was killed, and we remained to take the ivory from the dead beast; buffaloes and zebras were also killed. It was so cloudy that no observations could be taken to determine our position, but Chiséra rises in Lopéré. Further west it is free of papyrus, and canoes are required to cross it.

28th September, 1867.—Two hours north brought us to the Kamosenga, a river eight yards wide, of clear water which ran strongly among aquatic plants. Hippopotami, buffalo, and zebra abound. This goes into the Chiséra eastwards; country flat and covered with dense tangled bush. Cassias and another tree of the pea family are now in flower, and perfume the air. Other two hours took us round a large bend of this river.

30th September, 1867..—We crossed the Kamosenga or another, and reach Karungu's. The Kamosenga divides Lopéré from Itawa, the latter being Nsama's country; Lopéré is north-west of it.

1st October, 1867.—Karungu was very much afraid of us; he kept every one out of his stockade at first, but during the time the Arabs sent forward to try and conciliate other chiefs he gradually became more friendly. He had little ivory to sell, and of those who had, Mtété or Mtéma seemed inclined to treat the messengers roughly. Men were also sent to Nsama asking him to try and induce Mtéma and Chikongo to be friendly and sell ivory and provisions, but he replied that these chiefs were not men under him, and if they thought themselves strong enough to contend against guns he had nothing to say to them. Other chiefs threatened to run away as soon as they saw the Arabs approaching. These were assured that we meant to pass through the country alone, and if they gave us guides to show us how, we should avoid the villages altogether, and proceed to the countries where ivory was to be bought; however, the panic was too great, no one would agree to our overtures, and at last when we did proceed a chief on the River Choma fulfilled his threat and left us three empty villages. There were no people to sell though the granaries were crammed, and it was impossible to prevent the slaves from stealing.

3rd-4th October, 1867.—When Chikongo heard Tipo Tipo's message about buying ivory he said, "And when did Tipo Tipo place ivory in my country that he comes seeking it?" Yet he sent a tusk and said "That is all I have, and he is not to come here." Their hostile actions are caused principally by fear. "If Nsama could not stand before the Malongwana or traders, how can we face them?" I wished to go on to Moero, but all declare that our ten guns would put all the villages to flight: they are terror-struck. First rains of this season on the 5th.

10th October, 1867.—I had a long conversation with Syde, who thinks that the sun rises and sets because the Koran says so, and he sees it. He asserts that Jesus foretold the coming of Mohamad; and that it was not Jesus who suffered on the cross but a substitute, it being unlikely that a true prophet would be put to death so ignominiously. He does not understand how we can be glad that our Saviour died for our sins.

12th October, 1867.—An elephant killed by Tipo Tipo's men. It is always clouded over, and often not a breath of air stirring.

16th October, 1867.—A great many of the women of this district and of Lopéré have the swelled thyroid gland called *goitre* or Derbyshire neck; men, too, appeared with it, and they in addition have hydrocele of large size.

An Arab who had been long ill at Chitimba's died yesterday, and was buried in the evening. No women were allowed to come near. A long silent prayer was uttered over the corpse when it was laid beside the grave, and then a cloth was held over as men in it deposited the remains beneath sticks placed slanting on the side of the bottom of the grave; this keeps the earth from coming directly into contact with the body.

A feast was made by the friends of the departed, and portions sent to all who had attended the funeral: I got a good share.

18th October, 1867.—The last we hear of Nsama is that he will not interfere with Chikongo. Two wives beat drums and he dances to them; he is evidently in his dotage. We hear of many Arabs to the west of us.

20th October, 1867.—Very ill; I am always so when I have no work—sore bones—much headache; then lost power over the muscles of the back, as at Liemba; no appetite and much thirst. The fever uninfluenced by medicine.

21st October, 1867.—Syde sent his men to build a new hut in a better situation. I hope it may be a healthful one for me.

22nd October, 1867.—The final message from Chikongo was a discouraging one—no ivory. The Arabs, however, go west with me as far as Chisawé's, who, being accustomed to Arabs from Tanganyika, will give me men to take me on to Moero: the Arabs will then return, and we shall move on.

23rd October, 1867.—Tipo Tipo gave Karungu some cloth, and this chief is "looking for something" to give him in return; this detains us one day more.

When a slave wishes to change his master he goes to one whom he likes better and breaks a spear or a bow in his presence— the transference is irrevocable. This curious custom prevails on the Zambesi, and also among the Wanyamwesi; if the old master wishes to recover his slave the new one may refuse to part with him except when he gets his full price: a case of this kind happened here yesterday.

25th October, 1867.—Authority was found in the Koran for staying one day more here. This was very trying; but the fact was our guide from Hara hither had enticed a young slave girl to run away, and he had given her in charge to one of his countrymen, who turned round and tried to secure her for himself, and gave information about the other enticing her away. Nothing can be more tedious than the Arab way of travelling.

26th October, 1867.—We went S.W. for five hours through an undulating, well-wooded, well-peopled country, and quantities of large game. Several trees give out when burned very fine scents; others do it when cut. Euphorbia is abundant. We slept by a torrent which had been filled with muddy water by late rains. It thunders every afternoon, and rains somewhere as regularly as it thunders, but these are but partial rains; they do not cool the earth; nor fill the cracks made in the dry season.

27th October, 1867.—Off early in a fine drizzling rain, which continued for two hours, and came on to a plain about three miles broad, full of large game. These plains are swamps at times, and they are flanked by ridges of denudation some 200 or 300 feet above them, and covered with trees.

The ridges are generally hardened sandstone, marked with madrepores, and masses of brown haematite. It is very hot, and we become very tired. There is no system in the Arab marches. The first day was five hours, this 3-1/2 hours; had it been reversed—short marches during the first days and longer afterwards—the muscles would have become inured to the exertion. A long line of heights on our south points to the valley of Nsama.

28th October, 1867.—Five hours brought us to the Choma River and the villages of Chifupa, but, as already mentioned, the chief and people had fled, and no persuasion could prevail on them to come and sell us food. We showed a few who ventured to come among us what we were willing to give for flour, but they said, "Yes, we will call the women and they will sell." None came.

Rested all day on the banks of the Choma, which is a muddy stream coming from the north and going to the south-west to join the Chiséra. It has worn itself a deep bed in the mud of its banks, and is twenty yards wide and in some spots waist deep, at other parts it is unfordable, it contains plenty of fish, and hippopotami and crocodiles abound. I bought a few ground-nuts at an exorbitant price, the men evidently not seeing that it would have been better to part with more at a lower price than run off and leave all to be eaten by the slaves.

30th October, 1867.—Two ugly images were found in huts built for them: they represent in a poor way the people of the country, and are used in rain-making and curing the sick ceremonies; this is the nearest approach to idol worship I have seen in the country.[58]

31st October, 1867.—We marched over a long line of hills on our west, and in five and a half hours came to some villages where the people sold us food willingly, and behaved altogether in a friendly way. We were met by a herd of buffaloes, but Syde seized my gun from the boy who carried it, and when the animals came close past me I was powerless, and not at all pleased with the want of good sense shown by my usually polite Arab friend.

Note.—The Choma is said by Mohamad bin Saleh to go into Tanganyika (??). It goes to Kalongosi.

1st November, 1867.—We came along between ranges of hills considerably higher than those we have passed in Itawa or Nsama's country, and thickly covered with trees, some in full foliage, and some putting forth fresh red leaves; the hills are about 700 or 800 feet above the valleys. This is not a district of running rills: we crossed three sluggish streamlets knee deep. Buffaloes are very numerous.

The Ratel covers the buffalo droppings with earth in order to secure the scavenger beetles which bury themselves therein, thus he prevents them from rolling a portion away as usual.

We built our sheds on a hillside. Our course was west and 6-1/4 hours.

2nd November, 1867.—Still in the same direction, and in an open valley remarkable for the numbers of a small euphorbia, which we smashed at every step. Crossed a small but strong rivulet, the Lipandé, going south-west to Moero, then, an hour afterwards, crossed it again, now twenty yards wide and knee deep. After descending from the tree-covered hill which divides Lipandé from Luao, we crossed the latter to sleep on its western bank. The hills are granite now, and a range on our left, from 700 to 1500 feet high, goes on all the way to Moero.

These valleys along which we travel are beautiful. Green is the prevailing colour; but the clumps of trees assume a great variety of forms, and often remind one of English park scenery. The long line of slaves and carriers, brought up by their Arab employers, adds life to the scene, they are in three bodies, and number 450 in all. Each party has a guide with a flag, and when that is planted all that company stops till it is lifted, and a drum is beaten, and a kudu's horn sounded. One party is headed by about a dozen leaders, dressed with fantastic head-gear of feathers and beads, red cloth on the bodies, and skins cut into strips and twisted: they take their places in line, the drum beats, the horn sounds harshly, and all fall in. These sounds seem to awaken a sort of *esprit de corps* in those who have once been slaves. My attendants now jumped up, and would scarcely allow me time to dress when they heard the-sounds of their childhood, and all day they were among the foremost. One said to me "that his feet were rotten with marching," and this though told that they were not called on to race along like slaves.

The Africans cannot stand sneers. When any mishap occurs in the march (as when a branch tilts a load off a man's shoulder) all who see it set up a yell of derision; if anything is accidentally spilled, or if one is tired and sits down, the same yell greets him, and all are excited thereby to exert themselves. They hasten on with their loads, and hurry with the sheds they build, the masters only bringing up the rear, and helping anyone who may be sick. The distances travelled were quite as much as the masters or we could bear. Had frequent halts been made—as, for instance, a half or a quarter of an hour at the end of every hour or two—but little distress would have been felt; but five hours at a stretch is more than men can bear in a hot climate. The female slaves held on bravely; nearly all carried loads on their heads, the head, or lady of the party, who is also the wife of the Arab, was the only exception. She had a fine white shawl, with ornaments of gold and silver on her head. These ladies had a jaunty walk, and never gave in on the longest march; many pounds' weight of fine copper leglets above the ankles seemed only to help the sway of their walk: as soon as they arrive at the sleeping-place they begin to cook, and in this art they show a good deal of expertness, making savoury dishes for their masters out of wild fruits and other not very likely materials.

3rd November, 1867.—The ranges of hills retire as we advance; the soil is very rich. At two villages the people did not want us, so we went on and encamped near a third, Kabwakwa, where a son of Mohamad bin Saleh, with a number of Wanyamwesi, lives. The chief of this part is Muabo, but we did not see him: the people brought plenty of food for us to buy. The youth's father is at Casembe's. The country-people were very much given to falsehood—every place inquired for was near—ivory abundant—provisions of all sorts cheap and plenty. Our headmen trusted to these statements of this young man rather, and he led them to desist going further. Rua country was a month distant, he said, and but little ivory there. It is but three days off. (We saw it after three days.) "No ivory at Casembe's or here in Buiré, or Kabuiré." He was right as to Casembe. Letters, however, came from Hamees, with news of a depressing nature. Chitimba is dead, and so is Mambwé. Chitimba's people are fighting for the chieftainship: great hunger prevails there now, the Arabs having bought up all the food. Moriri, a chief dispossessed of his country by Nsama, wished Hamees to restore his possessions, but Hamees said that he had made peace, and would not interfere.

This unfavourable news from a part where the chief results of their trading were deposited, made Syde and Tipo Tipo decide to remain in Buiré only ten or twenty days, send out people to buy what ivory they could find, and then, retire.

As Syde and Tipo Tipo were sending men to Casembe for ivory, I resolved to go thither first, instead of shaping my course for Ujiji.

Very many cases of goitre in men and women here: I see no reason for it. This is only 3350 feet above the sea.

7th November, 1867.—Start for Moero, convoyed by all the Arabs for some distance: they have been extremely kind. We draw near to the mountain-range on our left, called Kakoma, and sleep at one of Kaputa's villages, our course now being nearly south.

8th November, 1867.—Villages are very thickly studded over the valley formed by Kakoma range, and another at a greater distance on our right; 100 or 200 yards is a common distance between these villages, which, like those in Londa, or Lunda, are all shaded with trees of a species of *Ficus indica*. One belongs to Puta, and this Puta, the paramount chief, sent to say that if we slept there, and gave him a cloth, he would send men to conduct us next day, and ferry us across: I was willing to remain, but his people would not lend a hut, so we came on to the Lake, and no ferry. Probably he thought that we were going across the Lualaba into Rua.

Lake Moero seems of goodly size, and is flanked by ranges of mountains on the east and west. Its banks are of coarse sand, and slope gradually down to the water: outside these banks stands a thick belt of tropical vegetation, in which fishermen build their huts. The country called Rua lies on the west, and is seen as a lofty range of dark mountains: another range of less height, but more broken, stands along the eastern shore, and in it lies the path to Casembe. We slept in a fisherman's hut on the north shore. They brought a large fish, called "mondé," for sale; it has a slimy skin, and no scales, a large head, with tentaculae like the Siluridie, and large eyes: the great gums in its mouth have a brush-like surface, like a whale's in miniature: it is said to eat small fish. A bony spine rises on its back (I suppose for defence), which is 2-1/2 inches long, and as thick as a quill. They are very retentive of life.

The northern shore has a fine sweep like an unbent bow, and round the western end flows the water that makes the river Lualaba, which, before it enters Moero, is the Luapula, and that again (if the most intelligent reports speak true) is the Chambezé before it enters Lake Bemba, or Bangweolo.

We came along the north shore till we reached the eastern flanking range, then ascended and turned south, the people very suspicious, shutting their gates as we drew near. We were alone, and only nine persons in all, but they must have had reason for fear. One headman refused us admission, then sent after us, saying that the man who had refused admission was not the chief: he had come from a distance, and had just arrived. It being better to appear friendly than otherwise, we went back, and were well entertained.

Provisions were given when we went away. Flies abound, and are very troublesome; they seem to be attracted by the great numbers of fish caught. The people here are Babemba, but beyond the river Kalongosi they are all Balunda.

A trade in salt is carried on from different salt springs and salt mud to Lunda and elsewhere. We meet parties of salt-traders daily, and they return our salutations very cordially, rubbing earth on the arms. We find our path lies between two ranges of mountains, one flanking the eastern shore, the other about three miles more inland, and parallel to it: these are covered thickly with trees, and are of loosely-coherent granite: many villages are in the space enclosed by these ranges, but all insecure.

12th November, 1867..—We came to the Kalongosi, or, as the Arabs and Portuguese pronounce it, Karungwesi, about 60 yards wide, and flowing fast over stones. It is deep enough, even now when the rainy season is not commenced, to requite canoes. It is said to rise in Kumbi, or Afar, a country to the south-east of our ford. Fish in great numbers are caught when ascending to spawn: they are secured by weirs, nets, hooks. Large strong baskets are placed in the rapids, and filled with stones, when the water rises these baskets are standing-places for the fishermen to angle or throw their nets. Having crossed the Kalongosi we were now in Lunda, or Londa.

13th November, 1867.—We saw that the Kalongosi went north till it met a large meadow on the shores of Moero, and, turning westwards, it entered there. The fishermen gave us the names of 39 species of fish in the Lake; they said that they never cease ascending the Kalongosi, though at times they are more abundant than at others: they are as follows.

Mondé; Mota; Lasa; Kasibé; Molobé; Lopembé; Motoya; Chipansa; Mpifu; Manda; Mpala; Moombo; Mfeu; Mendé; Seusé; Kadia nkololo; Etiaka; Nkomo; Lifisha; Sambamkaka; Ntondo; Sampa; Bongwé; Mabanga; Kisé; Kuanya; Nkosu; Palé; Mosungu; Litembwa; Mecheberé; Koninchia; Sipa; Lomembé; Molenga; Mirongé; Nfindo; Pende.

14th November, 1867.—Being doubtful as to whether we were in the right path, I sent to a village to inquire. The headman, evidently one of a former Casembe school, came to us full of wrath. "What right had we to come that way, seeing the usual path was to our left?" He mouthed some sentences in the pompous Lunda style, but would not show us the path; so we left him, and after going through a forest of large trees, 4-1/2 hours south, took advantage of some huts on the Kifurwa River, built by bark-cloth cutters.

15th November, 1867.—Heavy rains, but we went on, and found a village, Kifurwa, surrounded by cassava fields, and next day crossed the Muatozé, 25 yards wide, and running strongly towards Moero, knee deep. The River Kabukwa, seven yards wide, and also knee deep, going to swell the Muatozé.

We now crossed a brook, Chirongo, one yard wide and one deep; but our march was all through well-grown forest, chiefly gum-copal trees and bark-cloth trees. The gum-copal oozes out in abundance after or during the rains, from holes a quarter of an inch in diameter, made by an insect: it falls, and in time sinks into the soil, a supply for future generations. The small well-rounded features of the people of Nsama's country are common here, as we observe in the salt-traders and villages; indeed, this is the home of the Negro, and the features such as we see in pictures of ancient Egyptians, as first pointed out by Mr. Winwood Reade. We sleep by the river Mandapala, 12 yards wide, and knee deep.

18th November, 1867.—We rest by the Kabusi, a sluggish narrow rivulet. It runs into the Chungu, a quarter of a mile off. The Chungu is broad, but choked with trees and aquatic plants: Sapotas, Eschinomenas, Papyrus, &c. The free stream is 18 yards wide, and waist deep. We had to wade about 100 yards, thigh and waist deep, to get to the free stream.

On this, the Chungu, Dr. Lacerda died; it is joined by the Mandapala, and flows a united stream into Moero. The statements of the people are confused, but the following is what I have gleaned from many. There were some Ujiji people with the Casembe of the time. The Portuguese and Ujijians began to fight, but Casembe said to them and the Portuguese, "You are all my guests, why should you fight and kill each other?" He then gave Lacerda ten slaves, and men to live with him and work at building huts, bringing firewood, water, &c. He made similar presents to the Ujijians, which quieted them. Lacerda was but ten days at Chungu when he died. The place of his death was about 9° 32', and not 8° 43' as in Mr. Arrowsmith's map. The feud arose from one of Lacerda's people killing an Ujijian at the water: this would certainly be a barrier to their movements.

Palm-oil trees are common west of the Chungu, but none appeared east of it. The oil is eaten by the people, and is very nice and sweet. This is remarkable, as the altitude above the sea is 3350 feet.

Allah is a very common exclamation among all the people west of Nsama. By advice of a guide whom we picked up at Kifurwa, we sent four fathoms of calico to apprise Casembe of our coming: the Arabs usually send ten fathoms; in our case it was a very superfluous notice, for Casembe is said to have been telegraphed to by runners at every stage of our progress after crossing the Kalongosi.

We remain by the Chungu till Casembe sends one of his counsellors to guide us to his town. It has been so perpetually clouded over that we have been unable to make out our progress, and the dense forest prevented us seeing Moero as we wished: rain and thunder perpetually, though the rain seldom fell where we were.

I saw pure white-headed swallows (*Psalidoprocne albiceps*) skimming the surface of the Chungu as we crossed it. The soil is very rich. Casembe's ground-nuts are the largest I have seen, and so is the cassava. I got over a pint of palm oil for a cubit of calico.

A fine young man, whose father had been the Casembe before this one, came to see us; he is in the background now, otherwise he would have conducted us to the village: a son or heir does not succeed to the chieftainship here.

21st November, 1867.—The River Lundé was five miles from Chungu. It is six yards wide where we crossed it, but larger further down; springs were oozing out of its bed: we then entered on a broad plain, covered with bush, the trees being all cleared off in building a village. When one Casembe dies, the man who succeeds him invariably removes and builds his pembwé, or court, at another place: when Dr. Lacerda died, the Casembe moved to near the north end of the Mofwé. There have been seven Casembes in all. The word means a *general*.

The plain extending from the Lundé to the town of Casembe is level, and studded pretty thickly with red anthills, from 15 to 20 feet high. Casembe has made a broad path from his town to the Lundé, about a mile-and-a-half long, and as broad as a carriage-path. The chief's residence is enclosed in a wall of reeds, 8 or 9 feet high, and 300 yards square, the gateway is ornamented with about sixty human skulls; a shed stands in the middle of the road before we come to the gate, with a cannon dressed in gaudy cloths. A number of noisy fellows stopped our party, and demanded tribute for the cannon; I burst through them, and the rest followed without giving anything: they were afraid of the English. The town is on the east bank of the Lakelet Mofwé, and one mile from its northern end. Mohamad bin Saleh now met us, his men firing guns of welcome; he conducted us to his shed of reception, and then gave us a hut till we could build one of our own. Mohamad is a fine portly black Arab, with a pleasant smile, and pure white beard, and has been more than ten years in these parts, and lived with four Casembes: he has considerable influence here, and also on Tanganyika.

An Arab trader, Mohamad Bogharib, who arrived seven days before us with an immense number of slaves, presented a meal of vermicelli, oil, and honey, also cassava meal cooked, so as to resemble a sweet meat (I had not tasted honey or sugar since we left Lake Nyassa, in September 1866): they had coffee too.

Neither goats, sheep, nor cattle thrive here, so the people are confined to fowls and fish. Cassava is very extensively cultivated, indeed, so generally is this plant grown, that it is impossible to know which is town and which is country: every hut has a plantation around it, in which is grown cassava, Holcus sorghum, maize, beans, nuts.

Mohamad gives the same account of the River Luapula and Lake Bemba that Jumbé did, but he adds, that the Chambezé, where we crossed it, *is* the Luapula before it enters Bemba or Bangweolo: on coming out of that Lake it turns round and comes away to the north, as Luapula, and, without touching the Mofwé, goes into Moero; then, emerging thence at the north-west end it becomes Lualaba, goes into Rua, forms a lake there, and afterwards goes into another lake beyond Tanganyika.

The Lakelet Mofwé fills during the rains and spreads westward, much beyond its banks. Elephants wandering in its mud flats when covered are annually killed in numbers: if it were connected with the Lake Moero the flood would run off.

Many of Casembe's people appear with the ears cropped and hands lopped off: the present chief has been often guilty of this barbarity. One man has just come to us without ears or hands: he tries to excite our pity making a chirruping noise, by striking his cheeks with the stumps of his hands.

A dwarf also, one Zofu, with backbone broken, comes about us: he talks with an air of authority, and is present at all public occurrences: the people seem to bear with him. He is a stranger from a tribe in the north, and works in his garden very briskly: his height is 3 feet 9 inches.

FOOTNOTES:

56. Chéfu amongst the Manganja. Any animal possessing strength, has the terminal "fu" or "vu;" thus Njobvu, an elephant; M'vu, the hippopotamus.—ED.

57. The natives are quick to detect a peculiarity in a man, and give him a name accordingly: the conquerors of a country try to forestall them by selecting one for themselves. Susi states that when Tipo Tipo stood over the spoil taken from Nsama, he gathered it closer together and said, "Now I am Tipo Tipo," that is, "the gatherer together of wealth." Kumba Kumba, of whom we shall hear much, took his name from the number of captives he gathered in his train under similar circumstances; it might be translated, "the collector of people."—ED.

58. It is on the West Coast alone that idols are really worshipped in Africa.—ED.

* * * * *

CHAPTER X.

Grand reception of the traveller. Casenibe and his wife. Long stay in the town. Goes to explore Moero. Despatch to Lord Clarendon, with notes on recent travels. Illness at the end of 1867. Further exploration of Lake Moero. Flooded plains. The River Luao. Visits Kabwawata. Joy of Arabs at Mohamad bin Saleh's freedom. Again ill with fever. Stories of underground dwellings.

24th November, 1867.—We were called to be presented to Casembe in a grand reception.

The present Casembe has a heavy uninteresting countenance, without beard or whiskers, and somewhat of the Chinese type, and his eyes have an outward squint. He smiled but once during the day, and that was pleasant enough, though the cropped ears and lopped hands, with human skulls at the gate, made me indisposed to look on anything with favour. His principal wife came with her attendants, after he had departed, to look at the Englishman (Moenge-résé). She was a fine, tall, good-featured lady, with two spears in her hand; the principal men who had come around made way for her, and called on me to salute: I did so; but she, being forty yards off, I involuntarily beckoned her to come nearer: this upset the gravity of all her attendants; all burst into a laugh, and ran off.

Casembe's smile was elicited by the dwarf making some uncouth antics before him. His executioner also came forward to look: he had a broad Lunda sword on his arm, and a curious scizzor-like instrument at his neck for cropping ears. On saying to him that his was nasty work, he smiled, and so did many who were not sure of their ears a moment: many men of respectability show that at some former time they have been thus punished. Casembe sent us another large basket of fire-dried fish in addition to that sent us at Chungu, two baskets of flour, one of dried cassava, and a pot of pombe or beer. Mohamad, who was accustomed to much more liberal Casembes, thinks this one very stingy, having neither generosity nor good sense; but as we cannot consume all he gives, we do not complain.

27th November, 1867.—Casembe's chief wife passes frequently to her plantation, carried by six, or more commonly by twelve men in a sort of palanquin: she has European features, but light-brown complexion. A number of men run before her, brandishing swords and battle-axes, and one beats a hollow instrument, giving warning to passengers to clear the way: she has two enormous pipes ready filled for smoking. She is very attentive to her agriculture; cassava is the chief product; sweet potatoes, maize, sorghum, pennisetum, millet, ground-nuts, cotton. The people seem more savage than any I have yet seen: they strike each other barbarously from mere wantonness, but they are civil enough to me.

Mohamad bin Saleh proposes to go to Ujiji next month. He waited when he heard of our coming, in order that we might go together: he has a very low opinion of the present chief. The area which has served for building the chief town at different times is about ten miles in diameter.

Mofwé is a shallow piece of water about two miles broad, four or less long, full of sedgy islands, the abodes of waterfowl, but some are solid enough to be cultivated. The bottom is mud, though sandy at the east shore: it has no communication with the Luapula. (*28th November, 1867.*) The Lundé, Chungu, and Mandapala are said to join and flow into Moero. Fish are in great abundance (perch). On the west side there is a grove of palm-oil palms, and beyond west rises a long range of mountains of the Rua country 15 or 20 miles off.

1st December, 1867.—An old man named Pérémbé is the owner of the land on which Casembe has built. They always keep up the traditional ownership. Munongo is a brother of Pérémbé, and he owns the country east of the Kalongosi: if any one wished to cultivate land he would apply to these aboriginal chiefs for it.

I asked a man from Casembe to guide me to south end of Moero, but he advised me not to go as it was so marshy. The Lundé forms a marsh on one side, and the Luapula lets water percolate through sand and mud, and so does the Robukwé, which makes the path often knee deep. He said he would send men to conduct me to Moero, a little further down, and added that we had got very little to eat from him, and he wanted to give more. Moero's south end is about 9° 30' S.

Old Pérémbé is a sensible man: Mohamad thinks him 150 years old. He is always on the side of liberality and fairness; he says that the first Casembe was attracted to Mofwé by the abundance of fish in it. He has the idea of all men being derived from a single pair.

7th December, 1867.—It is very cloudy here; no observations can be made, as it clouds over every afternoon and night. *(8th and 11th December, 1867.)* Cleared off last night, but intermittent fever prevented my going out.

13th December, 1867.—Set-in rains. A number of fine young girls who live in Casembe's compound came and shook hands in their way, which is to cross the right over to your left, and clasp them; then give a few claps with both hands, and repeat the crossed clasp: they want to tell their children that they have seen me.

15th December, 1867.—To-day I announced to Casembe our intention of going away. Two traders got the same return present from him that I did, namely, one goat and some fish, meal and cassava. I am always ill when not working; I spend my time writing letters, to be ready when we come to Ujiji. *(18th December, 1867.)* We have been here a month, and I cannot get more than two lunars: I got altitudes of the meridian of stars north and south soon after we came, but not lunars. Casembe sent a big basket of fire-dried fish, two pots of beer, and a basket of cassava, and says we may go when we choose.

19th December, 1867.—On going to say good-bye to Casembe, he tried to be gracious, said that we had eaten but little of his food; yet he allowed us to go. He sent for a man to escort us; and on the *22nd December, 1867.* we went to Lundé River, crossed it, and went on to sleep at the Chungu, close by the place where Casembe's court stood when Dr. Lacerda came, for the town was moved further west as soon as the Doctor died. There are many palm-oil palms about, but no tradition exists of their introduction.

23rd December, 1867.—We crossed the Chungu. Rain from above, and cold and wet to the waist below, as I do not lift my shirt, because the white skin makes all stare. I saw black monkeys at this spot. The Chungu is joined by the Kaleusi and the Mandapala before it enters Moero. Casembe said that the Lundé ran into Mofwé; others denied this, and said that it formed a marsh with numbers of pools in long grass; but it may ooze into Mofwé thus. Casembe sent three men to guide me to Moero.

24th December, 1867.—Drizzly rain, and we are in a miserable spot by the Kabusi, in a bed of brakens four feet high. The guides won't stir in this weather. I gave beads to buy what could be got for Christmas.

25th December, 1867.—Drizzly showers every now and then; soil, black mud.

About ten men came as guides and as a convoy of honour to Mohamad.

27th December, 1867.—In two hours we crossed Mandapala, now waist deep. This part was well stocked with people five years ago, but Casembe's severity in cropping ears and other mutilations, selling the children for slight offences, &c., made them all flee to neighbouring tribes; and now, if he sent all over the country, he could not collect a thousand men.

[Livingstone refers (on the 15th Dec.) to some writings he was engaged upon, and we find one of them here in his journal which takes the form of a despatch to Lord Clarendon, with a note attached to the effect that it was not copied or sent, as he had no paper for the purpose. It affords an epitomised description of his late travels, and the stay at Casembe, and is inserted here in the place of many notes written daily, but which only repeat the same events and observations in a less readable form. It is especially valuable at this stage of his journal, because it treats on the whole geography of the district between Lakes Nyassa and Moero, with a broad handling which is impossible in the mere jottings of a diary.]

Town Of Casembe, *10th December, 1867.*.
Lat. 9° 37' 13" South; long. 28° East.
The Right Honourable the Earl of Clarendon.

My Lord,—The first opportunity I had of sending a letter to the coast occurred in February last, when I was at a village called Molemba (lat. 10° 14' S.; long. 31° 46' E.), in the country named Lobemba. Lobisa, Lobemba, Ulungu and Itawa-Lunda are the names by which the districts of an elevated region between the parallels 11° and 8° south, and meridians 28°-33° long. east, are known. The altitude of this upland is from 4000 to 6000 feet above the level of the sea. It is generally covered with forest, well watered by numerous rivulets, and comparatively cold. The soil is very rich, and yields abundantly wherever cultivated. This is the watershed between the Loangwa, a tributary of the Zambesi, and several rivers which flow towards the north. Of the latter, the most remarkable is the Chambezé, for it assists in the formation of three lakes, and changes its name three times in the five or six hundred miles of its course.

On leaving Lobemba we entered Ulungu, and, as we proceeded northwards, perceived by the barometers and the courses of numerous rivulets, that a decided slope lay in that direction. A friendly old Ulungu chief, named Kasonso, on hearing that I wished to visit Lake Liemba, which lies in his country, gave his son with a large escort to guide me thither; and on the 2nd April last we reached the brim of the deep cup-like cavity in which the Lake reposes. The descent is 2000 feet, and still the surface of the water is upwards of 2500 feet above the level of the sea. The sides of the hollow are very steep, and sometimes the rocks run the whole 2000 feet sheer down to the water. Nowhere is there three miles of level land from the foot of the cliffs to the shore, but top, sides, and bottom are covered with well-grown wood and grass, except where the bare rocks protrude. The scenery is extremely beautiful. The "Aeasy," a stream of 15 yards broad and thigh deep, came down alongside our precipitous path, and formed cascades by leaping 300 feet at a time. These, with the bright red of the clay schists among the greenwood-trees, made the dullest of my attendants pause and remark with wonder. Antelopes, buffaloes, and elephants abound on the steep slopes; and hippopotami, crocodiles, and fish swarm in the water. Gnus are here unknown, and these animals may live to old age if not beguiled into pitfalls. The elephants sometimes eat the crops of the natives, and flap their big ears just outside the village stockades. One got out of our way on to a comparatively level spot, and then stood and roared at us. Elsewhere they make clear off at sight of man.

The first village we came to on the banks of the Lake had a grove of palm-oil and other trees around it. This palm tree was not the dwarf species seen on Lake Nyassa. A cluster of the fruit passed the door of my hut which required two men to carry it. The fruit seemed quite as large as those on the West Coast. Most of the natives live on two islands, where they cultivate the soil, rear goats, and catch fish. The Lake is not large, from 15 to 20 miles broad, and from 30 to 40 long. It is the receptacle of four considerable streams, and sends out an arm two miles broad to the N.N.W., it is said to Tanganyika, and it may be a branch of that Lake. One of the streams, the Lonzua, drives a smooth body of water into the Lake fifty yards broad and ten fathoms deep, bearing on its surface duckweed and grassy islands. I could see the mouths of other streams, but got near enough to measure the Lofu only; and at a ford fifty miles from the confluence it was 100 yards wide and waist deep in the dry season.

We remained six weeks on the shores of the Lake, trying to pick up some flesh and strength. A party of Arabs came into Ulungu after us in search of ivory, and hearing that an Englishman had preceded them, naturally inquired where I was. But our friends, the Bäulungu, suspecting that mischief was meant, stoutly denied that they had ever seen anything of the sort; and then became very urgent that I should go on to one of the inhabited islands for safety. I regret that I suspected them of intending to make me a prisoner there, which they could easily have done by removing the canoes; but when the villagers who deceived the Arabs told me afterwards with an air of triumph how nicely they had managed, I saw that they had only been anxious for my safety. On three occasions the same friendly disposition was shown; and when we went round the west side of the Lake in order to examine the arm or branch above referred to, the headman at the confluence of the Lofu protested so strongly against my going—the Arabs had been fighting, and I might be mistaken for an Arab, and killed—that I felt half-inclined to believe him. Two Arab slaves entered the village the same afternoon in search of ivory, and confirmed all he had said. We now altered our course, intending to go south about the district disturbed by the Arabs. When we had gone 60 miles we heard that the head-quarters of the Arabs were 22 miles further. They had found ivory very cheap, and pushed on to the west, till attacked by a chief named, Nsama, whom they beat in his own stockade. They were now at a loss which way to turn. On reaching Chitimba's village (lat. 8° 57' 55" S.; long. 30° 20' E.), I found them about 600 in all; and, on presenting a letter I had from the Sultan of Zanzibar, was immediately supplied with provisions, beads, and cloth. They approved of my plan of passing to the south of Nsama's country, but advised waiting till the effects of punishment, which the Bäulungu had resolved to inflict on Nsama for breach of public law, were known. It had always been understood that whoever brought goods into the country was to be protected; and two hours after my arrival at Chitimba's, the son of Kasonso, our guide, marched in with his contingent. It was anticipated that Nsama might flee; if to the north, he would leave me a free passage through his country; if to the south, I might be saved from walking into his hands. But it turned out that Nsama was anxious for peace. He had sent two men with elephants' tusks to begin a negotiation; but treachery was suspected, and they were shot down. Another effort was made with ten goats, and repulsed. This was much to the regret of the head Arabs. It was fortunate for me that the Arab goods were not all sold, for Lake Moero lay in Nsama's country, and without peace no ivory could be bought, nor could I reach the Lake. The peace-making between the people and Arabs was, however, a tedious process, occupying three and a half months— drinking each other's blood. This, as I saw it west of this in 1854, is not more horrible than the thirtieth dilution of deadly night-shade or strychnine is in homoeopathy. I thought that had I been an Arab I could easily swallow that, but not the next means of cementing the peace— marrying a black wife. Nsama's daughter was the bride, and she turned out very pretty. She came riding pickaback on a man's shoulders: this is the most dignified conveyance that chiefs and their families can command. She had ten maids with her, each carrying a basket of provisions, and all having the same beautiful features as herself. She was taken by the principal Arab, but soon showed that she preferred her father to her husband, for seeing preparations made to send off to purchase ivory, she suspected that her father was to be attacked, and made her escape. I then, visited Nsama, and, as he objected to many people coming near him, took only three of my eight attendants. His people were very much afraid of fire-arms, and felt all my clothing to see if I had any concealed on my person. Nsama is an old man, with head and face like those sculptured on the Assyrian monuments. He has been a great conqueror in his time, and with bows and arrows was invincible. He is said to have destroyed many native traders from Tanganyika, but twenty Arab guns made him flee from his own stockade, and caused a great sensation in the country. He was much taken with my hair and woollen clothing; but his people, heedless of his scolding, so pressed upon us that we could not converse, and, after promising to send for me to talk during the night, our interview ended. He promised guides to Moero, and sent us more provisions than we could carry; but showed so much distrust, that after all we went without his assistance.

Nsama's people are particularly handsome. Many of the men have as beautiful heads as one could find in an assembly of Europeans. All have very fine forms, with small hands and feet. None of the West-coast ugliness, from which most of our ideas of the Negroes are derived, is here to be seen. No prognathous jaws nor lark-heels offended the sight. My observations deepened the impression first obtained from the remarks of Winwood Reade, that the typical Negro is seen in the ancient Egyptian, and not in the ungainly forms; which grow up in the unhealthy swamps of the West Coast. Indeed it is probable that this upland forest region is the true home of the Negro. The women excited the admiration of the Arabs. They have fine, small, well-formed features: their great defect is one of fashion, which does not extend to the next tribe; they file their teeth to points, the hussies, and that makes their smile like that of the crocodile.

Nsama's country is called Itawa, and his principal town is in lat. 8° 55' S., and long. 29° 21' E. From the large population he had under him, Itawa is in many parts well cleared of trees for cultivation, and it is lower than Ulungu, being generally about 3000 feet above the sea. Long lines of tree-covered hills raised some 600 or 700 feet above these valleys of denudation, prevent the scenery from being monotonous. Large game is abundant. Elephants, buffaloes, and zebras grazed in large numbers on the long sloping, banks of a river called Chiséra, a mile and a half broad. In going north we crossed this river, or rather marsh, which is full of papyrus plants and reeds. Our ford was an elephant's path; and the roots of the papyrus, though a carpet to these animals, were sharp and sore to feet usually protected by shoes, and often made us shrink and flounder into holes chest deep. The Chiséra forms a larger marsh west of this, and it gives off its water to the Kalongosi, a feeder of Lake Moero.

The Arabs sent out men in all directions to purchase ivory; but their victory over Nsama had created a panic among the tribes which no verbal assurances could allay. If Nsama had been routed by twenty Arab guns no one could stand before them but Casembe; and Casembe had issued strict orders to his people not to allow the Arabs who fought Nsama to enter his country. They did not attempt to force their way, but after sending friendly messages and presents to different chiefs, when these were not cordially received, turned off in some other direction, and at last, despairing of more ivory, turned homewards. From first to last they were extremely kind to me, and showed all due respect to the Sultan's letter. I am glad that I was witness to their mode of trading in ivory and slaves. It formed a complete contrast to the atrocious dealings of the Kilwa traders, who are supposed to be, but are not, the subjects of the same Sultan. If one wished to depict the slave-trade in its most attractive, or rather least objectionable, form, he would accompany these gentlemen subjects of the Sultan of Zanzibar. If he would describe the land traffic in its most disgusting phases he would follow the Kilwa traders along the road to Nyassa, or the Portuguese half-castes from Tette to the River Shiré.

Keeping to the north of Nsama altogether, and moving westwards, our small party reached the north end of Moero on the 8th November last. There the Lake is a goodly piece of water twelve or more miles broad, and flanked on the east and west by ranges of lofty tree-covered mountains. The range on the west is the highest, and is part of the country called Rua-Moero; it gives off a river at its north-west end called Lualaba, and receives the River Kalongosi (pronounced by the Arabs Karungwesi) on the east near its middle, and the rivers Luapula and Rovukwé at its southern extremity. The point of most interest in Lake Moero is that it forms one of a chain of lakes, connected by a river some 500 miles in length. First of all the Chambezé rises in the country of Mambwé, N.E. of Molemba. It then flows south-west and west till it reaches lat. 11° S., and long. 29° E., where it forms Lake Bemba or Bangweolo, emerging thence it assumes the new name Luapula, and comes down here to fall into Moero. On going out of this Lake it is known by the name Lualaba, as it flows N.W. in Rua to form another Lake with many islands called Urengé or Ulengé. Beyond this, information is not positive as to whether it enters Tanganyika or another Lake beyond that. When I crossed the Chambezé, the similarity of names led me to imagine that this was a branch of the Zambesi. The natives said, "No. This goes south-west, and forms a very large water there." But I had become prepossessed with the idea that Lake Liemba was that Bemba of which I had heard in 1863, and we had been so starved in the south that I gladly set my face north. The river-like prolongation of Liemba might go to Moero, and where I could not follow the arm of Liemba. Then I worked my way to this Lake. Since coming to Casembe's the testimony of natives and Arabs has been so united and consistent, that I am but ten days from Lake Bemba, or Bangweolo, that I cannot doubt its accuracy. I am so tired of exploration without a word from home or anywhere else for two years, that I must go to Ujiji on Tanganyika for letters before doing anything else. The banks and country adjacent to Lake Bangweolo are reported to be now very muddy and very unhealthy. I have no medicine. The inhabitants suffer greatly from swelled thyroid gland or Derbyshire neck and elephantiasis, and this is the rainy season and very unsafe for me.

When at the lower end of Moero we were so near Casembe that it was thought well to ascertain the length of the Lake, and see Casembe too. We came up between the double range that flanks the east of the Lake; but mountains and plains are so covered with well-grown forest that we could seldom see it. We reached Casembe's town on the 28th November. It stands near the north end of the Lakelet Mofwé; this is from one to three miles broad, and some six or seven long: it is full of sedgy islands, and abounds in fish. The country is quite level, but fifteen or twenty miles west of Mofwé we see a long range of the mountains of Rua. Between this range and Mofwé the Luapula flows past into Moero, the Lake called Moero okata = the great Moero, being about fifty miles long. The town of Casembe covers a mile square of cassava plantations, the huts being dotted over that space. Some have square enclosures of reeds, but no attempt has been made at arrangement: it might be called a rural village rather than a town. No estimate could be formed by counting the huts, they were so irregularly planted, and hidden by cassava; but my impression from other collections of huts was that the population was under a thousand souls. The court or compound of Casembe— some would call it a palace—is a square enclosure of 300 yards by 200 yards. It is surrounded by a hedge of high reeds. Inside, where Casembe honoured me with a grand reception, stands a gigantic hut for Casembe, and a score of small huts for domestics. The Queen's hut stands behind that of the chief, with a number of small huts also. Most of the enclosed space is covered with a plantation of cassava, *Curcus purgaris*, and cotton. Casembe sat before his hut on a equate seat placed on lion and leopard skins. He was clothed in a coarse blue and white Manchester print edged with red baize, and arranged in large folds so as to look like a crinoline put on wrong side foremost. His arms, legs and head were covered with sleeves, leggings and cap made of various coloured beads in neat patterns: a crown of yellow feathers surmounted his cap. Each of his headmen came forward, shaded by a huge, ill-made umbrella, and followed by his dependants, made obeisance to Casembe, and sat down on his right and left: various bands of musicians did the same. When called upon I rose and bowed, and an old counsellor, with his ears cropped, gave the chief as full an account as he had been able to gather during our stay of the English in general, and my antecedents in particular. My having passed through Lunda to the west of Casembe, and visited chiefs of whom he scarcely knew anything, excited most attention. He then assured me that I was welcome to his country, to go where I liked, and do what I chose. We then went (two boys carrying his train behind him) to an inner apartment, where the articles of my present were exhibited in detail. He had examined them privately before, and we knew that he was satisfied. They consisted of eight yards of orange-coloured serge, a large striped tablecloth; another large cloth made at Manchester in imitation of West Coast native manufacture, which never fails to excite the admiration of Arabs and natives, and a large richly gilded comb for the back hair, such as ladies wore fifty years ago: this was given to me by a friend at Liverpool, and as Casembe and Nsama's people cultivate the hair into large knobs behind, I was sure that this article would tickle the fancy. Casembe expressed himself pleased, and again bade me welcome.

I had another interview, and tried to dissuade him from selling his people as slaves. He listened awhile, then broke off into a tirade on the greatness of his country, his power and dominion, which Mohamad bin Saleh, who has been here for ten years, turned into ridicule, and made the audience laugh by telling how other Lunda chiefs had given me oxen and sheep, while Casembe had only a poor little goat and some fish to bestow. He insisted also that there were but two sovereigns in the world, the Sultan of Zanzibar and Victoria. When we went on a third occasion to bid Casembe farewell, he was much less distant, and gave me the impression that I could soon become friends with him;

but he has an ungainly look, and an outward squint in each eye. A number of human skulls adorned the entrance to his courtyard; and great numbers of his principal men having their ears cropped, and some with their hands lopped off, showed his barbarous way of making his ministers attentive and honest. I could not avoid indulging a prejudice against him.

The Portuguese visited Casembe long ago; but as each new Casembe builds a new town, it is not easy to fix on the exact spot to which strangers came. The last seven Casembes have had their towns within seven miles of the present one. Dr. Lacerda, Governor of Tette, on the Zambesi, was the only visitor of scientific attainments, and he died at the rivulet called Chungu, three or four miles from this. The spot is called Nshinda, or Inchinda, which the Portuguese wrote Lucenda or Ucenda. The latitude given is nearly fifty miles wrong, but the natives say that he lived only ten days after his arrival, and if, as is probable, his mind was clouded with fever when he last observed, those who have experienced what that is will readily excuse any mistake he may have made. His object was to accomplish a much-desired project of the Portuguese to have an overland communication between their eastern and western possessions. This was never made by any of the Portuguese nation; but two black traders succeeded partially with a part of the distance, crossing once from Cassangé, in Angola, to Tette on the Zambesi, and returning with a letter from the Governor of Mosambique. It is remarkable that this journey, which was less by a thousand miles than from sea to sea and back again, should have for ever quenched all white Portuguese aspirations for an overland route.

The different Casembes visited by the Portuguese seem to have varied much in character and otherwise. Pereira, the first visitor, said (I quote from memory) that Casembe had 20,000 trained soldiers, watered his streets daily, and sacrificed twenty human victims every day. I could hear nothing of human sacrifices now, and it is questionable if the present Casembe could bring a thousand stragglers into the field. When he usurped power five years ago, his country was densely peopled; but he was so severe in his punishments—cropping the ears, lopping off the hands, and other mutilations, selling the children for very slight offences, that his subjects gradually dispersed themselves in the neighbouring countries beyond his power. This is the common mode by which tyranny is cured in parts like these, where fugitives are never returned. The present Casembe is very poor. When he had people who killed elephants he was too stingy to share the profits of the sale of the ivory with his subordinates. The elephant hunters have either left him or neglect hunting, so he has now no tusks to sell to the Arab traders who come from Tanganyika. Major Monteiro, the third Portuguese who visited Casembe, appears to have been badly treated by this man's predecessor, and no other of his nation has ventured so far since. They do not lose much by remaining away, for a little ivory and slaves are all that Casembe ever can have to sell. About a month to the west of this the people of Katanga smelt copper-ore (malachite) into large bars shaped like the capital letter I. They may be met with of from 50 lbs. to 100 lbs. weight all over the country, and the inhabitants draw the copper into wire for armlets and leglets. Gold is also found at Katanga, and specimens were lately sent to the Sultan of Zanzibar.

As we come down from the watershed towards Tanganyika we enter an area of the earth's surface still disturbed by internal igneous action. A hot fountain in the country of Nsama is often used to boil cassava and maize. Earthquakes are by no means rare. We experienced the shock of one while at Chitimba's village, and they extend as far as Casembe's. I felt as if afloat, and as huts would not fall there was no sense of danger; some of them that happened at night set the fowls a cackling. The most remarkable effect of this one was that it changed the rates of the chronometers; no rain fell after it. No one had access to the chronometers but myself, and, as I never heard of this effect before, I may mention that one which lost with great regularity 1.5 sec. daily, lost 15 sec.; another, whose rate since leaving the coast was 15 sec., lost 40 sec.; and a third, which gained 6 sec. daily, stopped altogether. Some of Nsama's people ascribed the earthquakes to the hot fountain, because it showed unusual commotion on these occasions; another hot fountain exists near Tanganyika than Nsama's, and we passed one on the shores of Moero.

We could not understand why the natives called Moero much larger than Tanganyika till we saw both. The greater Lake lies in a comparatively narrow trough, with highland on each side, which is always visible; but when we look at Moero, to the south of the mountains of Rua on the west, we have nothing but an apparently boundless sea horizon. The Luapula and Rovukwé form a marsh at the southern extremity, and Casembe dissuaded me from entering it, but sent a man to guide me to different points of Moero further down. From the heights at which the southern portions were seen, it must be from forty to sixty miles broad. From the south end of the mountains of Rua (9° 4' south lat.) it is thirty-three miles broad. No native ever attempts to cross it even there. Its fisheries are of great value to the inhabitants, and the produce is carried to great distances.

Among the vegetable products of this region, that which interested me most was a sort of potato. It does not belong to the solanaceous, but to the papilionaceous or pea family, and its flowers have a delightful fragrance. It is easily propagated by small cuttings of the root or stalk. The tuber is oblong, like our kidney potato, and when boiled tastes exactly like our common potato. When unripe it has a slight degree of bitterness, and it is believed to be wholesome; a piece of the root eaten raw is a good remedy in nausea. It is met with on the uplands alone, and seems incapable of bearing much heat, though I kept some of the roots without earth in a box, which was carried in the sun almost daily for six months, without destroying their vegetative power.

It is remarkable that in all the central regions of Africa visited, the cotton is that known as the Pernambuco variety. It has a long strong staple, seeds clustered together, and adherent to each other. The bushes eight or ten feet high have woody stems, and the people make strong striped black and white shawls of the cotton.

It was pleasant to meet the palm-oil palm (*Elais Guineaensis*) at Casembe's, which is over 3000 feet above the level of the sea. The oil is sold cheap, but no tradition exists of its introduction into the country.

I send no sketch of the country, because I have not yet passed over a sufficient surface to give a connected view of the whole watershed of this region, and I regret that I cannot recommend any of the published maps I have seen as giving even a tolerable idea of the country. One bold constructor of maps has tacked on 200 miles to the north-west end of Lake Nyassa, a feat which no traveller has ever ventured to imitate. Another has placed a river in the same quarter running 3000 or 4000 feet up hill, and named it the "NEW ZAMBESI," because I suppose the old Zambesi runs down hill. I have walked over both these mental abortions, and did not know that I was walking on water till I saw them in the maps.

[The despatch breaks off at this point. The year concludes with health impaired. As time goes on we shall see how ominous the conviction was which made him dread the swamps of Bangweolo.]

28-31st December, 1867.—We came on to the rivulet Chirongo, and then to the Kabukwa, where I was taken ill. Heavy rains kept the convoy back. I have had nothing but coarsely-ground sorghum meal for some time back, and am weak; I used to be the first in the line of march, and am now the last; Mohamad presented a meal of finely-ground porridge and a fowl, and I immediately felt the difference, though I was not grumbling at my coarse dishes. It is well that I did not go to Bangweolo Lake, for it is now very unhealthy to the natives, and I fear that without medicine continual wettings by fording rivulets might have knocked me up altogether. As I have mentioned, the people suffer greatly from swelled thyroid gland or Derbyshire neck and Elephantiasis scroti.

1st January, 1868.—Almighty Father, forgive the sins of the past year for Thy Son's sake. Help me to be more profitable during this year. If I am to die this year prepare me for it.

* * * * *

I bought five hoes at two or three yards of calico each: they are 13-1/2 inches by 6-1/2 inches; many are made in Casembe's country, and this is the last place we can find them: when we come into Buiré we can purchase a good goat for one; one of my goats died and the other dried up. I long for others, for milk is the most strengthening food I can get.

My guide to Moero came to-day, and I visited the Lake several times, so as to get a good idea of its size. The first fifteen miles in the north are from twelve or more to thirty-three miles broad. The great mass of the Rua Mountains confines it. Thus in a clear day a lower range is seen continued from the high point of the first mass away to the west south-west, this ends, and sea horizon is alone visible away to the south and west; from the height we viewed it at, the width must be over forty, perhaps sixty miles. A large island, called Kirwa,[59] is situated between the Mandapala and Kabukwa Rivers, but nearest to the other shore. The natives never attempt to cross any part of the Lake south of this Kirwa. Land could not be seen with a good glass on the clearest day we had. I can understand why the natives pronounced Moero to be larger than Tanganyika: in the last named they see the land always on both sides; it is like a vast trough flanked with highlands, but at Moero nothing but sea horizon can be seen when one looks south-west of the Rua Mountains.

At the Kalongosi meadow one of Mohamad's men shot a buffalo, and he gave me a leg of the good beefy flesh. Our course was slow, caused partly by rains, and partly by waiting for the convoy. The people at Kalongosi were afraid to ferry us or any of his people in the convoy out of Casembe's country; but at last we gave a good fee, and their scruples yielded: they were influenced also by seeing other villagers ready to undertake the job; the latter nearly fought over us on seeing that their neighbours got all the fare.

We then came along the Lake, and close to its shores. The moisture caused a profusion of gingers, ferns, and tropical forest: buffaloes, zebras and elephants are numerous, and the villagers at Chukosi's, where we slept, warned us against lions and leopards.

12th January, 1868.—Sunday at Karembwé's village. The mountains east of him are called Makunga. We went yesterday to the shore, and by protraction Rua point was distant thirty-three miles. Karembwé sent for us, to have an audience; he is a large man with a gruff voice, but liked by his people and by strangers. I gave him a cloth, and he gave me a goat. The enthusiasm with which I held on to visit Moero had communicated itself to Tipo Tipo and Syde bin Alle, for they followed me up to this place to see the Lake, and remained five days while we were at Casembe's. Other Arabs, or rather Suahelis, must have seen it, but never mentioned it as anything worth looking at; and it was only when all hope of ivory was gone that these two headmen found time to come. There is a large population here.

13th January, 1868.—Heavy rains. Karembé mentioned a natural curiosity as likely to interest me: a little rivulet, Chipamba, goes some distance underground, but is uninteresting.

Next day we crossed the Vuna, a strong torrent, which, has a hot fountain close by the ford, in which maize and cassava may be boiled. A large one in Nsama's country is used in the same way, maize and cassava being tied to a string and thrown in to be cooked: some natives believe that earthquakes are connected with its violent ebullitions. We crossed the Katétté, another strong torrent, before reaching the north end of Moero, where we slept in some travellers' huts.

Leaving the Lake, and going north, we soon got on to a plain flooded by the Luao. We had to wade through very adhesive black mud, generally ankle deep, and having many holes in it much deeper: we had four hours of this, and then came to the ford of the Luao itself. We waded up a branch of it waist deep for at least a quarter of a mile, then crossed a narrow part by means of a rude bridge of branches and trees, of about forty yards width. The Luao, in spreading over the plains, confers benefits on the inhabitants, though I could not help concluding it imparts disease too, for the black mud in places smells horribly. Great numbers of Siluridae, chiefly *Clarias Capensis*, often three feet in length, spread over the flooded portions of the country, eating the young of other fishes, and insects, lizards, and worms, killed by the waters. The people make weirs for them, and as the waters retire kill large numbers, which they use as a relish to their farinaceous food.

16th January, 1868.—After sleeping near the Luao we went on towards the village, in which Mohamad's son lives. It is on the Kakoma Eiver, and is called Kabwabwata, the village of Mubao. In many of the villages the people shut their stockades as soon as we appear, and stand bows and arrows in hand till we have passed: the reason seems to be that the slaves when out of sight of their masters carry things with a high hand, demanding food and other things as if they had power and authority. One slave stole two tobacco pipes yesterday in passing through a village; the villagers complained to me when I came up, and I waited till Mohamad came and told him; we then went forward, the men keeping close to me till we got the slave and the pipes. They stole cassava as we went along, but this could scarcely be prevented. They laid hold of a plant an inch-and-a-half thick, and tore it out of the soft soil with its five or six roots as large as our largest carrots, stowed the roots away in their loads, and went on eating them; but the stalk thrown among those still growing shows the theft. The raw roots are agreeable and nutritious. No great harm is done by this, for the gardens are so large, but it inspires distrust in the inhabitants, and makes it dangerous for Arabs to travel not fully manned and armed.

On reaching the village Kabwabwata a great demonstration was made by Mohamad's Arab dependants and Wanyamwesi: the women had their faces all smeared with pipeclay, and lullilooed with all their might. When we came among the huts, they cast handfuls of soil on their heads, while the men fired off their guns as fast as they could load them. Those connected with Mohamad ran and kissed his hands, and fired, till the sound of shouting, lullilooing, clapping of hands, and shooting was deafening: Mohamad was quite overcome by this demonstration, and it was long before he could still them.

On the way to this village from the south we observed an extensive breadth of land, under ground-nuts which are made into oil: a large jar of this is sold for a hoe. The ground-nuts were now in flower, and green maize ready to be eaten. People all busy planting, transplanting, or weeding; they plant cassava on mounds prepared for it, on which they have sown beans, sorghum, maize, pumpkins: these ripen, and leave the cassava a free soil. The sorghum or dura is sown thickly, and when about a foot high—if the owner has been able to prepare the soil elsewhere—it is transplanted, a portion of the leaves being cut off to prevent too great evaporation and the death of the plant.

17th January, 1868.—The Wanyamwesi and people of Garaganza say that we have thirteen days' march from this to the

Tanganyika Lake. It is often muddy, and many rivulets are to be crossed.

Mohamad is naturally anxious to stay a little while with his son, for it is a wet season, and the mud is disagreeable to travel over: it is said to be worse near Ujiji: he cooks small delicacies for me with the little he has, and tries to make me comfortable. Vinegar is made from bananas, and oil from ground-nuts. I am anxious to be off, but chiefly to get news.

I find that many Unyamwesi people are waiting here, on account of the great quantity of rainwater in front: it would be difficult, they say, to get canoes on Tanganyika, as the waves are now large.

24th January, 1868.—Two of Mohamad Bogharib's people came from Casembe's to trade here, and a body of Syde bin Habib's people also from Garaganza, near Kazé, they report the flooded lands on this side of Lake Tanganyika as waist and chest deep. Bin Habib, being at Katanga, will not stir till the rains are over, and I fear we are storm-stayed till then too. The feeders of the Marungu are not fordable just now, and no canoes are to be had.

26th and 27th January, 1868.—I am ill with fever, as I always am when stationary.

28th January, 1868.—Better, and thankful to Him of the Greatest Name. We must remain; it is a dry spot, and favourable for ground-nuts. *Hooping-cough* here.

30th January, 1868.—The earth cooled by the rain last night sets all to transplanting dura or sorghum; they cut the leaves till only about eighteen inches of them are left, but it grows all the better for the change of place.

Mohamad believes that Tanganyika flows through Rusizi to Lohindé. (Chuambo.)

Seyd Seyd is said to have been the first Arab Sultan who traded, and Seyed Majid follows the example of his father, and has many Arab traders in his employment. He lately sent eight buffaloes to Mtéza, king of Uganda, son of Sunna, by way of increasing his trade, but if is not likely that he will give up the lucrative trade in ivory and slaves.

Susi bought a hoe with a little gunpowder, then a cylinder of dura, three feet long by two feet in diameter, for the hoe: it is at least one hundredweight.

Stone underground houses are reported in Rua, but whether natural or artificial Mohamad could not say. If a present is made to the Rua chiefs they never obstruct passengers.

Chikosi, at whose village we passed a night, near Kalongosi, and Chiputa are both dead.

The Mofwé fills during the greater rains, and spreads over a large district; elephants then wander in its marshes, and are killed easily by people in canoes: this happens every year, and Mohamad Bogharib waits now for this ivory.

7th to 21st February, 1868.—On inquiring of men who have seen the underground houses in Rua, I find that they are very extensive, ranging along mountain sides for twenty miles, and in one part a rivulet flows inside. In some cases the doorways are level with the country adjacent: in others, ladders are used to climb up to them; inside they are said to be very large, and not the work of men, but of God. The people have plenty of fowls, and they too obtain shelter in these Troglodyte habitations.

23rd February, 1868.—I was visited by an important chief called Chapé, who said that he wanted to make friends with the English. He, Chisapi, Sama, Muabo, Karembwé, are of one tribe or family, the Oanza: he did not beg anything, and promised to send me a goat.

FOOTNOTES:

59. Kirwa and its various corruptions, such as Shirwa, Chirua, and Kiroa, perpetually recur in Africa, and would almost seem to stand for "the island."—ED.

* * * * *

CHAPTER XI.

Riot in the camp. Mohamad's account of his long imprisonment. Superstitions about children's teeth. Concerning dreams. News of Lake Chowambé. Life of the Arab slavers. The Katanga gold supply. Muabo. Ascent of the Rua Mountains. Syde bin Habib. Birthday 19th March, 1868. Hostility of Mpwéto. Contemplates visiting Lake Bemba. Nile sources. Men desert. The shores of Moero. Visits Fungafunga. Beturn to Casembe's. Obstructiveness of "Cropped-ears." Accounts of Pereira and Dr. Lacerda. Major Monteiro. The line of Casembe's. Casembe explains the connection of the Lakes and the Luapula. Queen Moäri. Arab sacrifice. Kapika gets rid of his wife.

24th February, 1868.—Some slaves who came with Mohamad Bogharib's agent, abused my men this morning, as bringing unclean meat into the village to sell, though it had been killed by a man of the Wanyamwesi. They called out, "Kaffir, Kaffir!" and Susi, roused by this, launched forth with a stick; the others joined in the row, and the offenders were beat off, but they went and collected all their number and renewed the assault. One threw a heavy block of wood and struck Simon on the head, making him quite insensible and convulsed for some time. He has three wounds on the head, which may prove serious. This is the first outburst of Mohamadan bigotry we have met, and by those who know so little of the creed that it is questionable if one of them can repeat the formula: "La illaha illa lahu Mohamad Rasulela salla lahu, a leihi oa Salama." Simon recovered, but Gallahs are in general not strong.

25th February, 1868.—Mohamad called on me this morning to apologise for the outrage of yesterday, but no one was to blame except the slaves, and I wanted no punishment inflicted if they were cautioned for the future. It seems, plain that if they do not wish to buy the unclean meat they can let it alone,—no harm is done. The Wanyamwesi kill for all, and some Mohamadans say that they won't eat of it, but their wives and people do eat it privately.

I asked Mohamad to-day if it were true that he was a prisoner at Casembe's. He replied, "Quite so." Some Garaganza people, now at Katanga, fought with Casembe, and Mohamad was suspected of being connected with them. Casembe attacked his people, and during the turmoil a hundred frasilahs of copper were stolen from him, and many of his people killed. Casembe kept him a prisoner till sixty of his people were either killed or died, among these Mohamad's eldest son: he was thus reduced to poverty. He gave something to Casembe to allow him to depart, and I suspect that my Sultan's letter had considerable influence in inducing Casembe to accede to his request, for he repeated again and again in my hearing that he must pay respect to my letter, and see me safe at least as far as Ujiji. Mohamad says that he will not return to Casembe again, but will begin to trade with some other chief: it is rather hard for a man at his age to begin *de novo*. He is respected among the Arabs, who pronounce him to be a good man. He says that he has been twenty-two years in Africa, and never saw an outburst like that of yesterday among the Wanyamwesi: it is, however, common for the people at Ujiji to drink palm toddy, and then have a general row in the bazaar, but no bad feeling exists next day.

If a child cuts the upper front teeth before the lower, it is killed, as unlucky: this is a widely-spread superstition. When I was amongst the Makololo in 1859 one of Sekelétu's wives would not allow her servant's child to be killed for this, but few would have the courage to act in opposition to public feeling as she did. In Casembe's country if a child is seen to turn from one side to the other in sleep it is killed. They say of any child who has what they consider these defects "he is an Arab child," because the Arabs have none of this class of superstitions, and should any Arab be near they give the child to him: it would bring ill-luck, misfortunes, "milando," or guilt, to the family. These superstitions may account for the readiness with which one tribe parted with their children to Speke's followers. Mohamad says that these children must have been taken in war, as none sell their own offspring.

If Casembe dreams of any man twice or three times he puts the man to death, as one who is practising secret arts against his life: if any one is pounding or cooking food for him he must preserve the strictest silence; these and other things show extreme superstition and degradation.

During, his enforced detention Mohamad's friends advised him to leave Casembe by force, offering to aid him with their men, but he always refused. His father was the first to open this country to trade with the Arabs, and all his expenses while so doing were borne by himself; but Mohamad seems to be a man of peace, and unwilling to break the appearance of friendship with the chiefs. He thinks that this Casembe poisoned his predecessor: he certainly killed his wife's mother, a queen, that she might be no obstacle to him in securing her daughter.

We are waiting in company with a number of Wanyamwesi for the cessation of the rains, which have flooded the country between this and Tanganyika. If there were much slope this water would flow off: this makes me suspect that Tanganyika is not so low as Speke's measurement. The Arabs are positive that water flows from that Lake to the Victoria Nyanza, and assert that Dagara, the father of Rumanyika, was anxious to send canoes from his place to Ujiji, or, as some say, to dig a canal to Ujiji. The Wanyamwesi here support themselves by shooting buffaloes, at a place two days distant, and selling the meat for grain and cassava: no sooner is it known that an animal is killed, than the village women crowd in here, carrying their produce to exchange it for meat, which they prefer to beads or anything else. Their farinaceous food creates a great craving for flesh: were my shoes not done I would go in for buffaloes too.

A man from the upper part of Tanganyika gives the same account of the river from Rusisi that Burton and Speke received when they went to its mouth. He says that the water of the Lake goes up some distance, but is met by Rusisi water, and driven back thereby. The Lake water, he adds, finds an exit northwards and eastwards by several small rivers which would admit small canoes only. They pour into Lake Chowambé—probably that discovered by Mr. Baker. This Chowambé is in Hundi, the country of cannibals, but the most enlightened informants leave the impression on the mind of groping in the dark: it may be all different when we come to see it.

The fruit of the palm, which yields palm-oil, is first of all boiled, then pounded in a mortar, then put into hot or boiling water, and the oil skimmed off. The palm-oil is said to be very abundant at Ujiji, as much as 300 gallons being often brought into the bazaar for sale in one morning; the people buy it eagerly for cooking purposes. Mohamad says that the Island of Pemba, near Zanzibar, contains many of these palms, but the people are ignorant of the mode of separating the oil from the nut: they call the palm Nkoma at Casembe's, and Chikichi at Zanzibar.[60]

No better authority for what has been done or left undone by Mohamadans in this country can be found than Mohamad bin Saleh, for he is very intelligent, and takes an interest in all that happens, and his father was equally interested in this country's affairs. He declares that no attempt was ever made by Mohamadans to proselytize the Africans: they teach their own children to read the Koran, but them only; it is never translated, and to servants who go to the Mosque it is all dumb show. Some servants imbibe Mohamadan bigotry about eating, but they offer no prayers. Circumcision, to make *halel*, or fit to slaughter the animals for their master, is the utmost advance any have made. As the Arabs in East Africa never feel themselves called on to propagate the doctrines of Islam, among the heathen Africans, the statement of Captain Burton that they would make better missionaries to the Africans than Christians, because they would not insist on the abandonment of polygamy, possesses the same force as if he had said Mohamadans would catch more birds than Christians, because they would put salt on their tails. The indispensable requisite or qualification for any kind of missionary is that he have some wish to proselytize: this the Arabs do not possess in the slightest degree.

As they never translate the Koran, they neglect the best means of influencing the Africans, who invariably wish to understand what they are about. When we were teaching adults the alphabet, they felt it a hard task. "Give me medicine, I shall drink it to make me understand it," was their earnest entreaty. When they have advanced so far as to form clear conceptions of Old Testament and Gospel histories, they tell them to their neighbours; and, on visiting distant tribes, feel proud to show how much they know: in this way the knowledge of Christianity becomes widely diffused. Those whose hatred to its self-denying doctrines has become developed by knowledge, propagate slanders; but still they speak of Christianity, and awaken attention. The plan, therefore, of the Christian missionary in imparting knowledge is immeasurably superior to that of the Moslem in dealing with dumb show. I have, however, been astonished to see that none of the Africans imitate the Arab prayers: considering their great reverence of the Deity, it is a wonder that they do not learn to address prayers to Him except on very extraordinary occasions.

My remarks referring to the education by Mohamadans do not refer to the Suahelis, for they teach their children to read, and even send them to school. They are the descendants of Arab and African women and inhabit the coast line. Although they read, they understand very little Arabic beyond the few words which have been incorporated into Suaheli. The establishment of Moslem missions among the heathen is utterly unknown, and this is remarkable, because the Wanyamwesi, for instance, are very friendly with the Arabs—are great traders, too, like them, and are constantly employed as porters and native traders, being considered very trustworthy. They even acknowledge Seyed Majid's authority. The Arabs speak of all the Africans as *"Gumu"* that is hard or callous to the Mohamadan religion.

Some believe that Kilimanjaro Mountain has mummies, as in Egypt, and that Moses visited it of old.

Mungo Park mentions that he found the Africans in the far interior of the west in possession of the stories of Joseph and his brethren, and others. They probably got them from the Koran, as verbally explained by some liberal Mullah, and showed how naturally they spread any new ideas they obtained: they were astonished to find that Park knew the stories.

The people at Katanga are afraid to dig for the gold in their country because they believe that it has been hidden where it is by "Ngolu," who is the owner of it. The Arabs translate Ngolu by Satan: it means Mézimo, or departed spirits, too. The people are all oppressed by their superstitions; the fear of death is remarkably strong. The Wagtails are never molested, because, if they were killed, death would visit the village; this too is the case with the small Whydah birds, the fear of death in the minds of the people saves them from molestation. But why should we be so prone to criticise? A remnant of our own superstitions is seen in the prejudice against sitting down thirteen to dinner, spilling the salt, and not throwing a little of it over the left shoulder. Ferdinand I., the King of Naples, in passing through the streets, perpetually put one hand into his pockets to cross the thumb over the finger in order to avert the influence of the evil eye!

On the 6th, Muabo, the great chief of these parts, came to call on Mohamad: several men got up and made some antics before him, then knelt down and did obeisance, then Muabo himself jumped about a little, and all applauded. He is a good-natured-looking man, fond of a joke, and always ready with a good-humoured smile: he was praised very highly, Mpwéto was nothing to Muabo mokolu, the great Muabo; and he returned the praise by lauding Tipo Tipo and Mpamari, Mohamad's native name, which means, "Give me wealth, or goods." Mohamad made a few of the ungainly antics like the natives, and all were highly pleased, and went off rejoicing.

Some Arabs believe that a serpent on one of the islands in the Nyanza Lake has the power of speaking, and is the same that beguiled Eve. It is a crime at Ujiji to kill a serpent, even though it enters a house and kills a kid! The native name, for the people of Ujiji is Wayeiyé, the very same as the people on the Zouga, near Lake Ngami. They are probably an offshoot from Ujiji.[61]

There are underground stone houses in Kabiuré, in the range called Kakoma, which is near to our place of detention. *15th March, 1868.*—The roots of the Nyumbo or Noombo open in four or five months from the time of planting, those planted by me on the 6th February have now stalks fifteen inches long. The root is reported to be a very wholesome food, never disagreeing with the stomach; and the raw root is an excellent remedy in obstinate vomiting and nausea; four or five tubers are often given by one root, in Marungu they attain a size of six inches in length by two in diameter.

16th March, 1868.—We started for Mpwéto's village, which is situated on the Lualaba, and in our course crossed the Lokinda, which had a hundred yards of flood water on each side of it. The river itself is forty yards wide, with a rude bridge over it, as it flows fast away into Moero.

Next day we ascended the Rua Mountains, and reached the village of Mpwéto, situated in a valley between two ridges, about one mile from the right bank of the Lualaba, where it comes through the mountains. It then flows about two miles along the base of a mountain lying east and west before it begins to make northing: its course is reported to be very winding, this seems additional evidence that Tanganyika is not in a depression of only 1844 feet above the sea, otherwise the water of Lualaba would flow faster and make a straighter channel. It is said to flow into the Lufira, and that into Tanganyika.

18th March, 1868.—On reaching Mpwéto's yesterday we were taken up to the house of Syde bin Habib, which is built on a ridge overhanging the chiefs village, a square building of wattle and plaster, and a mud roof to prevent it being fired by an enemy. It is a very pretty spot among the mountains. Sariama is Bin Habib's agent, and he gave us a basket of flour and leg of kid. I sent a message to Mpwéto, which he politely answered by saying that he had no food ready in his village, but if we waited two days he would have some prepared, and would then see us. He knew what we should give him, and he need not tell us I met a man from Seskéké, left sick at Kirwa by Bin Habib and now with him here.

A very beautiful young woman came to look at us, perfect in every way, and nearly naked, but unconscious of indecency; a very Venus in black. The light-grey, red-tailed parrot seen on the West Coast is common in Rua, and tamed by the natives.[62]

19th March, 1868.[63]—(Grant, Lord, grace to love Thee more and serve Thee better.)

The favourite son of Mpwéto called on us; his father is said to do nothing without consulting him; but he did not seem to be endowed with much wisdom.

20th and 21st March, 1868.—Our interview was put off; and then a sight of the cloth we were to give was required. I sent a good large cloth, and explained that we were nearly out of goods now, having been travelling two years, and were going to Ujiji to get more. Mpwéto had prepared a quantity of pombe, a basket of meal, and a goat; and when he looked at them and the cloth, he seemed to feel that it would be a poor bargain, so he sent to say that we had gone to Casembe and given him many cloths, and then to Muabo, and if I did not give another cloth he would not see me. "He had never slept with only one cloth." "I had put medicine on this one to kill him, and must go away."

It seems he was offended because we went to his great rival, Muabo, before visiting him. He would not see Syde bin Habib for eight days; and during that time was using charms to try if it would be safe to see him at all: on the ninth day he peeped past a door for some time to see if Bin Habib were a proper person, and then came out: he is always very suspicious.

At last he sent an order to us to go away, and if we did not move, he would come with all his people and drive us off. Sariamo said if he were not afraid for Syde bin Habib's goods, he would make a stand against Mpwéto; but I had no wish to stay or to quarrel with a worthless chief, and resolved to go next day. (*24th March.*) He abused a native trader with his tongue for coming to trade, and sent him away too. We slept again at our half-way village, Kapemba, just as a party of salt-traders from Rua came into it: they were tall, well-made men, and rather dark.

25th March, 1868.—Reached Kabwabwata at noon, and were welcomed by Mohamad and all the people. His son, Sheikh But, accompanied us; but Mohamad told us previously that it was likely Mpwéto would refuse to see us.

The water is reported to be so deep in front that it is impossible to go north: the Wanyamwesi, who are detained here as well as we, say it is often more than a man's depth, and there are no canoes. They would not stop here if a passage home could be made. I am thinking of going to Lake Bemba, because at least two months must be passed here still before a passage can be made; but my goods are getting done, and I cannot give presents to the chiefs on our way.

This Lake has a sandy, not muddy bottom, as we were at first informed, and there are four islands in it, one, the Bangweolo, is very large, and many people live on it; they have goats and sheep in abundance: the owners of canoes demand three hoes for the hire of one capable of carrying eight or ten persons; beyond this island it is sea horizon only. The tsébula and nzoé antelopes abound. The people desire salt and not beads for sale.

2nd April, 1868.—If I am not deceived by the information I have received from various reliable sources, the springs of the Nile rise between 9° and 10° south latitude, or at least 400 or 500 miles south of the south end of Speke's Lake, which he considered to be the sources of the Nile. Tanganyika is declared to send its water through north into Lake Chowambé or Baker's Lake; if this does not prove false, then Tanganyika is an expansion of the Nile, and so is Lake Chowambé; the two Lakes being connected by the River Loanda. Unfortunately the people on the east side of the Loanda are constantly at war with the people on the west of it, or those of Rusisi. The Arabs have been talking of opening up a path through to Chowambé, where much ivory is reported; I hope that the Most High may give me a way there.

11th April, 1868.—I had a long oration from Mohamad yesterday against going off for Bemba to-morrow. His great argument is the extortionate way of Casembe, who would demand cloth, and say that in pretending to go to Ujiji I had told him lies: he adds to this argument that this is the last month of the rains; the Masika has begun, and our way north will soon be open. The fact of the matter is that Mohamad, by not telling me of the superabundance of water in the country of the Marungu, which occurs every year, caused me to lose five months. He knew that we should be detained here, but he was so eager to get out of his state of durance with Casembe that he hastened my departure by asserting that we should be at Ujiji in one month. I regret this deception, but it is not to be wondered at, and in a Mohamadan and in a Christian too it is thought clever. Were my goods not nearly done I would go, and risk the displeasure of Casembe for the chance of discovering the Lake Bemba. I thought once of buying from Mohamad Bogharib, but am afraid that his stock may be getting low too: I fear that I must give up this Lake for the present.

12th April, 1868.—I think of starting to-morrow for Bangweolo, even if Casembe refuses a passage beyond him: we shall be better there than we are here, for everything at Kabwabwata is scarce and dear. There we can get a fowl for one string of beads, here it costs six: there fish may be bought, here none. Three of Casembe's principal men are here, Kakwata, Charley, and Kapitenga; they are anxious to go home, and would be a gain to me, but Mohamad detains them, and when I ask his reason he says "Muabo refuses," but they point to Mohamad's house and say, "It is he who refuses."

[A very serious desertion took place at this time amongst Dr. Livingstone's followers. Not to judge them too harshly they had become to a great extent demoralised by camp life with Mohamad and his horde of slaves and slavers. The Arab tried all he could to dissuade the traveller from proceeding south instead of homewards through Ujiji, and the men seem to have found their own breaking-point where this disappointment occurred.]

13th April, 1868.—On preparing to start this morning my people refused to go: the fact is, they are all tired, and Mohamad's opposition encourages them. Mohamad, who was evidently eager to make capital out of their refusal, asked me to remain over to-day, and then demanded what I was going to do with those who had absconded. I said, "Nothing: if a magistrate were on the spot, I would give them over to him." "Oh," said he, "I am magistrate, shall I apprehend them?" To this I assented. He repeated this question till it was tiresome: I saw his reason long afterwards, when he asserted that I "came to him and asked him to bind them, but he had refused:" he wanted to appear to the people as much better than I am.

14th April, 1868.—I start off with five attendants, leaving most of the luggage with Mohamad, and reach the Luao to spend the night. Headman Ndowa.

15th April, 1868.—Amoda ran away early this morning. "Wishes to stop with his brothers." They think that, by refusing to go to Bemba, they will force me to remain with them, and then go to Ujiji: one of them has infused the idea into their minds that I will not pay them, and exclaims "Look at the sepoys!"—not knowing that they are paid by the Indian Government; and as for the Johanna men, they were prepaid *29l. 4s.* in cash, besides clothing. I sent Amoda's bundle back to Mohamad: my messenger got to Kabwabwata before Amoda did, and he presented himself to my Arab friend, who, of course, scolded him: he replied that he was tired of carrying, and no other fault had he; I may add that I found out that Amoda wished to come south to me with one of Mohamad Bogharib's men, but "Mpamari" told him not to return. Now that I was fairly started, I told my messenger to say to Mohamad that I would on no account go to Ujiji, till I had done all in my power to reach the Lake I sought: I would even prefer waiting at Luao or Moero, till people came to me from Ujiji to supplant the runaways. I did not blame them very severely in my own mind for absconding: they were tired of tramping, and so verily am I, but Mohamad, in encouraging them to escape to him, and talking with a double tongue, cannot be exonerated from blame. Little else can be expected from him, he has lived some thirty-five years in the country, twenty-five being at Casembe's, and there he had often to live by his wits. Consciousness of my own defects makes me lenient.

16th April, 1868.—Ndowa gives Mita or Mpamañkanana as the names of the excavations in Muabo's hills, he says that they are sufficient to conceal all the people of this district in case of war: I conjecture that this implies room for ten thousand people: provisions are stored in them, and a perennial rivulet runs along a whole street of them. On one occasion, when the main entrance was besieged by an enemy, someone who knew all the intricacies of the excavations led a party out by a secret passage, and they, coming over the invaders, drove them off with heavy loss. Their formation is universally ascribed to the Deity. This may mean that the present inhabitants have succeeded the original burrowing race, which dug out many caves adjacent to Mount Hor—the *Jebel Nébi Harin*, Mount of the Prophet Aaron, of the Arabs—and many others; and even the Bushman caves, a thousand miles south of this region.

A very minute, sharp-biting mosquito is found here: the women try to drive them out of their huts by whisking bundles of green leaves all round the walls before turning into them.

17th August, 1868.—Crossed the Luao by a bridge, thirty yards long, and more than half a mile of flood on each side; passed many villages, standing on little heights, which overlook plains filled with water. Some three miles of grassy plains abreast of Moero were the deepest parts, except the banks of Luao. We had four hours of wading, the bottom being generally black tenacious mud. Ruts had been formed in the paths by the feet of passengers: these were filled with soft mud, and, as they could not be seen, the foot was often placed on the edge, and when the weight came on it, down it slumped into the mud, half-way up the calves; it was difficult to draw it out, and very fatiguing. To avoid these ruts we encroached on the grass at the sides of the paths, but often stepping on the unseen edge of a rut, we floundered in with both feet to keep the balance, and this was usually followed by a rush of bubbles to the surface, which, bursting, discharged foul air of frightful faecal odour. In parts, the black mud and foul water were cold, in others hot, according as circulation went on or not. When we came near Moero, the water became half-chest and whole-chest deep; all perishable articles had to be put on the head. We found a party of fishermen on the sands, and I got a hut, a bath in the clear but tepid waters, and a delicious change of dress. Water of Lake, 83° at 3 P.M.

18th April, 1868.—We marched along the north end of Moero, which has a south-east direction. The soft yielding sand which is flanked by a broad belt of tangled tropical vegetation and trees, added to the fatigues of yesterday, so finding a deserted fisherman's village near the eastern hills, we gladly made it our quarters for Sunday (19th). I made no mark, but the Lake is at least twenty feet higher now than it was on our first visits, and there are banks showing higher rises even than this.

Large fish-baskets made of split reeds are used in trios for catching small fish; one man at each basket drives fish ashore.

20th April, 1868.—Went on to Katétté River, and then to a strong torrent; slept at a village on the north bank of the River Vuna, where, near the hills, is a hot fountain, sometimes used to cook cassava and maize.

21st April, 1868.—Crossed the Vuna and went on to Kalembwé's village, meeting the chief at the gate, who guided us to a hut, and manifested great curiosity to see all our things; he asked if we could not stop next day and drink beer, which would then be ready. Leopards abound here. The Lake now seems broader than ever.

I could not conceive that a hole in the cartilage of the nose could be turned to any account except to hold an ornament, though that is usually only a bit of grass, but a man sewing the feathers on his arrows used his nose-hole for holding a needle! In coming on to Kangalola we found the country swimming: I got separated from the company, though I saw them disappear in the long grass not a hundred yards off and shouted, but the splashing of their feet prevented any one hearing. I could not find a path going south, so I took one to the east to a village; the grass was so long and tangled, I could scarcely get along, at last I engaged a man to show me the main path south, and he took me to a neat village of a woman— Nyinakasangaand would go no further, "Mother Kasanga," as the name means, had been very handsome, and had a beautiful daughter, probably another edition of herself, she advised my waiting in the deep shade of the Ficus indica, in which her houses were placed. I fired a gun, and when my attendants came gave her a string of beads, which made her express distress at my "leaving without drinking anything of hers." People have abandoned several villages on account of the abundance of ferocious wild beasts.

23rd April, 1868.—Through very thick tangled Nyassi grass to Chikosi's burned village; Nsama had killed him. We spent the night in a garden hut, which the fire of the village had spared. Turnips were growing in the ruins. The Nyassi, or long coarse grass, hangs over the paths, and in pushing it aside the sharp seeds penetrate the clothes and are very annoying. The grass itself rubs on the face and eyes disagreeably: when it is burned off and greensward covers the soil it is much more pleasant walking.

24th *April, 1868.*—We leave Chikosi's ruins and make for the ford of the Kalungosi. Marigolds are in full bloom all over the forest, and so are foxgloves. The river is here fully 100 yards broad with 300 yards of flood on its western bank; so deep we had to remain in the canoes till within 50 yards of the higher ground. The people here chew the pith of the papyrus, which is three inches in diameter and as white as snow: it has very little sweetness or anything else in it. The headman of the village to which we went was out cutting wood for a garden, and his wife refused us a hut, but when Kansabala came in the evening he scolded his own spouse roundly and all the wives of the village, and then pressed me to come indoors, but I was well enough in my mosquito curtain without, and declined: I was free from insects and vermin, and few huts are so.

25th April, 1868.—Off early west, and then on to an elevated forest land, in which our course was S.S.W. to the great bend of the rivulet Kifurwa, which enters Moero near to the mouth of the Kalungosi.

26th April, 1868.—Here we spent Sunday in our former woodcutters' huts. Yesterday we were met by a party of the same occupation, laden with bark-cloth, which they had just been stripping off the trees. Their leader would not come along the path because I was sitting near it: I invited him to do so, but it would have been disrespectful to let his shadow fall on any part of my person, so he went a little out of the way: this politeness is common.

27th April, 1868.—But a short march to Fungafunga's village: we could have gone on to the Muatizé, but no village exists there, and here we could buy food. Fungafunga's wife gave a handsome supper to the stranger: on afterwards acknowledging it to her husband he said, "That is your village; always go that way and eat my provisions." He is a Monyamwezi trading in the country for copper, hoes, and slaves. Parrots are here in numbers stealing Holcus sorghum in spite of the shouts of the women.

We cross Muatizé by a bridge of one large tree, getting a good view of Moero from a hill near Kabukwa, and sleep at Chirongo River.

29th April, 1868.—At the Mandapala River. Some men here from the Chungu, one of whom claimed to be a relative of Casembe, made a great outcry against our coming a second time to Casembe without waiting at the Kalungosi for permission. One of them, with his ears cropped short off, asked me when I was departing north if I should come again. I replied, "Yes, I think I shall." They excited themselves by calling over the same thing again and again. "The English come the second time!" "The second time—the second time—the country spoiled! Why not wait at the Kalungosi? Let him return thither." "Come from Mpamari too, and from the Bagaraganza or Banyamwezi!!" "The second time—the second time!" Then all the adjacent villagers were called in to settle this serious affair. I look up to that higher Power to influence their minds as He has often done before. I persuaded them to refer the matter to Casembe himself by sending a man with one of mine up to the town. They would not consent to go on to the Chungu, as the old cropped-eared man would have been obliged to come back the distance again, he having been on the way to the Kalungosi as a sentinel of the ford. Casembe is reasonable and fair, but his people are neither, and will do anything to mulct either strangers or their own countrymen.

30th April, 1868.—The cold of winter has begun, and dew is deposited in great quantities, but all the streams are very high in flood, though the rains have ceased here some time.

1st May, 1868.—At the Mandapala River. I sent a request to Mohamad Bogharib to intercede with Casembe for me for a man to show the way to Chikumbi, who is near to Bangweolo. I fear that I have become mixed up in the Lunda mind with Mpamari

(Mohamad bin Saleh), from having gone off with him and returning ere we reached Ujiji, whither ostensibly we were bound. I may be suspected of being in his confidence, and of forwarding his plans by coming back. A deaf and dumb man appears among the people here, making signs exactly as I have seen such do in England, and occasionally emitting a low unmodulated guttural drawl like them.

3rd May, 1868.—Abraham, my messenger, came back, while we were at afternoon prayers, with good news for us, but what made Cropped-ears quite chopfallen was that Casembe was quite gracious! He did not wish me to go away, and now I am welcome back; and as soon as we hear of peace at Chikumbi's we shall have a man to conduct us thither. The Mazitu were reported to have made an inroad into Chikumbi's country; and it was said that chief had fled, and Casembe had sent messengers to hear the truth. Thanks to the Most High for His kindness and influence.

4th May, 1868.—We leave the Mandapala. Cropped-ears, whose name I never heard, collapsed at once on hearing the message of Casembe: before that I never heard such a babbler, to every one passing, man or woman, he repeated the same insinuations about the English, and "Mpamari," and the Banyamwezi,—conspiracy—guilt—return a second time,—till, like a meddling lawyer, he thought that he had really got an important case in hand!

The River Chungu we found to be from fifteen to eighteen yards broad and breast deep, with at least one hundred yards of flood, before we reached the main stream, the Mandapala. The Chungu and the Lundi join in the country called Kimbafuma, about twelve miles from our crossing-place of Mandapala, and about west of it. The Lundi was now breast deep too, and twelve yards broad.

On reaching Casembe's, on the Mofwé, we found Mohamad Bogharib digging and fencing up a well to prevent his slaves being taken away by the crocodiles, as three had been eaten already. A dog bit the leg of one of my goats so badly that I was obliged to kill it: they are nasty curs here, without courage, and yet they sometimes bite people badly. I met some old friends, and Mohamad Bogharib cooked a supper, and from this time forward never omitted sharing his victuals with me.

6th May, 1868.—Manoel Caetano Pereira visited Casembe in 1796, or seventy-two years ago: his native name was Moendo-mondo, or the world's leg—"world-wide traveller!" He came to

Mandapala, for there the Casembe of the time resided, and he had a priest or "Kasisé" with him, and many people with guns. Pérémbé, the oldest man now in Lunda, had children even then: if Pérémbé were thirty years of age at that period he would now be 102 years old, and he seems quite that, for when Dr. Lacerda came he had forty children. He says that Pereira fired off all his guns on his arrival, and Casembe asking him what he meant by that, he replied, "These guns ask for slaves and ivory," both of which were liberally given.

I could not induce Pérémbé to tell anything of times previous to his own. Moendo-mondo, the world's leg (Pereira), told Dr. Lacerda that the natives called him "The Terror!"—a bit of vanity, for they have no such word or abstract term in their language.

When Major Monteiro was here the town of Casembe was on the same spot as now, but the Mosumba, or enclosure of the chief, was about 500 yards S.E. of the present one. Monteiro went nowhere and did nothing, but some of his attendants went over to the Luapula, some six miles distant. He complains in his book of having been robbed by the Casembe of the time. On asking the present occupant of the office why Monteiro's goods were taken from him, he replied, that he was then living at another village and did not know of the affair. Mohamad bin Saleh was present, and he says that Monteiro's statement is false: no goods were forced from him; but it was a year of scarcity, and Monteiro had to spend his goods in buying food instead of slaves and ivory, and made up the tale of Casembe plundering him to appease his creditors.

A number of men were sent with Monteiro as an honorary escort. Kapika, an old man now living, was the chief or one of the chiefs of this party, and he says that he went to Tette, Senna, and Quillimane with Monteiro: this honorary escort seems confirmatory of Mohamad's explanation, for had Casembe robbed the Major none would have been granted or received.

It is warmer here than we found it in the way; clouds cover the sky and prevent radiation. The sorghum is now in full ear. People make very neat mats of the leaves of the Shuaré palm. I got lunars this time.

9th May, 1868.—Eight or ten men went past us this morning, sent by the chief to catch people whom he intends to send to his paramount chief, Matiamvo, as a tribute of slaves. Pérémbé gives the following list of the Casembes:—

I.   KANYIMBE, came from Lunda, attracted by the fish of Mofwé and Moero, and conquered Pérémbé's forefather, Katéré, who planted the first palm-oil palms here from seeds got in Lunda. It is probable that the intercourse then set afoot led to Kanyimbé's coming and conquest.
II.   KINYANTA.
III.   NGUANDA MILONDA.
IV.   KANYEMBO.
V.   LEKWISA.
VI.   KIRÉKA.
VII.   KAPUMBA.
VIII.   KINYANTA.
IX.   LEKWISA, still alive, but a fugitive at Nsama's.
X.   MUONGA, the present ruler, who drove Lékwisa away.

The Portuguese came to Kiréka, who is said to have been very liberal with presents of ivory, slaves, and cattle. The present man has good sense, and is very fair in his judgments, but stingy towards his own people as well as strangers: nevertheless I have had good reason to be satisfied with his conduct to me. Maiyé, not in the list, and 7, 8, 9, 10 are the children of Kiréka. Muonga is said by the others to be a slave "born out of the house," that is, his mother was not of the royal line; she is an ugly old woman, and greedy. I got rid of her begging by giving her the beads she sought, and requesting her to cook some food for me; she begged no more, afraid that I would press my claim for provisions!

10th May, 1868.—I sent to Casembe for a guide to Luapula, he replied that he had not seen me nor given me any food; I must come to-morrow: but next day he was occupied in killing a man for witchcraft and could not receive us, but said that he would on the 12th. He sent 15 fish (perch) from Mofwé, and a large basket of dried cassava. I have taken lunars several times, measuring both sides of the moon about 190 times, but a silly map-maker may alter the whole for the most idiotic of reasons.

13th May, 1868.—Mohamad Bogharib has been here some seven months, and bought three tusks only; the hunting, by Casembe's people, of elephants in the Mofwé has been unsuccessful.

We did not get an audience from Casembe; the fault lay with Kapika—Monteiro's escort—being afraid to annoy Casembe by putting him in mind of it, but on the 15th Casembe sent for me, and told me that as the people had all fled from Chikumbi's, he would therefore send guides to take us to Kabaia, where there was still a population; he wished me to wait a few days till he had looked out good men as guides, and ground some flour for us to use in the journey. He understood that I wished to go to Bangweolo; and it was all right to do what my own chief had sent me for, and then come back to him. It was only water—the same as Luapula, Mofwé, and Moero; nothing to be seen. His people must not molest me again, but let me go where I liked. This made me thank Him who has the hearts of all in His hand.

Casembe also admitted that he had injured "Mpamari," but he would send him some slaves and ivory in reparation: he is better than his people, who are excessively litigious, and fond of milandos or causes—suits. He asked if I had not the leopard's skin he gave me to sit on, as it was bad to sit on the ground; I told him it had so many holes in it people laughed at it and made me ashamed, but he did not take the hint to give me another. He always talks good sense when he has not swilled beer or pombe: all the Arabs are loud in his praises, but they have a bad opinion of the Queen Moäri or Ngombé or Kifuta. The Garaganza people at Katanga killed a near relative of Casembe and herself, and when the event happened, Fungafunga, one of the Garaganza or Banyamwezi being near the spot, fled and came to the Mofwé: he continued his flight as soon as it was dark without saying anything to anyone, until he got north to Kabiuré. The Queen and Casembe suspected Mpamari of complicity with the Banyamwezi, and believed that Fungafunga had communicated the news to him before fleeing further. A tumult was made; Mpamari's eldest son was killed; and he was plundered of all his copper, ivory, and slaves: the Queen loudly demanded his execution, but Casembe restrained his people as well as he was able and it is for this injury that he now professes to be sorry.

The Queen only acted according to the principles of her people. "Mpamari killed my son, kill his son—himself." It is difficult to get at the truth, for Mohamad or Mpamari never tells the whole truth. He went to fight Nsama with Muonga, and was wounded in the foot and routed, and is now glad to get out of Lunda back to Ujiji. *(16th May.)* Complete twenty sets of lunars.

11th May, 1868.—Mohamad Bogharib told Casembe that he could buy nothing, and therefore was going away, Casembe replied that he had no ivory and he might go: this was sensible; he sent far and near to find some, but failed, and now confesses a truth which most chiefs hide from unwillingness to appear poor before foreigners.

18th and 19th May, 1868.—It is hot here though winter; but cold by night. Casembe has sent for fish for us. News came that one of Syde bin Habib's men had come to Chikumbi on his way to Zanzibar.

20th May, 1868.—A thunder-shower from the east laid the dust and cooled the ground: the last shower of this season, as a similar slight shower was the finish up of the last on the 12th of May. *(21st May.)* This cannot be called a rainy month: April is the last month of the wet season, and November the first.

22nd May, 1868.—Casembe is so slow with his fish, meal, and guides, and his people so afraid to hurry him, that I think of going off as soon as Mohamad Bogharib moves; he is going to Chikumbi's to buy copper, and thence he will proceed to Uvira to exchange that for ivory; but this is at present kept as a secret from his slaves. The way seems thus to be opening for me to go to the large Lake west of Uvira.

I told Casembe that we were going; he said to me that if in coming back I had found no travelling party, I must not risk going by Nsama's road with so few people, but must go to his brother Moenempanda, and he would send men to guide me to him, and thence he would send me safely by his path along Lake Moero: this was all very good.

23rd May, 1868.—The Arabs made a sort of sacrifice of a goat which was cooked all at once; they sent a good dish of it to me. They read the Koran very industriously, and prayed for success or luck in leaving, and seem sincerely religious, according to the light that is in them. The use of incense and sacrifices brings back the old Jewish times to mind.

A number of people went off to the Kanengwa, a rivulet an hour south of this, to build huts; there they are to take leave of Casembe, for the main body goes off to-morrow, after we have seen the new moon. They are very particular in selecting lucky days, and anything unpleasant that may have happened in one month is supposed to be avoided by choosing a different day for beginning an enterprise in the next. Mohamad left Uvira on the third day of a new moon, and several fires happened in his camp; he now considers a third day inauspicious.

Casembe's dura or sorghum is ripe to-day: he has eaten mapemba or dura, and all may thereafter do the same: this is just about the time when it ripens and is reaped at Kolobeng, thus the difference in the seasons is not great.

24th May, 1868.—Detained four days yet. Casembe's chief men refuse to escort Mohamad Bogharib; they know him to be in debt, and fear that he may be angry, but no dunning was intended. Casembe was making every effort to get ivory to liquidate it, and at last got a couple of tusks, which he joyfully gave to Mohamad: he has risen much in the estimation of us all.

26th May, 1868.—Casembe's people killed five buffaloes by chasing them into the mud and water of Mofwé, so he is seeing to the division of the meat, and will take leave to-morrow.

28th May, 1868.—We went to Casembe; he was as gracious as usual. A case of crim. con. was brought forward against an Arab's slave, and an attempt was made to arrange the matter privately by offering three cloths, beads, and another slave, but the complainant refused everything. Casembe dismissed the case by saying to the complainant, "You send your women to entrap the strangers in order to get a fine, but you will get nothing:" this was highly applauded by the Arabs, and the owner of the slave heaped dust on his head, as many had done before for favours received. Casembe, still anxious to get ivory for Mohamad, proposed another delay of four days to send for it; but all are tired, and it is evident that it is not want of will that prevents ivory being produced.

His men returned without any, and he frankly confessed inability: he is evidently very poor.

30th May, 1868.—We went to the Kanengwa rivulet at the south end of Mofwé, which forms a little lagoon there fifty yards broad and thigh deep; but this is not the important feeder of the

Lagoon, which is from two to three miles broad, and nearly four long: that has many large flat sedgy islands in it, and its water is supplied by the Mbérézé from south-east.

31st May, 1868.—Old Kapika sold his young and good-looking wife for unfaithfulness, as he alleged. The sight of a lady in the chain-gang shocked the ladies of Lunda, who ran to her, and having ascertained from her own mouth what was sufficiently apparent, that she was a slave now, clapped their hands on their mouths in the way that they express wonder, surprise, and horror: the hand is placed so that the fingers are on one cheek and the thumb on the other.

The case of the chieftainess excited great sympathy among the people; some brought her food, Kapika's daughters brought her pombe and bananas; one man offered to redeem her with two, another with three slaves, but Casembe, who is very strict in punishing infidelity, said, "No, though ten slaves be offered she must go." He is probably afraid of his own beautiful queen should the law be relaxed. Old Kapika came and said to her, "You refused me, and I now refuse you." A young wife of old Pérémbé was also sold as a punishment, but redeemed.

There is a very large proportion of very old and very tall men in this district. The slave-trader is a means of punishing the wives which these old fogies ought never to have had.

Casembe sent me about a hundredweight of the small fish Nsipo, which seems to be the whitebait of our country; it is a little bitter when cooked alone, but with ground-nuts is a tolerable relish: we can buy flour with these at Chikumbi's.

FOOTNOTES:

60. Chikichi nuts have been an article of trade and export for some time from Zanzibar. The oil-palm grows wild in Pemba.

61. A chief named Moené Ungu, who admires the Arabs, sent his children to Zanzibar to be instructed to read and write.

62. This bird is often brought to Zanzibar by the Ivory Caravans.

63. The Doctor's birthday.

* * * * *

CHAPTER XII.

Prepares to examine Lake Bemba. Starts from Casembe's 11th June, 1868. Dead leopard. Moenampanda's reception. The River Luongo. Weird death-song of slaves. The forest grave. Lake Bembo changed to Lake Bangweolo. Chikumbi's. The Imbozhwa people. Kombokombo's stockade. Mazitu difficulties. Discovers Lake Bangweolo on 18th July, 1868. The Lake Chief Mapuni. Description of the Lake. Prepares to navigate it. Embarks for Lifungé Island. Immense size of Lake. Reaches Mpabala Island. Strange dream. Fears of canoe men. Return to shore. March back. Sends letters. Meets Banyamweze. Reviews recent explorations at length. Disturbed state of country.

1st June, 1868.—Mohamad proposes to go to Katanga to buy copper, and invites me to go too. I wish to see the Lufra Kiver, but I must see Bemba or Bangweolo. Grant guidance from above!

2nd June, 1868.—In passing a field of cassava I picked the pods of a plant called Malumbi, which climbs up the cassava bushes; at the root it has a number of tubers with eyes, exactly like the potato. One plant had sixteen of these tubers, each about 2 inches long and 1-1/2 inch in diameter: another tuber was 5 inches long and 2 in diameter, it would be difficult for anyone to distinguish them from English potatoes. When boiled they are a little waxy, and, compared with our potato, hard. There are colours inside, the outer part reddish, the inner whiter. At first none of the party knew them, but afterwards they were recognised as cultivated at Zanzibar by the name "Men," and very good when mashed with fish: if in Zanzibar, they are probably known in other tropical islands,

4th June, 1868.—From what I see of slaving, even in its best phases, I would not be a slave-dealer for the world.

5th June, 1868.—The Queen Moäri passed us this morning, going to build a hut at her plantation; she has a pleasant European countenance, clean light-brown skin, and a merry laugh, and would be admired anywhere. I stood among the cassava to see her pass; she twirled her umbrella as she came near, borne by twelve men, and seemed to take up the laugh which made her and her maids bolt at my reception, showing that she laughs not with her mouth only, but with her eyes and cheeks: she said, "Yambo" (how are you)? To which I replied, "Tambo sana" (very well). One of her attendants said, "Give her something of what you have at hand, or in the pockets." I said, "I have nothing here," and asked her if she would come back near my hut. She replied that she would, and I duly sent for two strings of red beads, which I presented. Being lower than she, I could see that she had a hole through the cartilage, near the point of her slightly aquiline nose; and a space was filed between the two front teeth, so as to leave a triangular hole.

Filed Teeth of Queen Moäri.

After delay had grown vexatious, we march three hours on the 9th, and reach the Katofia River, covered with aquatic trees and running into the Mbérézé: five yards wide and knee deep.

10th June, 1868.—Detained again, for business is not finished with the people of Casembe. The people cannot esteem the slave-trader, who is used as a means of punishing those who have family differences, as those of a wife with her husband, or a servant with his master. The slaves are said to be generally criminals, and are sold in revenge or as punishment. Kapika's wife had an ornament of the end of a shell called the cone; it was borrowed and she came away with it in her hair: the owner, without making any effort to recover it, seized one of Kapika's daughters as a pledge that Kapika would exert himself to get it back!

[At last the tedious delay came to an end and we must now follow the Doctor on his way south to discover Lake Bemba.]

11th June, 1868.—Crossed the Mbérézé, ten yards broad and thigh deep, ascending a range of low hills of hardened sandstone, covered, as the country generally is, with forest. Our course S.E. and S.S.E. Then descended into a densely-wooded valley, having a rivulet four yards wide and knee deep. Buffaloes and elephants very numerous.

12th June, 1868.—We crossed the Mbérézé again twice; then a very deep narrow rivulet, and stopped at another in a mass of trees, where we spend the night, and killing an ox remained next day to eat it. When at Kanengwa a small party of men came past, shouting as if they had done something of importance: on going to them, I found that two of them carried a lion slung to a pole. It was a small maneless variety, called "the lion of *Nyassi*," or long grass. It had killed a man and they killed it. They had its mouth carefully strapped, and the paws tied across its chest, and were taking it to Casembe. *Nyassi* means long grass, such as towers overhead, and is as thick in the stalk as a goose-quill; and is erroneously applied to Nyassa. Other lions—Thambwé, Karamo, Simba, are said to stand 5 feet high, and some higher: this seemed about 3 feet high, but it was too dark to measure it.

13th June, 1868.—The Arabs distinguish the Suaheli, or Arabs of mixed African blood, by the absence of beard and whiskers: these are usually small and stunted in the Suaheli.

Birds, as the Drongo shrike, and a bird very like the grey linnet, with a thick reddish bill, assemble in very large flocks now that it is winter, and continue thus till November, or period of the rains.

A very minute bee goes into the common small holes in wormeaten wood to make a comb and lay its eggs, with a supply of honey. There are seven or eight honey-bees of small size in this country.

A sphex may be seen to make holes in the ground, placing stupified insects in them with her eggs; another species watches when she goes off to get more insects, and every now and then goes in too to lay her eggs, I suppose without any labour: there does not appear to be any enmity between them. We remained a day to buy food for the party, and eat our ox.

14th June, 1868.—March over well-wooded highlands with dolomite rocks cropping out and trees all covered with lichens, the watershed then changed to the south.

15th June, 1868.—Yery cold in mornings now (43°). Found Moenempanda, Casembe's brother, on the Luluputa, a stream twenty yards wide and flowing west. The Moenempanda visited by the Portuguese was grandfather to this one, and not at the same spot; it is useless to put down the names of chiefs as indicating geographical positions, for the name is often continued, but at a spot far distant from the dwelling of the original possessor. A slave tried to break out of his slave-stick, and actually broke half an inch of tough iron with his fingers; the end stuck in the wood, or he would have freed himself.

The chief gave me a public reception, which was like that of Casembe, but better managed. He is young, and very handsome but for a defect in his eyes, which makes him keep them half shut or squinting. He walked off in the jaunty way all chiefs do in this country, to show the weight of rings and beads on the legs, and many imitate this walk who have none, exactly as our fathers imitated the big cravat of George IV., who thereby hid defects in his neck: thousands carried their cravats over the chin who had no defects to hide. Moenempanda carried his back stiffly, and no wonder, he had about ten yards of a train carried behind it. About 600 people were present. They kept rank, but not step; were well armed; marimbas and square drums formed the bands, and one musician added his voice: "I have been to Syde" (the Sultan); "I have been to Meereput" (King of Portugal); "I have been to the sea." At a private reception, where he was divested of his train, and had only one umbrella instead of three, I gave him a cloth. The Arabs thought highly of him; but his graciousness had been expended on them in getting into debt; he now showed no inclination to get out of it, but offered about a twentieth part of the value of the goods in liquidation. He sent me two pots of beer, which I care not to drink except when very thirsty on a march, and promised a man to guide me to Chikumbi, and then refused. Casembe rose in the esteem of all as Moenempanda sank, and his people were made to understand how shabbily he had behaved.

The Lulaputa is said to flow into the Luéna, and that into the Luongo: there must be two Luénas.

22nd June, 1868.—March across a grassy plain southerly to the Luongo, a deep river embowered in a dense forest of trees, all covered with lichens—some flat, others long and thready, like old men's beards, and waving in the wind, just as they do on the mangrove-swamp trees on the coast. The Luongo here is fifty yards broad and three fathoms deep; near its junction with the Luapula it is 100 yards; it rises here to eight fathoms' depth. A bridge of forty yards led us over to an island, and a branch of the river was ten yards beyond: the bridge had been broken, some thought on purpose, but it was soon mended with trees eighteen to twenty yards long. We went a little way beyond, and then halted for a day at a rivulet flowing into the Luongo, 200 yards off.

23rd June, 1868.—We waited for copper here, which was at first refused as payment of debt. I saw now that the Luongo had steep clay banks fifteen feet down, and many meadows, which must be swimming during the rains. The Luéna is said to rise east of this.

[In a private letter Livingstone shows that he had seldom been more affected by the sufferings of slaves than at this time, and it would perhaps be difficult to imagine any scene more calculated to excite misery and distress of mind.

The following incident deals with the firm belief in a future state, which enters so largely into the minds of all Africans, and which for very lack of guidance assumes all the distorted growths of superstition.

He must be of a thankless spirit who does not long to substitute the great vision of future peace afforded by Christianity, in lieu of the ghastly satisfaction which cheered these men, when he sees by the light of this story the capacity that exists for realising a life beyond the grave.]

24th June, 1868.—Six men slaves were singing as if they did not feel the weight and degradation of the slave-sticks. I asked the cause of their mirth, and was told that they rejoiced at the idea "of coming back after death and haunting and killing those who had sold them." Some of the words I had to inquire about; for instance, the meaning of the words "to haunt and kill by spirit power;" then it was, "Oh, you sent me off to Manga (sea-coast), but the yoke is off when I die, and back I shall come to haunt and to kill you." Then all joined in the chorus, which was the name of each vendor. It told not of fun, but of the bitterness and tears of such as were oppressed, and on the side of the oppressors there was a power: there be higher than they!

Pérémbé was one of the culprits thus menaced. The slave-owner asked Kapika's wife if she would return to kill Kapika. The others answered to the names of the different men with laughter. Her heart was evidently sore: for a lady to come so low down is to her grievous. She has lost her jaunty air, and is, with her head shaved, ugly; but she never forgets to address her captors with dignity, and they seem to fear her.

25th June, 1868.—We went over flat forest with patches of brown haematite cropping out; this is the usual iron ore, but I saw in a village pieces of specular iron-ore which had been brought for smelting. The Luongo flowed away somewhat to our right or west, and the villagers had selected their site where only well-water could be found: we went ten minutes towards the Luongo and got abundance.

A Forest Grave.

The gardens had high hedges round to keep off wild beasts. We came to a grave in the forest; it was a little rounded mound as if the occupant sat in it in the usual native way: it was strewed over with flour, and a number of the large blue beads put on it: a little path showed that it had visitors. This is the sort of grave I should prefer: to lie in the still, still forest, and no hand ever disturb my bones. The graves at home always seemed to me to be miserable, especially those in the cold damp clay, and without elbow room; but I have nothing to do but wait till He who is over all decides where I have to lay me down and die. Poor Mary lies on Shupanga brae, "and beeks fornent the sun."[64]

Came to the Chando River, which is the boundary between Casembe and Chikumbi; but Casembe is over all.

27th June, 1868.—We crossed a flooded marsh with the water very cold, and then the Chando itself twelve feet broad and knee deep, then on to another strong brook Nsénga.

28th June, 1868.—After service we went on up hills to a stockade of Banyamwezi, on the Kalomina River, and here we built our sheds; the spot is called Kizinga, and is on the top of a sandstone range covered as usual with forest. The Banyamwezi beat off the Mazitu with their guns, while all the country people fled. The Banyamwezi are decidedly uglier than the Balonda and Baitawa: they eat no fish, though they come from the east side of Tanganyika, where fish are abundant and cheap; but though uglier, they have more of the sense of honour with traders than the aborigines.

29th June, 1868.—Observed the "smokes" to-day, the first of the season:[65] they obscured the whole country.

1st July, 1868.—I went over to Chikumbi, the paramount chief of this district, and gave him a cloth, begging a man to guide me to Bangweolo. He said that I was welcome to his country; all were so: I had better wait two days till he had selected a *good* man as a guide, and he would send some food for me to eat in the journey—he would not say ten days, but only two, and his man would take me to the smaller part of the Lake, and leave others to forward me to the greater or Bangweolo. The smaller part is named Bemba, but that name is confusing, because Bemba is the name of the country in which a portion of the Lake lies. When asking for Lake Bemba, Kasongo's son said to me, "Bemba is not a lake, but a country:" it is therefore better to use the name BANGWEOLO, which is applied to the great mass of the water, though I fear that our English folks will bogle at it, or call it Bungyhollow! Some Arabs say Bambeolo as easier of pronunciation, but Bangweolo is the correct word. Chikumbi's stockade is 1-1/2 hour S.E. of our camp at Kizinga.

2nd July, 1868.—Writing to the Consul at Zanzibar to send supplies of cloth to Ujiji—120 pieces, 40 Kiniki; 80 merikano 34 inches broad, or samsam. Fine red beads—Talaka, 12 frasilas. I ask for soap, coffee, sugar, candles, sardines, French preserved meats, a cheese in tin, Nautical Almanac for 1869 and 1870, shoes (two or four pairs), ruled paper, pencils, sealing-wax, ink, powder, flannel-serge, 12 frasila beads, 6 of Talaka; added 3 F. pale red, 3 W. white.

3rd July, 1868.—The summary of the sources which I have resolved to report as flowing into the central line of drainage formed by the Chambezé, Luapula, and Lualaba are thirteen in all, and each is larger than the Isis at Oxford, or Avon at Hamilton. Five flow into the eastern line of drainage going through Tanganyika, and five more into the western line of drainage or Lufira, twenty-three or more in all. The Lualaba and the Lufira unite in the Lake of the chief Kinkonza.

5th July, 1868.—I borrowed some paper from Mohamad Bogharib to write home by some Arabs going to the coast. I will announce my discovery to Lord Clarendon; but I reserve the parts of the Lualaba and Tanganyika for future confirmation. I have no doubts on the subject, for I receive the reports of natives of intelligence at first hand, and they have no motive for deceiving me. The best maps are formed from the same sort of reports at third or fourth hand. Cold N.E. winds prevail at present.

6th July, 1868.—Divided our salt that each may buy provisions for himself: it is here of more value than beads. Chikumbi sent fine flour, a load for two stout men carried in a large basket slung to a pole, and a fine fat sheep, carried too because it was too fat to walk the distance from his stockade.

7th, 8th, and 9th July, 1868.—After delaying several days to send our guide, Chikumbi said that he feared the country people would say that the Ingleza brought the Mazitu to them, and so blame will be given to him. I set this down as "words of pombe," beery babble; but after returning from Bangweolo, I saw that he must have been preparing to attack a stockade of Banyamwezi in our path, and had he given us a guide, that man would have been in danger in coming back: he therefore preferred the safety of his man to keeping his promise to me. I got a Banyamwezi guide, and left on the *10th July, 1868*, going over gently rising sandstone hills, covered with forest and seeing many deserted villages, the effects of the Mazitu foray: we saw also the Mazitu sleeping-places and paths. They neglect the common paths of the country as going from one village to another, and take straight courses in the direction they wish to go, treading down the grass so as to make a well-marked route, The Banyamwezi expelled them, cutting off so many of them with their guns and arrows that the marauders retired. The effect of this success on the minds of the Imboshwa, or Imbozhwas, as Chikumbi's people are called, was not gratitude, but envy at the new power sprung up among them of those who came originally as traders in copper.

Kombokombo's stockade, the village to which we went this day, was the first object of assault, and when we returned, he told us that Chikumbi had assaulted him on three sides, but was repulsed. The Banyamwezi were, moreover, much too sharp as traders for the Imboshwa, cheating them unmercifully, and lying like Greeks. Kombokombo's stockade was on the Chibérasé River, which flows briskly, eight yards broad and deep, through a mile of sponge. We came in the midst of a general jollification, and were most bountifully supplied with pombe and food. The Banyamwezi acknowledge allegiance to the Sultan of Zanzibar, and all connected with him are respected. Kombokombo pressed food and drink on me, and when I told him that I had nothing to return for it, he said that he expected nothing: he was a child of the Sultan, and ought to furnish all I needed.

11th July, 1868.—On leaving the Chibérasé we passed up over a long line of hills with many villages and gardens, but mostly deserted during the Mazitu raid. The people fled into the forests on the hills, and were an easy prey to the marauders, who seem to have been unmerciful. When we descended into the valley beyond we came to a strong stockade, which had successfully resisted the onset of the Mazitu; we then entered on flat forest, with here and there sponges containing plenty of water; plains succeeded the hills, and continued all the way to Bangweolo. We made a fence in the forest; and next day *(12th July)* reached the Rofuba, 50 yards broad and 4-1/2 feet deep, full of aquatic plants, and flowing south-west into the Luongo: it had about a mile and a half of sponge on each side of it. We encamped a little south of the river.

13th July, 1868.—On resting at a deserted spot, the men of a village in the vicinity came to us excited and apparently drunk, and began to work themselves up still more by running about, poising their spears at us, taking aim with their bows and arrows, and making as if about to strike with their axes: they thought that we were marauders, and some plants of ground-nuts strewn about gave colour to the idea. There is usually one good soul in such rabbles. In this case a man came to me, and, addressing his fellows, said, "This is only your pombe. White man, do not stand among them, but go away," and then he placed himself between me and a portion of the assailants, about thirty of whom were making their warlike antics. While walking quietly away with my good friend they ran in front and behind bushes and trees, took aim with bow and arrow, but none shot: the younger men ran away with our three goats. When we had gone a quarter of a mile my friend told me to wait and he would bring the goats, which he did: I could not feel the inebriates to be enemies; but in that state they are the worst one can encounter, for they have no fear as they have when sober. One snatched away a fowl from our guide, that too was restored by our friend. I did not load my gun; for any accidental discharge would have inflamed them to rashness. We got away without shedding blood, and were thankful. The Mazitu raid has produced lawlessness in the country: every one was taken as an enemy.

14th July, 1868.—We remained a day at the stockade of Moiéggéa. A Banyamwezi or Garaganza man is settled here in Kabaia's district, and on the strong rivulet called Mato. We felt secure only among the strangers, and they were friendly with us.

15th July, 1868.—At the village on the south bank of the Mpanda we were taken by the headman as Mazitu. He was evidently intoxicated, and began to shut his gates with frantic gesticulations. I offered to go away; but others of his people, equally intoxicated, insisted on my remaining. I sat down a little, but seeing that the chief was still alarmed, I said to his people, "The chief objects and I can't stay:" they saw the reasonableness of this, but I could not get my cowardly attendants to come on, though one said to me, "Come, I shall show you the way: we must speak nice to them." This the wise boys think the perfection of virtue, speaking nice means adopting a childish treble tone of voice and words exactly similar to those of the little Scotch girl who, passing through a meadow, was approached by a cow, probably from curiosity. To appease this enemy, she said, "Oh, coo, coo, if you no hurt me, I no hurt you." I told them to come on and leave them quietly, but they remained babbling with them. The guide said that there was no water in front: this I have been told too often ever to believe, so I went on through the forest, and in an hour and a half came to a sponge where, being joined by my attendants, we passed the night.

16th July, 1868.—Crossing this sponge, and passing through flat forest, we came to another named Méshwé, when there, as a contrast, the young men volunteered to carry me across; but I had got off my shoes, and was in the water, and they came along with me, showing the shallower parts. We finished the day's march by crossing the Molongosi spongy ooze, with 150 paces of deep water, flowing N.E. The water in these oozes or sponges felt very cold, though only 60° in the mornings, and 65° at midday. The Molongosi people invited us into the village; but the forest, unless when infested with leopards and lions, is always preferable, for one is free from vermin, and free from curiosity gazers, who in the village think they have a right to stare, but in the forest feel that they are not on an equality with strangers.

[It was on the 18th of July, 1868, we see that Dr. Livingstone discovered one of the largest of the Central African Lakes. It is extraordinary to notice the total absence of all pride and enthusiasm, as—almost parenthetically—he records the fact.]

17th and 18th July, 1868.—Reached the chief village of Mapuni, near the north bank of Bangweolo. On the 18th I walked a little way out and saw the shores of the Lake for the first time, thankful that I had come safely hither.

I told the chief that my goods were all expended, and gave him a fathom of calico as all I could spare: I told him that as soon as I had seen and measured the Lake I would return north; he replied, that seeing our goods were done he could say nothing, he would give me guides, and what else he should do was known to himself. He gave a public reception at once. I asked if he had ever seen anyone like me, and he said, "Never." A Babisa traveller asked me why I had come so far; I said I wished to make the country and people better known to the rest of the world, that we were all children of one Father, and I was anxious that we should know each other better, and that friendly visits should be made in safety. I told him what the Queen had done to encourage the growth of cotton on the Zambezi, and how we had been thwarted by slave-traders and their abettors: they were pleased with this. When asked I showed them my note-book, watch, compass, burning-glass, and was loudly drummed home.

I showed them the Bible, and told them a little of its contents. I shall require a few days more at Bangweolo than I at first intended. The moon being in its last stage of waning I cannot observe till it is of some size.

19th July, 1868.—Went down to Masantu's village, which is on the shore of the Lake, and by a spring called Chipoka, which comes out of a mass of disintegrated granite. It is seldom that we see a spring welling out beneath a rock: they are covered by oozing sponges, if indeed they exist. Here we had as a spectator a man walking on stilts tied to his ankles and knees. There are a great many Babisa among the people. The women have their hair ornamented with strings of cowries, and well oiled with the oil and fat from the seeds of the Mosikisi trees. I sent the chief a fathom of calico, and got an audience at once. Masantu is an oldish man; had never prayed to the Great Father of all, though he said the footsteps of "Mungu," or Mulungu, could be seen on a part of Lifungé Island: a large footstep may also be seen on the rock at the Chambezé, about fifteen inches long. He informed us that the Lake is much the largest at the part called Bangweolo.

The country around the Lake is all flat, and very much denuded of trees, except the Motsikiri or Mosikisi, which has fine dark, dense foliage, and is spared for its shade and the fatty oil yielded by its seeds: we saw the people boiling large pots full of the dark brown fat, which they use to lubricate their hair. The islands, four in number, are all flat, but well peopled. The men have many canoes, and are all expert fishermen; they are called Mboghwa, but are marked on the forehead and chin as Babisa, and file the teeth to points. They have many children, as fishermen usually have.

21st July, 1868.—Canoe-men are usually extortionate, because one cannot do without them. Mapuni claims authority over them, and sent to demand another fathom that he may give orders to them to go with us: I gave a hoe and a string of beads instead, but he insisted on the cloth, and kept the hoe too, as I could not afford the time to haggle.

Chipoka spring water at 9 A.M. 75° }
Lake water at same time 71°   } air 72°.
Chipoka spring at 4 P.M. 74° 5'   }
Lake water at same time 75°   } air 71° 5'; wet bulb 70°.

Discovery of Lake Bangweolo.

No hot fountains or earthquakes are known in this region. The bottom of the Lake consists of fine white sand, and a broad belt of strong rushes, say 100 yards wide, shows shallow water. In the afternoons quite a crowd of canoes anchor at its outer edge to angle; the hooks are like ours, but without barbs. The fish are perch chiefly, but others similar to those that appear in the other Lakes are found, and two which attain the large size of 4 feet by 1-1/2 in. thickness: one is called Sampa.

22nd July, 1868.—A very high wind came with the new moon, and prevented our going, and also the fishermen from following their calling. Mapuni thought that we meant to make, an escape from him to the Babisa on the south, because we were taking our goats, I therefore left them and two attendants at Masantu's village to assure him.

23rd July, 1868.—Wind still too strong to go. Took lunars.

24th July, 1868.—Wind still strong.

25th July, 1868.—Strong S.E. wind still blowing, but having paid the canoe-men amply for four days with beads, and given Masantu a hoe and beads too, we embarked at 11.40 A.M. in a fine canoe, 45 feet long, 4 feet deep, and 4 feet broad. The waves were high, but the canoe was very dry and five stout men propelled her quickly towards an opening in Lifungé Island, on our S.E. Here we stopped to wood, and I went away to look at the island, which had the marks of hippopotami and a species of jackal on it: it had hard wiry grass, some flowers, and a species of Gapparidaceous tree. The trees showed well the direction of the prevailing wind to be south-east, for the branches on that side were stunted or killed, while those on the north-west ran out straight, and made the trees appear, as sailors say, lopsided: the trunks too were bent that way.

The canoe-men now said that they would start, then that they would sleep here, because we could not reach the Island Mpabala before dark, and would not get a hut. I said that it would be sleeping out of doors only in either case, so they went. We could see the island called Kisi on our east, apparently a double island, about 15 miles off, and the tops of the trees barely visible on Mpabala on our south-east. It was all sea horizon on our south and north, between Lifungé and Mpabala, and between Lifungé and Kisi. We could not go to Kisi, because, as the canoe-men told us, they had stolen their canoe thence. Though we decided to go, we remained awhile to let the sea go down. A hammerhead's nest on one of the trees was fully four feet high. Coarse rushes show the shoals near the islands. Only one shell was seen on the shores. The canoe ships much less water in this surf than our boat did in that of Nyassa. The water is of a deep sea-green colour, probably from the reflection of the fine white sand of the bottom; we saw no part having the deep dark blue of Nyassa, and conjecture that the depth is not great; but I had to leave our line when Amoda absconded. On Kisi we observed a dark square mass, which at first I took to be a low hill: it turned out to be a mass of trees (probably the place of sepulture, for the graveyards are always untouched), and shows what a dense forest this land would become were it not for the influence of men.

We reached Mpabala after dark. It was bitterly cold, from the amount of moisture in the air. I asked a man who came to see what the arrival was, for a hut; he said, "Do strangers require huts, or ask for them at night?" he then led us to the public place of meeting, called Nsaka, which is a large shed, with planks around and open spaces between, instead of walls; here we cooked a little porridge, and ate it, then I lay down on one side, with the canoe-men and my attendants at the fire in the middle, and was soon asleep, and dreamed that I had apartments in Mivart's Hotel. This made me feel much amused next day, for I never dream unless I am ill, or going to be ill; and of all places in the world, I never thought of Mivart's Hotel in my waking moments; a freak of the fancy surely, for I was not at all discontented with my fare, or apartment, I was only afraid of getting a stock of vermin from my associates.

26th July, 1868.—I have to stand the stare of a crowd of people at every new place for hours: all usually talk as quickly as their glib tongues can; these certainly do not belong to the tribes who are supposed to eke out their language by signs! A few indulge their curiosity in sight-seeing, but go on steadily weaving nets, or by beating bark-cloth, or in spinning cotton, others smoke their big tobacco pipes, or nurse a baby, or enjoy the heat of the bright morning sun. I walked across the north end of the island, and found it to be about one mile broad, I also took bearings of Chirubi Island from the eastern point of Mpabala, and found from the south-east point of Chirubi that there are 183° of sea horizon from it to the point of departure of the Luapula. Chirubi is the largest of the islands, and contains a large population, possessing many sheep and goats. At the highest part of Mpabala we could see the tops of the trees on Kasango, a small uninhabited islet, about thirty miles distant: the tops of the trees were evidently lifted up by the mirage, for near the shore and at other parts they were invisible, even with a good glass. This uninhabited islet would have been our second stage had we been allowed to cross the Lake, as it is of the people themselves; it is as far beyond it to the mainland, called Manda, as from Masantu's to Mpabala.

27th July, 1868.—Took lunars and stars for latitude.

The canoe-men now got into a flurry, because they were told here that the Kisi men had got an inkling that their canoe was here, and were coming to take it; they said to me that they would come back for me, but I could not trust thieves to be so honest. I thought of seizing their paddles, and appealing to the headmen of the island; but aware from past experience how easy it is for acknowledged thieves like them to get up a tale to secure the cheap sympathy of the soft-headed, or tender-hearted, I resolved to bear with meekness, though groaning inwardly, the loss of two of the four days for which I had paid them. I had only my coverlet to hire another canoe, and it was now very cold; the few beads left would all be required to buy food in the way back, I might have got food by shooting buffaloes, but that on foot and through grass, with stalks as thick as a goose quill, is dreadfully hard work; I had thus to return to Masantu's, and trust to the distances as deduced from the time taken by the natives in their canoes for the size of the Lake.

We had come to Mpabala at the rate of six knots an hour, and returned in the same time with six stout paddlers. The latitude was 12' in a south-east course, which may give 24' as the actual distance. To the sleeping-place, the Islet Kasango, there was at least 28' more, and from thence to the mainland "Manda," other 28'. This 24 + 28 + 28 = 80' as the breadth from Masantu village, looking south-east. It lies in 11° 0' S. If we add on the half distance to this we have 11° 40' as the latitude of Manda. The mainland to the south of Mpabala is called Kabendé. The land's end running south of Masantu's village is the entrance to the Luapula: the clearest eye cannot see across it there. I saw clouds as if of grass burning, but they were probably "Kungu," an edible insect, whose masses have exactly the same appearance as they float above and on the water. From the time the canoes take to go to Kabendé I believe the southern shore to be a little into 12° of south latitude: the length, as inferred from canoes taking ten days to go from Mpabala to the Chambezé, I take to be 150 miles, probably more. No one gave a shorter time than that. The Luapula is an arm of the Lake for some twenty miles, and beyond that is never narrower than from 180 to 200 yards, generally much broader, and may be compared with the Thames at London Bridge: I think that I am considerably within the mark in setting down Bangweolo as 150 miles long by 80 broad.

When told that it contained four large islands, I imagined that these would considerably diminish the watery acreage of the whole, as is said to be the case with five islands in Ukerewé; but even the largest island, Chirubi, does not in the least dwarf the enormous mass of the water of Bangweolo. A range of mountains, named Lokinga, extends from the south-east to the south-west: some small burns come down from them, but no river; this range joins the Koné, or Mokoné range, west of Katanga, from which on one side rises the Lufira, and on the other the Liambai, or Zambesi. The river of Manda, called Matanga, is only a departing and re-entering branch of the Lake, also the Luma and Loéla rivers—some thirty yards broad—have each to be examined as springs on the south of the Lake.

July 29th, 1868.—Not a single case of Derbyshire neck, or of Elephantiasis, was observed anywhere near the Lake, consequently the report we had of its extreme unhealthiness was erroneous: no muddy banks did we see, but in the way to it we had to cross so many sponges, or oozes, that the word *matopé*, mud, was quite applicable; and I suspect, if we had come earlier, that we should have experienced great difficulty in getting to the Lake at all.

30th July, 1868.—We commenced our march back, being eager to get to Chikumbi's in case Mohamad should go thence to Katanga. We touched at Mapuni's, and then went on to the Molongosi. Clouds now began to cover the sky to the Mpanda, which has fifteen yards of flood, though the stream itself is only five yards wide, then on to the Mato and Moiéggé's stockade, where we heard of Chikumbi's attack on Kombokombo's. Moiéggé had taken the hint, and was finishing a second line of defence around his village: we reached him on the 1st August, 1868, and stopped for Sunday the 2nd: on the 3rd back to the Rofubu, where I was fortunate enough to hire a canoe to take me over.

In examining a tsetse fly very carefully I see that it has a receptacle at the root of the piercer, which is of a black or dark-red colour; and when it is squeezed, a clear fluid is pressed out at its point: the other two parts of the proboscis are its shield, and have no bulb at the base. The bulb was pronounced at the Royal Society to be only muscle, but it is curious that muscle should be furnished where none is needed, and withheld in the movable parts of the shield where it is decidedly needed.

5th August, 1868.—Reach Kombokombo, who is very liberal, and pressed us to stay a day with him as well as with others; we complied, and found that Mohamad had gone nowhere.

7th August, 1868.—We found a party starting from Kizinga for the coast, having our letters with them; it will take five months to reach the sea. The disturbed state of the country prevented parties of traders proceeding in various directions, and one that set off on the same day with us was obliged to return. Mohamad has resolved to go to Manyuema as soon as parties of his men now out return: this is all in my favour; it is in the way I want to go to see the Lualaba and Lufira to Chowambé. The way seems opening out before me, and I am thankful. I resolved to go north by way of Casembe, and guides were ready to start, so was I; but rumours of war where we were going induced me to halt to find out the truth: the guides (Banyamwezi) were going to divine, by means of a cock, to see if it would be lucky to go with me at present. The rumours of danger became so circumstantial that our fence was needed: a well was dug inside, and the Banyamwezi were employed to smelt copper as for the market of Manyuema, and balls for war. Syde bin Omar soon came over the Luapula from Iramba, and the state of confusion induced the traders to agree to unite their forces and make a safe retreat out of the country. They objected very strongly to my going away down the right bank of the Luapula with my small party, though it was in sight, so I resolved to remain till all went.

13th August, 1868.—The Banyamwezi use a hammer shaped like a cone, without a handle. They have both kinds of bellows, one of goatskin the other of wood, with a skin over the mouth of a drum, and a handle tied to the middle of it; with these they smelt pieces of the large bars of copper into a pot, filled nearly full of wood ashes. The fire is surrounded by masses of anthills, and in these there are hollows made to receive the melted metal: the metal is poured while the pot is held with the hands, protected by wet rags.

15th August, 1868.—Bin Omar, a Suaheli, came from Muaboso on Chambezé in six days, crossing in that space twenty-two burns or oozes, from knee to waist deep.

Very high and cold winds prevail at present. It was proposed to punish Chikumbi when Syde bin Omar came, as he is in debt and refuses payment; but I go off to Casembe.

I learn that there is another hot fountain in the Baloba country, called Fungwé; this, with Kapira and Vana, makes three hot fountains in this region.

Some people were killed in my path to Casembe, so this was an additional argument against my going that way.

Some Banyamwezi report a tribe—the Bonyolo—that extract the upper front teeth, like Batoka; they are near Loanda, and Lake Chipokola is there, probably the same as Kinkonza. Feeling my way. All the trees are now pushing out fresh young leaves of different colours: winds S.E. Clouds of upper stratum N.W.

29th August, 1868.—Kaskas began to-day hot and sultry. This will continue till rains fall. Rumours of wars perpetual and near;

and one circumstantial account of an attack made by the Bausé. That again contradicted. *(31st August, 1868.)* Rain began here this evening, quite remarkable and exceptional, as it precedes the rains generally off the watershed by two months at least: it was a thunder shower, and it and another on the evening of the second were quite partial.

* * * * *

[As we shall see, he takes advantage of his late experience to work out an elaborate treatise on the climate of this region, which is exceedingly important, bearing, as it does, upon the question of the periodical floods on the rivers which drain the enormous cistern-lakes of Central Africa.]

* * * * *

The notion of a rainy zone, in which the clouds deposit their treasures in perpetual showers, has received no confirmation from my observations. In 1866-7, the rainfall was 42 inches. In 1867-8, it amounted to 53 inches: this is nearly the same as falls in the same latitudes on the West Coast. In both years the rains ceased entirely in May, and with the exception of two partial thunder showers on the middle of the watershed, no rain fell till the middle and end of October, and then, even in November, it was partial, and limited to small patches of country; but scarcely a day passed between October and May without a good deal of thunder. When the thunder began to roll or rumble, that was taken by the natives as an indication of the near cessation of the rains. The middle of the watershed is the most humid part: one sees the great humidity of its climate at once in the trees, old and young, being thickly covered with lichens; some flat, on the trunks and branches; others long and thready, like the beards of old men waving in the wind. Large orchids on the trees in company with the profusion of lichens are seen nowhere else, except in the mangrove swamps of the sea-coast.

I cannot account for the great humidity of the watershed as compared with the rest of the country, but by the prevailing winds and the rains being from the south-east, and thus from the Indian Ocean: with this wind generally on the surface one can observe an upper strong wind from the north-west, that is, from the low humid West Coast and Atlantic Ocean. The double strata of winds can easily be observed when there are two sheets of clouds, or when burning grass over scores of square miles sends up smoke sufficiently high to be caught by the upper or north-west wind. These winds probably meet during the heavy rains: now in August they overlap each other. The probability arises from all continued rains within the tropics coming in the opposite direction from the prevailing wind of the year. Partial rains are usually from the south-east.

The direction of the prevailing wind of this region is well marked on the islands in Lake Bangweolo: the trunks are bent away from the south-east, and the branches on that side are stunted or killed; while those on the north-west run out straight and make the trees appear lopsided. The same bend away from the south-east is seen on all exposed situations, as in the trees covering the brow of a hill. At Kizinga, which is higher than the Lake, the trees are covered with lichens, chiefly on the south-east sides, and on the upper surfaces of branches, running away horizontally to or from the north-west. Plants and trees, which elsewhere in Africa grow only on the banks of streams and other damp localities, are seen flourishing all over the country: the very rocks are covered with lichens, and their crevices with ferns.

But that which demonstrates the humidity of the climate most strikingly is the number of earthen sponges or oozes met with. In going to Bangweolo from Kizinga, I crossed twenty-nine of these reservoirs in thirty miles of latitude, on a south-east course: this may give about one sponge for every two miles. The word "Bog" conveys much of the idea of these earthen sponges; but it is inseparably connected in our minds with peat, and these contain not a particle of peat, they consist of black porous earth, covered with a hard wiry grass, and a few other damp-loving plants. In many places the sponges hold large quantities of the oxide of iron, from the big patches of brown haematite that crop out everywhere, and streams of this oxide, as thick as treacle, are seen moving slowly along in the sponge-like small red glaciers. When one treads on the black earth of the sponge, though little or no water appears on the surface, it is frequently squirted up the limbs, and gives the idea of a sponge. In the paths that cross them, the earth readily becomes soft mud, but sinks rapidly to the bottom again, as if of great specific gravity: the water in them is always circulating and oozing. The places where the sponges are met with are slightly depressed valleys without trees or bushes, in a forest country where the grass being only a foot or fifteen inches high, and thickly planted, often looks like a beautiful glade in a gentleman's park in England. They are from a quarter of a mile to a mile broad, and from two to ten or more miles long. The water of the heavy rains soaks into the level forest lands: one never sees runnels leading it off, unless occasionally a footpath is turned to that use. The water, descending about eight feet, comes to a stratum of yellow sand, beneath which there is another stratum of fine white sand, which at its bottom cakes, so as to hold the water from sinking further.

It is exactly the same as we found in the Kalahari Desert, in digging sucking places for water for our oxen. The water, both here and there, is guided by the fine sand stratum into the nearest valley, and here it oozes forth on all sides through the thick mantle of black porous earth, which forms the sponge. There, in the desert, it appears to damp the surface sands in certain valleys, and the Bushmen, by a peculiar process, suck out a supply. When we had dug down to the caked sand there years ago, the people begged us not to dig further, as the water would all run away; and we desisted, because we saw that the fluid poured in from the fine sand all round the well, but none came from the bottom or cake. Two stupid Englishmen afterwards broke through the cake in spite of the entreaties of the natives, and the well and the whole valley dried up hopelessly. Here the water, oozing forth from the surface of the sponge mantle, collects in the centre of the slightly depressed valley which it occupies, and near the head of the depression forms a sluggish stream; but further down, as it meets with more slope, it works out for itself a deeper channel, with perpendicular banks, with, say, a hundred or more yards of sponge on each side, constantly oozing forth fresh supplies to augment its size. When it reaches rocky ground it is a perennial burn, with many aquatic plants growing in its bottom. One peculiarity would strike anyone: the water never becomes discoloured or muddy. I have seen only one stream muddied in flood, the Choma, flowing through an alluvial plain in Lopéré. Another peculiarity is very remarkable; it is, that after the rains have entirely ceased, these burns have their largest flow, and cause inundations. It looks as if towards the end of the rainy season the sponges were lifted up by the water off their beds, and the pores and holes, being enlarged, are all employed to give off fluid. The waters of inundation run away. When the sponges are lifted up by superabundance of water, all the pores therein are opened: as the earthen mantle subsides again, the pores act like natural valves, and are partially closed, and by the weight of earth above them, the water is thus prevented from running away altogether; time also being required to wet all the sand through which the rains soak, the great supply may only find its way to the sponge a month or so after the great rains have fallen.

I travelled in Lunda, when the sponges were all supersaturated. The grassy sward was so lifted up that it was separated into patches or tufts, and if the foot missed the row of tufts of this wiry grass which formed the native path, down one plumped up to the thigh in slush. At that time we could cross the sponge only by the native paths, and the central burn only where they had placed bridges: elsewhere they were impassable, as they poured off the waters of inundation: our oxen were generally bogged—all four legs went down up to the body at once. When they saw the clear sandy bottom of the central burn they readily went in, but usually plunged right over head, leaving their tail up in the air to show the nervous shock they had sustained.

These sponges are a serious matter in travelling. I crossed the twenty-nine already mentioned at the end of the fourth month of the dry season, and the central burns seemed then to have suffered no diminution: they were then from calf to waist deep, and required from fifteen to forty minutes in crossing; they had many deep holes in the paths, and when one plumps therein every muscle in the frame receives a painful jerk. When past the stream, and apparently on partially dry ground, one may jog in a foot or more, and receive a squirt of black mud up the thighs: it is only when you reach the trees and are off the sour land that you feel secure from mud and leeches. As one has to strip the lower part of the person in order to ford them, I found that often four were as many as we could cross in a day. Looking up these sponges a bird's-eye view would closely resemble the lichen-like vegetation of frost on window panes; or that vegetation in Canada-balsam which mad philosophical instrument makers *will* put between the lenses of the object-glasses of our telescopes. The flat, or nearly flat, tops of the subtending and transverse ridges of this central country give rise to a great many: I crossed twenty-nine, a few of the feeders of Bangweolo, in thirty miles of latitude in one direction. Burns are literally innumerable: rising on the ridges, or as I formerly termed them mounds, they are undoubtedly the primary or ultimate sources of the Zambezi, Congo, and Nile: by their union are formed streams of from thirty to eighty or 100 yards broad, and always deep enough to require either canoes or bridges. These I propose to call the secondary sources, and as in the case of the Nile they are drawn off by three lines of drainage, they become the head waters (the *caput* Nili) of the river of Egypt.

Thanks to that all-embracing Providence, which has watched over and enabled me to discover what I have done. There is still much to do, and if health and protection be granted I shall make a complete thing of it.

[Then he adds in a note a little further on:—]

But few of the sponges on the watershed ever dry; elsewhere many do; the cracks in their surface are from 15 to 18 inches deep, with lips from 2 to 3 inches apart. Crabs and other animals in clearing out their runs reveal what I verified by actually digging wells at Kizinga and in Kabuiré, and also observed in the ditches 15 feet deep dug by the natives round many of their stockades, that the sponge rests on a stratum of fine white washed sand. These cracks afford a good idea of the effect of the rains: the partial thunder-showers of October, November, December, and even January, produce no effect on them; it is only when the sun begins to return from his greatest southern declination that the cracks close their large lips. The whole sponge is borne up, and covers an enormous mass of water, oozing forth in March and April forming the inundations. These floods in the Congo, Zambesi, and Nile require different times to reach the sea. The bulk of the Zambesi is further augmented by the greater rains finding many pools in the beds of its feeders filled in February, as soon as the sun comes north.

Mem.—In apparent contradiction of the foregoing, so far as touches the sources of the Zambesi, Syde bin Habib informed me a few days ago that he visited the sources of the Liambai and of the Lufira. Each comes out of a fountain; the Lufira one is called Changozi, and is small, and in a wood of large trees S.W. of Katanga;

the fountain of the Liambai is so large that one cannot call to a person on the other side, and he appears also very small there—the two fountains are just five hours distant from each other. He is well acquainted with the Liambai (Leeambye), where I first met him. Lunga, another river, comes out of nearly the same spot which goes into the Leuñge, Kafué (?). Lufira is less than Kalongosi up there; that is less than 80 or 200 yards, and it has deep waterfalls in it. The Koné range comes down north, nearly to Mpméto's. Mkana is the chief of the stone houses in the Baloba, and he may be reached by three days of hard travelling from Mpwéto's; Lufira is then one long day west. As Muabo refuses to show me his "mita," "miengelo," or "mpamankanana" as they are called, I must try and get to those of the Baloba of Mkana.

Senegal swallows pair in the beginning of December.

Note.—Inundation.

The inundation I have explained in the note on the climate as owing to the sponges being supersaturated in the greater rains, when the sun returns from his greatest southern declination, the pores are then all enlarged, and the water of inundation flows in great volume even after the rains have entirely ceased. Something has probably to be learned from the rainfall at or beyond the equator, as the sun pursues his way north beyond my beat, but the process I have named accounts undoubtedly for the inundations of the Congo and Zambesi. The most acute of the ancients ascribed the inundation with Strabo to summer rains in the south; others to snows melting on the Mountains of the Moon; others to the northern wind—the Etesian breezes blowing directly against the mouth of the river and its current: others, with less reason, ascribed the inundation to its having its source in the ocean: Herodotus and Pliny to evaporation following the course of the sun.

1st September, 1868.—Two men come from Casembe—I am reported killed. The miningo-tree distils water, which falls in large drops. The Luapula seen when the smoke clears off. Fifty of Syde bin Omar's people died of small-pox in Usafa. *Mem.* Vaccine virus. We leave on the 25th, east bank of Moisi River, and cross the Luongo on the 28th, the Lofubu on the 1st October, and the Kalongosi on the 7th.

[Dr. Livingstone seems to have been unable to find opportunity to make daily entries at this period. All was turmoil and panic, and his life appears to have been in imminent danger. Briefly we see that on his way back from the Lake he found that his Arab associates of the last few months had taken up Casembe's cause against the devastating hordes of Mazitu, who had swept down on these parts, and had repulsed them. But now a fresh complication arose! Casembe and Chikumbi became alarmed lest the Arabs, feeling their own power, should turn upon them and possess the whole country, so they joined forces and stormed Kombokombo, one of the leading Arabs, and with what success we shall see. It is a fair specimen of the unaccountable complications which dog the steps of the traveller, where war is afoot, and render life a misery. He writes as follows on the 5th October:—]

I was detained in the Imbozhwa country much longer than I relished. The inroad of the Mazitu, of which Casembe had just heard when we reached the Mofwé, was the first cause of delay: he had at once sent off men to verify the report, and requested me to remain till his messengers should return. This foray produced a state of lawlessness in the country, which was the main reason of our further detention.

The Imbozhwa fled before the marauders, and the Banyamwezi or Garaganza, who had come in numbers to trade in copper, took on themselves the duty of expelling the invaders, and this, by means of their muskets, they did effectually, then, building stockades they excited the jealousy of the Imbozhwa lords of the soil who, instead of feeling grateful, hated the new power thus sprung up among them! They had suffered severely from the sharp dealing of the strangers already, and Chikumbi made a determined assault on the stockade of Kombokombo in vain.

Confusion prevailed all over the country. Some Banyamwezi assumed the offensive against the Baüsi, who resemble the Imbozhwa, but are further south, and captured and sold some prisoners: it was in this state of things that, as already mentioned, I was surrounded by a party of furious Imbozhwa. A crowd stood within fifteen or twenty yards with spears poised and arrows set in the bowstrings, and some took aim at me: they took us for plunderers, and some plants of ground-nuts thrown about gave colour to their idea. One good soul helped us away—a blessing be on him and his. Another chief man took us for Mazitu! In this state of confusion Cazembe heard that my party had been cut off:

he called in Moenempanda and took the field in person, in order to punish the Banyamwezi, against whom he has an old grudge for killing a near relative of his family, selling Baüsi, and setting themselves up as a power in his country.

The two Arab traders now in the country felt that they must unite their forces, and thereby effect a safe retreat. Chikumbi had kept twenty-eight tusks for Syde bin Omar safely; but the coming of Casembe might have put it out of his power to deliver up his trust in safety, for an army here is often quite lawless: each man takes to himself what he can. When united we marched from Kizinga on 23rd September together, built fences every night to protect ourselves and about 400 Banyamwezi, who took the opportunity to get safely away. Kombokombo came away from his stockade, and also part of the way, but cut away by night across country to join the parties of his countrymen who still love to trade in Katanga copper. We were not molested, but came nearly north to the Kalongosi. Syde parted from us, and went away east to Mozamba, and thence to the coast.

FOOTNOTES:

64. The allusion is to Mrs. Livingstone's grave.

65. At one season the long grass which covers the face of the country catches fire. For some three months the air is consequently filled with smoke.— ED.

* * * * *

CHAPTER XIII.

Cataracts of the Kalongosi. Passage of the river disputed. Leeches and method of detaching them. Syde bin Habib's slaves escape. Enormous collection of tusks. III. Theory of the Nile sources. Tribute to Miss Tinné. Notes on climate. Separation of Lake Nyassa from the Nile system. Observations on Victoria Nyanza. Slaves dying. Repentant deserters. Mohamad Bogharib. Enraged Imbozhwa. An attack. Narrow escape. Renewed attack. A parley. Help arrives. Bin Juma. March from the Imbozhwa country. Slaves escape. Burial of Syde bin Habib's brother. Singular custom. An elephant killed. Native game-laws. Rumour of Baker's Expedition. Christmas dinners.

11th October, 1868.—From Kizinga north the country is all covered with forest, and thrown up into ridges of hardened sandstone, capped occasionally with fine-grained clay schist. Trees often appear of large size and of a species closely resembling the gum-copal tree; on the heights masukos and rhododendrons are found, and when exposed they are bent away from the south-east. Animals, as buffaloes and elephants, are plentiful, but wild. Rivulets numerous, and running now as briskly as brooks do after much rain in England. All on the south-western side of Kalongosi are subjects of Casembe, that is Balunda, or Imbozhwa.

It was gratifying to see the Banyamwezi carrying their sick in cots slung between two men: in the course of time they tired of this, and one man, who was carried several days, remained with Chuma. We crossed the Luongo far above where we first became acquainted with it, and near its source in Urungu or Usungu Hills, then the Lobubu, a goodly stream thirty yards broad and rapid with fine falls above our ford, which goes into Kalongosi.

6th October, 1868.—Cross the Papusi, and a mile beyond the Luéna of forty yards and knee deep; here we were met by about 400 of Kabanda's men, as if they were come to dispute our passage at the ford: I went over; all were civil; but had we shown any weakness they would no doubt have taken advantage of it.

7th October, 1868.—We came to the Kalongosi, flowing over five cataracts made by five islets in a place called Kabwérumé. Near the Mebamba a goodly rivulet joins it.

12th October, 1868.—We came to the Kalongosi at the ford named Mosolo: by pacing I found it to be 240 yards broad, and thigh deep at the end of the dry season, it ran so strongly that it was with difficulty I could keep my feet. Here 500 at least of Nsama's people stood on the opposite shore to know what we wanted. Two fathoms of calico were sent over, and then I and thirty guns went over to protect the people in the ford: as we approached they retired. I went to them, and told them that I had been to Nsama's, and he gave me a goat and food, and we were good friends: some had seen me there, and they now crowded to look till the Arabs thought it unsafe for me to be among them: if I had come with bared skin they would have fled. All became friendly: an elephant was killed, and we remained two days buying food. We passed down between the ranges of hills on the east of Moero, the path we followed when we first visited Casembe.

20th and 21st October, 1868.—From the Luao I went over to the chief village of Muabo, and begged him to show me the excavations in his country: he declined, by saying that I came from a crowd of people, and must go to Kabwabwata, and wait awhile there, meanwhile he would think what he should do, whether to refuse or invite me to come. He evidently does not wish me to see his strongholds. All his people could go into them, though over ten thousand: they are all abundantly supplied with water, and they form the storehouses for grain.

22nd October, 1868.—We came to Kabwabwata, and I hope I may find a way to other underground houses. It is probable that they are not the workmanship of the ancestors of the present occupants, for they ascribe their formation invariably to the Deity, Mulungu or

Réza: if their forefathers had made them, some tradition would have existed of them.

23rd October, 1868.—Syde bin Habib came over from Mpwéto's; he reports Lualaba and Lufira flowing into the Lake of Kinkonza. Lungabalé is paramount chief of Rua.

Mparahala horns measured three feet long and three inches in diameter at the base: this is the yellow kualata of Makololo, bastard gemsbuck of the Dutch.

27th, 29th, and 30th October, 1868.—Salem bin Habib was killed by the people in Rua: he had put up a tent and they attacked it in the night, and stabbed him through it. Syde bin Habib waged a war of vengeance all through Rua after this for the murder of his brother: Sef's raid may have led the people to the murder.

29th October, 1868.—In coming north in September and October, the last months of the dry season, I crossed many burns flowing quite in the manner of our brooks at home, after a great deal of rain; here, however, the water was clear, and the banks not abraded in the least. Some rivulets had a tinge of white in them, as if of felspar in disintegrating granite; some nearly stagnant burns had as if milk and water in them, and some red oxide of iron.

Where leeches occur they need no coaxing to bite, but fly at the white skin like furies, and refuse to let go: with the fingers benumbed, though the water is only 60°, one may twist them round the finger and tug, but they slip through. I saw the natives detaching them with a smart slap of the palm, and found it quite effectual.

Swifts, Senegal swallows, and common dark-bellied swallows appeared at Kizinga in the beginning of October: other birds, as drongo shrikes, a bird with a reddish bill, but otherwise like a grey linnet, keep in flocks yet. *(5th December.)* They pair now. The kite came sooner than the swallows; I saw the first at Bangweolo on the 20th July, 1868.

1st November, 1868.—At Kabwabwata; we are waiting till Syde comes up that we may help him. He has an enormous number of tusks and bars of copper, sufficient it seems for all his people to take forward, going and returning three times over. He has large canoes on the Lake, and will help us in return.

2nd November, 1868.—News came yesterday from Mpwéto's that twenty-one slaves had run away from Syde bin Habib at one time: they were Rua people, and out of the chains, as they were considered safe when fairly over the Lualaba, but they showed their love of liberty on the first opportunity. Mpwéto is suspected to have harboured them, or helped them over the river; this will probably lead to Syde attacking him, as he has done to so many chiefs in Rua. In this case Mpwéto will have no sympathy; he is so wanting in the spirit of friendliness to others.

3rd November, 1868.—Sent off men to hasten Syde onwards. We start in two or three days.

The oldest map known to be in existence is the map of the Ethiopian Goldmines, dating from the time of Sethos I., the father of Rameses II., long enough before the time of the bronze tablet of Aristagoras, on which was inscribed the circuit of the whole earth, and all the sea and all rivers. (Tylor, p. 90, quoted from Birch's *Archaeologia*, vol. xxxiv. p. 382.) Sesostris was the first to distribute his maps.

8th November, 1868.—Syde bin Habib is said to have amassed 150 frasilahs of ivory = 5250 lbs., and 300 frasilahs of copper = 10,500 lbs. With one hundred carriers he requires to make four relays, or otherwise make the journey four times over at every stage. Twenty-one of his slaves ran away in one night, and only four were caught again: they were not all bought, nor was the copper and ivory come at by fair means; the murder of his brother was a good excuse for plunder, murder, and capture. Mpwéto is suspected of harbouring them as living on the banks of the Lualaba, for they could not get over without assistance from his canoes and people. Mpwéto said, "Remove from me, and we shall see if they come this way." They are not willing to deliver fugitives up. Syde sen£ for Elmas, the only thing of the Mullam or clerical order here, probably to ask if the Koran authorizes him to attack Mpwéto. Mullam will reply, "Yes, certainly. If Mpwéto won't restore your slaves, take what you can by force." Syde's bloodshed is now pretty large, and he is becoming afraid for his own life; if he ceases not, he will himself be caught some day.

Ill of fever two days. Better and thankful.

[Whilst waiting to start for Ujiji, Livingstone was intently occupied on the great problem of the Nile and the important part he had taken so recently in solving it: he writes at this date as follows:—]

The discovery of the sources of the Nile is somewhat akin in importance to the discovery of the North-West Passage, which called forth, though in a minor degree, the energy, the perseverance, and the pluck of Englishmen, and anything that does that is beneficial to the nation and to its posterity. The discovery of the sources of the Nile possesses, moreover, an element of interest which the North-West Passage never had. The great men of antiquity have recorded their ardent desires to know the fountains of what Homer called "*Egypt's heaven-descended spring*." Sesostris, the first who in camp with his army made and distributed maps, not to Egyptians only, but to the Scythians, naturally wished to know the springs, says Eustathius, of the river on whose banks he flourished. Alexander the Great, who founded a celebrated city at this river's-mouth, looked up the stream with the same desire, and so did the Caesars. The great Julius Caesar is made by Lucan to say that he would give up the civil war if he might but see the fountains of this far-famed river. Nero Caesar sent two centurions to examine the "*Caput Nili*." They reported that they saw the river rushing with great force from two rocks, and beyond that it was lost in immense marshes. This was probably "native information," concerning the cataracts of the Nile and a long space above them, which had already been enlarged by others into two hills with sharp conical tops called Crophi and Mophi—midway between which lay the fountains of the Nile—fountains which it was impossible to fathom, and which gave forth half their water to Ethiopia in the south, and the other half to Egypt in the north: that which these men failed to find, and that which many great minds in ancient times longed to know, has in this late age been brought to light by the patient toil and laborious perseverance of Englishmen.[66]

In laying a contribution to this discovery at the feet of his countrymen, the writer desires to give all the honour to his predecessors which they deserve. The work of Speke and Grant is deserving of the highest commendation, inasmuch as they opened up an immense tract of previously unexplored country, in the firm belief they were bringing to light the head of the Nile. No one can appreciate the difficulties of their feat unless he has gone into new country. In association with Captain Burton, Speke came much nearer to the "coy fountains," than at the Victoria Nyanza, but they all turned their backs on them. Mr. Baker showed courage and perseverance worthy of an Englishman in following out the hints given by Speke and Grant. But none rises higher in my estimation than the Dutch lady Miss Tinné, who, after the severest domestic afflictions, nobly persevered in the teeth of every difficulty, and only turned away from the object of her expedition, after being assured by Speke and Grant that they had already discovered in Victoria Nyanza the sources she sought. Had they not given their own mistaken views, the wise foresight by which she provided a steamer, would inevitably have led her to pull up, and by canoes to reach Lake Bangweolo's sources full five hundred miles south of the most southerly part of Victoria Nyanza. She evidently possesses some of the indomitable pluck of Van Tromp, whose tomb every Englishman who goes to Holland must see.[67] Her doctor was made a baron—were she not a Dutch lady already we think she ought to be made a duchess.

By way of contrast with what, if I live through it, I shall have to give, I may note some of the most prominent ideas entertained of this world-renowned river. Ptolemy, a geographer who lived in the second century, and was not a king of Egypt, with the most ancient maps made the Nile rise from the "Montes Lunae," between ten and twelve south lat., by six several streams which flowed north into two Lakes, situated east and west of each other. These streams flowed about west of his river Rhapta, or Raptus, which is probably our Rovuma or Louma. This was very near the truth, but the Mountains of the Moon cannot be identified with the Lokinga, or mountains of Bisa, from which many of the springs do actually arise. Unless, indeed, we are nearer to the great alterations in climate which have taken place, as we are supposed to be nearer the epoch of the mammoth, aurochs, and others. Snow never lay in these latitudes, on altitudes of 6000 feet above the sea.

Some of the ancients supposed the river to have its source in the ocean. This was like the answer we received long ago from the natives on the Liambai or Upper Zambesi when inquiring for its source. "It rises in Leoatlé, the white man's sea, or Métséhula." The second name means the "*grazing water*," from the idea of the tides coming in to graze; as to the freshness of the Liambai waters, they could offer no explanation.

Some again thought that the Nile rose in Western Africa, and after flowing eastwards across the Continent, turned northwards to Egypt; others still thought that it rose in India! and others again, from vague reports collected from their slaves, made it and several other rivers rise but of a great inland sea. *Achélunda* was said to be the name of this Lake, and in the language of Angola, it meant the "sea." It means only "*of*" or "*belonging to Lunda*," a country. It might have been a sea that was spoken of on a whole, or anything. "*Nyassi, or the sea*," was another name and another blunder. "Nyassi" means long grass, and nothing else. Nyanza contracted into Nyassa, means lake, marsh, any piece of water, or even the dry bed of a lake. The N and *y* are joined in the mouth, and never pronounced separately. The "Naianza"!—it would be nearer the mark to say the Nancy!

Of all theoretical discoverers, the man who ran in 200 miles of Lake and placed them on a height of some 4000 feet at the north-west end of Lake Nyassa, deserves the highest place. Dr. Beke, in his guess, came nearer the sources than most others, but after all he pointed out where they would not be found. Old Nile played the theorists a pretty prank by having his springs 500 miles south of them all! I call mine a contribution, because it is just a hundred years (1769) since Bruce, a greater traveller than any of us, visited Abyssinia, and having discovered the sources of the Blue Nile, he thought that he had then solved the ancient problem. Am I to be cut out by some one discovering southern fountains of the river of Egypt, of which I have now no conception?

David Livingstone.

[The tiresome procrastination of Mohamad and his horde was not altogether an unmixed evil. With so many new discoveries in hand Livingstone had an opportunity for working out several problems, and instituting comparisons between the phenomena of Inner Africa and the well-marked changes which go on in other parts of the world. We find him at this time summing them up as follows:—]

The subject of change of climate from alteration of level has not received the investigation it deserves. Mr. Darwin saw reason to believe that very great alterations of altitude, and of course of climate, had taken place in South America and the islands of the Pacific; the level of a country above the sea I believe he thought to be as variable as the winds. A very great alteration of altitude has also taken place in Africa; this is apparent on the sea-coast of Angola, and all through the centre of the country, where large rivers which once flowed southwards and westwards are no longer able to run in these directions: the general desiccation of the country, as seen in the beds of large rivers and of enormous lakes, tells the same tale. Portions of the east coast have sunk, others have risen, even in the Historic Period. The upper or northern end of the Red Sea has risen, so that the place of the passage of the children of Israel is now between forty and fifty miles from Suez, the modern head of the Gulf. This upheaval, and not the sand from the desert, caused the disuse of the ancient canal across the Isthmus: it took place since the Mohamadan conquest of Egypt. The women of the Jewish captivities were carried past the end of the Red Sea and along the Mediterranean in ox-waggons, where such cattle would now all perish for want of water and pasture; in fact, the route to Assyria would have proved more fatal to captives then than the middle passage has been to Africans since. It may be true that, *as the desert is now*, it could not have been traversed by the multitude under Moses—the German strictures put forth by Dr. Colenso, under the plea of the progress of science, assume that no alteration has taken place in either desert or climate—but a scientific examination of the subject would have ascertained what the country was then when it afforded pasture to "flocks and herds, and even very much cattle." We know that Eziongeber was, with its docks, on the seashore, with water in abundance for the ship-carpenters: it is now far from the head of the Elaic Gulf in a parched desert. Aden, when visited by the Portuguese Balthazar less than 300 years ago, was a perfect garden; but it is now a vast conglomeration of black volcanic rocks, with so little vegetation, that, on seeing flocks of goats driven out, I thought of the Irish cabman at an ascent slamming the door of his cab and whispering to his fare, "Whish, it's to desave the baste: he thinks that you are out walking." Gigantic tanks in great numbers and the ruins of aqueducts appear as relics of the past, where no rain now falls for three or more years at a time. They have all dried up by a change of climate, possibly similar and cotemporaneous with that which has dried up the Dead Sea.

The journey of Ezra was undertaken after a fast at the River Ahava. With nearly 50,000 people he had only about 8000 beasts of burden. He was ashamed to ask a band of soldiers and horsemen for protection in the way. It took about four months to reach Jerusalem; this would give five and a half or six miles a day, as the crow flies, which is equal to twelve or fifteen miles of surface travelled over; this bespeaks a country capable of yielding both provisions and water, such as cannot now be found. Ezra would not have been ashamed to ask for camels to carry provisions and water had the country been as dry as it is now. The prophets, in telling all the woes and miseries of the captivities, never allude to suffering or perishing by thirst in the way, or being left to rot in the route as African slaves are now in a well-watered country. Had the route to Assyria been then as it is now, they could scarcely have avoided referring to the thirst of the way; but everything else is mentioned except that.

Respecting this system of Lakes in the centre of Africa, it will possibly occur to some that Lake Nyassa may give a portion of its water off from its northern end to the Nile, but this would imply a Lake giving off a river at both ends; the country, too, on the north-north-west and north-east rises to from 4000 to 6000 feet above the sea, and there is not the smallest indication that Nyassa and Tanganyika were ever connected. Lake Liemba is the most southerly part of Tanganyika; its latitude is 8° 46' south; the most northerly point of Lake Nyassa is probably 10° 56'-8° 46' = 2° 10'. Longitude of Liemba 34° 57'-31° 57' = 3° 00' = 180' of longitude. Of latitude 130' + 180' = 310', two-thirds of which is about 206', the distance between two Lakes; and no evidence of fissure, rent, or channel now appears on the highland between.

Again, Liemba is 3000 feet above the sea. The altitude of Nyassa is 1200/x800 feet. Tanganyika would thus go to Nyassa— down the Shiré into the Zambesi and the sea, if a passage existed even below ground.

The large Lake, said to exist to the north-west of Tanganyika might, however, send a branch to the Nile; but the land rises up into a high ridge east of this Lake.

It is somewhat remarkable that the impression which intelligent Suaheli, who have gone into Karagwé, have received is, that the Kitangulé flows from Tanganyika into Lake Ukerewé. One of Syde bin Omar's people put it to me very forcibly the other day by saying, "Kitangulé is an arm of Tanganyika!" He had not followed it out; but that Dagara, the father of Rumanyika, should have in his lifetime seriously proposed to deepen the upper part of it, so as to allow canoes to pass from his place to Ujiji, is very strong evidence of the river being large on the Tanganyika side. We know it to be of good size, and requiring canoes on the Ukerewé side. Burton came to the very silly conclusion that when a native said a river ran one way, he meant that it flowed in the opposite direction. Ujiji, in Rumanyika's time, was the only mart for merchandise in the country. Garaganza or Galaganza has most trade and influence now. (*14th Sept., 1868.*)

Okara is the name by which Victoria Nyanza is known on the eastern side, and an arm of it, called Kavirondo, is about forty miles broad. Lake Baringo is a distinct body of water, some fifty miles broad, and giving off a river called Ngardabash, which flows eastwards into the Somauli country. Lake Naibash is more to the east than Kavirondo, and about fifty miles broad too: it gives off the River Kidété, which is supposed to flow into Lufu. It is south-east of Kavirondo; and Kilimanjaro can be seen from its shores; in the south-east Okara, Naibash and Baringo seem to have been run by Speke into one Lake. Okara, in the south, is full of large islands, and has but little water between them; that little is encumbered with aquatic vegetation called "Tikatika," on which, as in lakelet Gumadona, a man can walk. Waterlilies and duckweed are not the chief part of this floating mass. In the north Okara is large. Burukineggé land is the boundary between the people of Kavirondo and the Gallahs with camels and horses.

9th November, 1868.—Copied several Notes written at Kizinga and elsewhere, and at Kabwabwata resume Journal. Some slight showers have cooled the air a little: this is the hottest time of the year.

10th November, 1868.—A heavier shower this morning will have more of the same effect.

11th November, 1868.—Muabo visited this village, but refuses to show his underground houses.

13th November, 1868.—I was on the point of starting without Mohamad Bogharib, but he begged me not to go till he had settled some weighty matter about a wife he is to get at Ujiji from Mpamari; we must have the new moon, which will appear in three days, for lucky starting, and will leave Syde bin Habib at Chisabi's. Meanwhile two women slaves ran away, and Syde has got only five back of his twenty-one fugitives. Mullam was mild with his decisions, and returned here; he informed me that many of Syde's slaves, about forty, fled. Of those who cannot escape many die, evidently broken-hearted; they are captives, and not, as slaves often are, criminals sold for their guilt, hence the great mortality caused by being taken to the sea to be, as they believe, fatted and eaten. Poor things! Heaven help them!

Ujiji is the pronunciation of the Banyamwezi; and they call the people Wayeiyé, exactly as the same people styled themselves on the River Zougha, near Ngami.

[It will be remembered that several of his men refused to go to Lake Bangweolo with him: they seem now to have thought better of it, and on his return are anxious to come back to their old master who, for his part, is evidently willing to overlook a good deal.]

I have taken all the runaways back again; after trying the independent life they will behave better. Much of their ill conduct may be ascribed to seeing that after the flight of the Johanna men I was entirely dependent on them: more enlightened people often take advantage of men in similar circumstances; though I have seen pure Africans come out generously to aid one abandoned to their care. I have faults myself.

15th November, 1868.—The Arabs have some tradition of the Emir Musa coming as far south as the Jagga country. Some say he lived N.E. of Sunna, now Mtéza; but it is so mixed up with fable and tales of the Genii (Mageni), that it cannot refer to the great Moses, concerning whose residence at Meröe and marriage of the king of Ethiopia's daughter there is also some vague tradition further north: the only thing of interest to me is the city of Meröe, which is lost, and may, if built by ancient Egyptians, still be found.

The Africans all beckon with the hand, to call a person, in a different way from what Europeans do. The hand is held, as surgeons say, *prone*, or palm down, while we beckon with the hand held *supine*, or palm up: it is quite natural in them, for the idea in their mind is to lay the hand on the person and draw him towards them. If the person wished for is near, say forty yards off, the beckoner puts out his right hand on a level with his breast, and makes the motion of catching the other by shutting the fingers and drawing him to himself: if the person is further off, this motion is exaggerated by lifting up the right hand as high as he can; he brings it down with a sweep towards the ground, the hand being still held prone as before. In nodding assent they differ from us by lifting up the chin instead of bringing it down as we do. This lifting up. the chin looks natural after a short usage therewith, and is perhaps purely conventional, not natural, as the other seems to be.

16th November, 1868.—I am tired out by waiting after finishing the Journal, and will go off to-morrow north. Simon killed a zebra after I had taken the above resolution, and this supply of meat makes delay bearable, for besides flesh, of which I had none, we can buy all kinds of grain and pulse for the next few days. The women of the adjacent villages crowd into this as soon as they hear of an animal killed, and sell all the produce of their plantations for meat.

17th November, 1868.—It is said that on the road to the Great Salt Lake in America the bones and skulls of animals lie scattered everywhere, yet travellers are often put to great straits for fuel: this, if true, is remarkable among a people so apt in turning everything to account as the Americans. When we first steamed up the River Shiré our fuel ran out in the elephant marsh, where no trees exist, and none could be reached without passing through many miles on either side of impassable swamp, covered with reeds, and intersected everywhere with deep branches of the river. Coming to a spot where an elephant had been slaughtered, I at once took the bones on board, and these, with the bones of a second elephant, enabled us to steam briskly up to where wood abounded. The Scythians, according to Herodotus, used the bones[68] of the animal sacrificed to boil the flesh, the Guachos of South America do the same when they have no fuel: the ox thus boils himself.

18th November, 1868.—A pretty little woman ran away from her husband, and came to "Mpamari." Her husband brought three hoes, a checked cloth, and two strings of large neck beads to redeem her; but this old fellow wants her for himself, and by native law he can keep her as his slave-wife. Slave-owners make a bad neighbourhood, for the slaves, are always running away and the headmen are expected to restore the fugitives for a bit of cloth. An old woman of Mpmari fled three times; she was caught yesterday, and tied to a post for the young slaves to plague her. Her daughter burst into an agony of tears on seeing them tying her mother, and Mpamari ordered her to be tied to the mother's back for crying; I interceded for her, and she was let go. He said, "You don't care, though Sayed Majid loses his money." I replied, "Let the old woman go, she will be off again to-morrow." But they cannot bear to let a slave have freedom. I don't understand what effect his long prayers and prostrations towards the "Kibla" have on his own mind, they cannot affect the minds of his slaves favourably, nor do they mine, though I am as charitable as most people.

19th November, 1868.—I prepared to start to-day, but Mohamad Bogharib has been very kind, and indeed cooked meals for me from my arrival at Casembe's, 6th May last, till we came here, 22nd October; the food was coarse enough, but still it was food; and I did not like to refuse his genuine hospitality. He now begged of me not to go for three days, and then he would come along with me! Mpamari also entreated. I would not have minded him, but they have influence with the canoe-men on Tanganyika, and it is well not to get a bad name if possible.

20th November, 1868.—Mohamad Bogharib purposed to attack two villages near to this, from an idea that the people there concealed his runaway slaves; by remaining I think that I have put a stop to this, as he did not like to pillage while I was in company: Mpamari also turned round towards peace, though he called all the riff-raff to muster, and caracoled among them like an old broken-winded horse. One man became so excited with yelling, that the others had to disarm him, and he then fell down as if in a fit; water poured on his head brought him to calmness. We go on the 22nd.

22nd November, 1868.—This evening the Imbozhwa, or Babemba, came at dusk, and killed a Wanyamwezi woman on one side of the village, and a woman and child on the other side of it. I took this to be the result of the warlike demonstration mentioned above; but one of Mohamad Bogharib's people, named Bin Juma, had gone to a village on the north of this and seized two women and two girls, in lieu of four slaves who had run away. The headman, resenting this, shot an arrow into one of Bin Junta's party, and Bin Juma shot a woman with his gun.

This, it turned out, had roused the whole country, and next morning we were assailed by a crowd of Imbozhwa on three sides: we had no stockade, but the men built one as fast as the enemy allowed, cutting down trees and carrying them to the line of defence, while others kept the assailants at bay with their guns. Had it not been for the crowd of Banyamwezi which we have, who shot vigorously with their arrows, and occasionally chased the Imbozhwa, we should have been routed. I did not go near the fighting, but remained in my house to defend my luggage if necessary. The women went up and down the village with sieves, as if winnowing, and singing songs, and lullilooing, to encourage their husbands and friends who were fighting, each had a branch of the Ficus indica in her hand, which she waved, I suppose as a charm. About ten of the Imbozhwa are said to have been killed, but dead and wounded were at once carried off by their countrymen. They continued the assault from early dawn till 1 P.M., and showed great bravery, but they wounded only two with their arrows. Their care to secure the wounded was admirable: two or three at once seized the fallen man, and ran off with him, though pursued by a great crowd of Banyamwezi with spears, and fired at by the Suaheli—Victoria-cross fellows truly many of them were! Those who had a bunch of animals' tails, with medicine, tied to their waists, came sidling and ambling up to near the unfinished stockade, and shot their arrows high up into the air, to fall among the Wanyamwezi, then picked up any arrows on the field, ran back, and returned again. They thought that by the ambling gait they avoided the balls, and when these whistled past them they put down their heads, as if to allow them to pass over; they had never encountered guns before. We did not then know it, but Muabo, Phuta, Ngurué, Sandaruko, and Chapi, were the assailants, for we found it out by the losses each of these five chiefs sustained.

It was quite evident to me that the Suaheli Arabs were quite taken aback by the attitude of the natives; they expected them to flee as soon as they heard a gun fired in anger, but instead of this we were very nearly being cut off, and should have been but for our Banyamwezi allies. It is fortunate that the attacking party had no success in trying to get Mpwéto and Karembwé to join them against us, or it would have been more serious still.

24th November, 1868.—The Imbozhwa, or Babemba rather, came early this morning, and called on Mohamad to come out of his stockade if he were a man who could fight, but the fence is now finished, and no one seems willing to obey the taunting call: I have nothing to do with it, but feel thankful that I was detained, and did not, with my few attendants, fall into the hands of the justly infuriated Babemba. They kept up the attack to-day, and some went out to them, fighting till noon: when a man was killed and not carried off, the Wanyamwezi brought his head and put it on a pole on the stockade—six heads were thus placed. A fine young man was caught and brought in by the Wanyamwezi, one stabbed him behind, another cut his forehead with an axe, I called in vain to them not to kill him. As a last appeal, he said to the crowd that surrounded him, "Don't kill me, and I shall take you to where the women are." "You lie," said his enemies; "you intend to take us where we may be shot by your friends;" and they killed him. It was horrible: I protested loudly against any repetition of this wickedness, and the more sensible agreed that prisoners ought not to be killed, but the Banyamwezi are incensed against the Babemba because of the women killed on the 22nd.

25th November, 1868.—The Babemba kept off on the third day, and the Arabs are thinking it will be a good thing if we get out of the country unscathed. Men were sent off on the night of the 23rd to Syde bin Habib for powder and help. Mohamad Bogharib is now unwilling to take the onus of the war: he blames Mpamari, and Mpamari blames him; I told Mohamad that the war was undoubtedly his work, inasmuch as Bin Juma is his man, and he approved of his seizing the women.

He does not like this, but it is true; he would not have entered a village of Casembe or Moamba or Chikumbi as he did Chapi's man's village: the people here are simply men of more metal than he imagined, and his folly in beginning a war in which, if possible, his slaves will slip through his hands is apparent to all, even to himself. Syde sent four barrels of gunpowder and ten men, who arrived during last night.

27th November, 1868.—Two of Muabo's men came over to bring on a parley; one told us that he had been on the south side of the village before, and heard one man say to another "mo pigé" (shoot him). Mpamari gave them a long oration in exculpation, but it was only the same everlasting, story of fugitive slaves. The slave-traders cannot prevent them from escaping, and impudently think that the country people ought to catch them, and thus be their humble servants, and also the persecutors of their own countrymen! If they cannot keep them, why buy them—why put their money into a bag with holes?

It is exactly what took place in America—slave-owners are bad neighbours everywhere. Canada was threatened, England browbeaten, and the Northerners all but kicked on the same score, and all as if property in slaves had privileges which no other goods have. To hear the Arabs say of the slaves after they are fled, "Oh, they are bad, bad, very bad!" (and they entreated me too to free them from the yoke), is, as the young ladies say, "too absurd." The chiefs also who do not apprehend fugitives, they too are "bad."

I proposed to Mohamad Bogharib to send back the women seized by Bin Juma, to show the Babemba that he disapproved of the act and was willing to make peace, but this was too humiliating; I added that their price as slaves was four barrels of gunpowder or 160 dollars, while slaves lawfully bought would have cost him only eight or ten yards of calico each. At the conclusion of Mpamari's speech the four barrels of gunpowder were exhibited, and so was the Koran, to impress them (Muabo's people) with an idea of their great power.

28th and 29th November, 1868.—It is proposed to go and force our way if we can to the north, but all feel that that would be a fine opportunity for the slaves to escape, and they would not be loth to embrace it; this makes it a serious matter, and the Koran is consulted at hours which are auspicious.

30th November, 1868.—Messengers sent to Muabo to ask a path, or in plain words protection from him; Mpamari protests his innocence of the whole affair.

1st December, 1868.—Muabo's people over again; would fain send them to make peace with Chapi!

2nd December, 1868.—The detention is excessively vexatious to me. Muabo sent three slaves as offers of peace—a fine self-imposed, but he is on our south side, and we wish to go north.

3rd December, 1868.—A party went to-day to clear the way to the north, but were warmly received by Babemba with arrows; they came back with one woman captured, and they say that they killed one man: one of themselves is wounded, and many others in danger: others who went east were shot at, and wounded too.

4th December, 1868.—A party went east, and were fain to flee from the Babemba, the same thing occurred on our west, and to-day *(5th)* all were called to strengthen the stockade for fear that the enemy may enter uninvited. The slaves would certainly flee, and small blame to them though they did. Mpamari proposed to go off north by night, but his people objected, as even a child crying would arouse the Babemba, and reveal the flight, so finally he sent off to ask Syde what he ought to do, whether to retire by day or by night; probably entreating Syde to come and protect him.

A sort of idol is found in every village in this part, it is of wood, and represents the features, markings and fashion of the hair of the inhabitants: some have little huts built for them—others are in common houses. The Babemba call them *Nkisi* ("Sancan" of the Arabs): the people of Rua name one *Kalubi*; the plural, *Tulubi*; and they present pombe, flour, bhang, tobacco, and light a fire for them to smoke by.

They represent the departed father or mother, and it is supposed that they are pleased with the offerings made to their representatives, but all deny that they pray to them. Casembe has very many of these Nkisi; one with long hair, and named *Motombo*, is carried in front when he takes the field; names of dead chiefs are sometimes given to them. I have not met with anyone intelligent enough to explain if prayers are ever made to anyone; the Arabs who know their language, say they have no prayers, and think that at death there is an end of the whole man, but other things lead me to believe this is erroneous. Slaves laugh at their countrymen, in imitation of their masters, and will not reveal their real thoughts: one said that they believed in two Superior Beings—Réza above, who kills people, and Réza below, who carries them away after death.

6th December, 1868.—Ten of Syde bin Habib's people came over, bringing a letter, the contents of which neither Mpamari nor Mohamad cares to reveal. Some think, with great probability, that he asks, "Why did you begin a war if you wanted to leave so soon? Did you not know that the country people would take advantage of your march, encumbered as you will be by women and slaves?" Mohamad Bogharib called me to ask what advice I could give him, as all his own advice, and devices too, had been lost or were useless, and he did not know what to do. The Banyamwezi threatened to go off by night and leave him, as they are incensed against the Babemba, and offended because the Arabs do not aid them in wreaking their vengeance upon them.

I took care not to give any advice, but said, if I had been or was in his place, I would have sent or would send back Bin Juma's captives, to show that I disapproved of his act—the first in the war—and was willing to make peace with Chapi. He said that he did not know that Bin Juma would capture these people; that Bin Juma had met some natives with fish, and took ten by force, that the natives, in revenge, caught three Banyamwezi slaves, and Bin Juma then gave one slave to them as a fine, but Mohamad did not know of this affair either. I am of opinion, however, that he was fully aware of both matters, and Mpamari's caracoling showed that he knew it all, though now he denies it.

Bin Juma is a long, thin, lanky Suaheli, six feet two high, with a hooked nose and large lips: I told Mohamad that if he were to go with us to Manyuema, the whole party would be cut off. He came here, bought a slave-boy, and allowed him to escape; then browbeat Chapi's man about him (and he says, three others); and caught ten in lieu of him, of which Mohamad restored six: this was the origin of the war. Now that we are in the middle of it, I must do as Mohamad does in going off either by day or by night. It is unreasonable to ask my advice now, but it is felt that they have very unjustifiably placed me in a false position, and they fear that Syed Majid will impute blame to them, meanwhile Syde bin Habib sent a private message to me to come with his men to him, and leave this party.

I perceive that the plan now is to try and clear our way of Chapi, and then march, but I am so thoroughly disgusted with this slave-war, that I think of running the risk of attack by the country people, and go off to-morrow without Mohamad Bogharib, though I like him much more than I do Mpamari or Syde bin Habib. It is too glaring hypocrisy to go to the Koran for guidance while the stolen women, girls, and fish, are in Bin Juma's hands.

8th and 9th December, 1868.—I had to wait for the Banyamwezi preparing food: Mohamad has no authority over them, or indeed over anyone else. Two Babemba men came in and said that they had given up fighting, and begged for their wives, who had been captured by Syde's people on their way here: this reasonable request was refused at first, but better counsels prevailed, and they were willing to give something to appease the anger of the enemy, and sent back six captives, two of whom were the wives prayed for.

[At last he makes a start on the 11th of December with the Arabs, who are bound eastwards for Ujiji. It is a motley group, composed of Mohamad and his friends, a gang of Unyamwezi hangers-on, and strings of wretched slaves yoked together in their heavy slave-sticks. Some carry ivory, others copper, or food for the march, whilst hope and fear, misery and villainy, may be read off on the various faces that pass in line out of this country, like a serpent dragging its accursed folds away from the victim it has paralysed with its fangs.]

* * * * *

11th December, 1868.—We marched four hours unmolested by the natives, built a fence, and next day crossed the Lokinda River and its feeder the Mookosi; here the people belonged to Chisabi, who had not joined the other Babemba. We go between two ranges of tree-covered mountains, which are continuations of those on each side of Moero.

12th December, 1868.—The tiresome tale of slaves running away was repeated again last night by two of Mpamari's making off, though in the yoke, and they had been with him from boyhood. Not one good-looking slave-woman is now left of Mohamad Bogharib's fresh slaves; all the pretty ones obtain favour by their address, beg to be unyoked, and then escape. Four hours brought us to many villages of Chisabi and the camp of Syde bin Habib in the middle of a set-in rain, which marred the demonstration at meeting with his relative Mpamari; but the women braved it through, wet to the skin, and danced and lullilooed with "draigled" petticoats with a zeal worthy of a better cause, as the "penny-a-liners" say. It is the custom for the trader who receives visitors to slaughter goats, and feed all his guests for at least two days, nor was Syde wanting in this hospitality, though the set-in rain continuing, we did not enjoy it as in fine weather.

14th December, 1868.—Cotton-grass and brackens all over the country show the great humidity of Marungu. Rain daily; but this is not the great rain which falls when the sun comes back south over our heads.

15th December, 1868.—March two hours only to the range of Tamba. A pretty little light-grey owl, called "nkwékwé," was killed by a native as food; a black ring round its face and its black ears gave it all the appearance of a cat, whose habits it follows.

16th to 18th December, 1868.—A brother of Syde bin Habib died last night: I had made up my mind to leave the whole party, but Syde said that Chisabi was not to be trusted, and the death of his brother having happened, it would not be respectful to leave him to bury his dead alone. Six of his slaves fled during the night—one, the keeper of the others. A Mobemba man, who had been to the coast twice with him, is said to have wished a woman who was in the chain, so he loosed five out, and took her off; the others made clear heels of it, and now that the grass is long and green, no one can trace their course.

Syde told me that the slaves would not have detained him, but his brother's death did. We buried the youth, who has been ill three months. Mpamari descended into the grave with four others; a broad cloth was held over them horizontally, and a little fluctuation made, as if to fan those who were depositing the body in the side excavation made at the bottom: when they had finished they pulled in earth, and all shoved it towards them till the grave was level. Mullam then came and poured a little water into and over the grave, mumbled a few prayers, at which Mpamari said aloud to me, "Mullam does not let his voice be heard;" and Mullam smiled to me, as if to say, "Loud enough for all I shall get:" during the ceremony the women were all wailing loudly. We went to the usual sitting-place, and shook hands with Syde, as if receiving him back again into the company of the living.

Syde told me previously to this event that he had fought the people who killed his elder brother Salem bin Habib, and would continue to fight them till all their country was spoiled and a desolation: there is no forgiveness with Moslems for bloodshed. He killed many, and took many slaves, ivory, and copper: his tusks number over 200, many of large size.

19th and 20th December, 1868.—To Chisabi's village stockade, on the left bank of the Lofunso, which flows in a marshy valley three miles broad. Eight of Mohamad Bogharib's slaves fled by night, one with his gun and wife; a, large party went in search, but saw nothing of them.

To-day an elephant was killed, and they sent for the meat, but Chisabi ordered the men to let his meat alone: experience at Kabwabwata said, "Take the gentle course," so two fathoms of calico and two hoes were sent to propitiate the chief; Chisabi then demanded half the meat and one tusk: the meat was given, but the tusk was mildly refused: he is but a youth, and this is only the act of his counsellors. It was replied that Casembe, Chikumbi, Nsama, Meréré, made no demand at all: his counsellors have probably heard of the Portuguese self-imposed law, and wish to introduce it here, but both tusks were secured.

22nd December, 1868.—We crossed the Lofunso River, wading three branches, the first of forty-seven yards, then the river itself, fifty yards, and neck deep to men and women of ordinary size. Two were swept away and drowned; other two were rescued by men leaping in and saving them, one of whom was my man Susi. A crocodile bit one person badly, but was struck, and driven off. Two slaves escaped by night; a woman loosed her husband's yoke from the tree, and got clear off.

24th December, 1868.—Five sick people detain us to-day; some cannot walk from feebleness and purging brought on by sleeping on the damp ground without clothes.

Syde bin Habib reports a peculiar breed of goats in Rua, remarkably short in the legs, so much so, that they cannot travel far; they give much milk, and become very fat, but the meat is indifferent. Gold is found at Katanga in the pool of a waterfall only: it probably comes from the rocks above this. His account of the Lofu, or, as he says, West Lualaba, is identical with that of his cousin, Syde bin Omar; it flows north, but west of Lufira, into the Lake of Kinkonza, so named after the chief. The East Lualaba becomes very large, often as much as six or eight miles broad, with many inhabited islands, the people of which, being safe from invasion, are consequently rapacious and dishonest, and their chiefs, Moengé and Nyamakunda, are equally lawless. A hunter, belonging to Syde, named Kabwebwa, gave much information gleaned during his hunting trips; for instance, the Lufira has nine feeders of large size; and one, the Lekulwé, has also nine feeders; another, the Kisungu, is covered with, "tikatika," by which the people cross it, though it bends under their weight; he also ascribes the origin of the Lufira and the Lualaba West, or Lofu, with the Liambai to one large earthen mound, which he calls "segulo," or an anthill!

25th December, 1868, Christmas Day.—We can buy nothing except the very coarsest food—not a goat or fowl—while Syde, having plenty of copper, can get all the luxuries. We marched past Mount Katanga, leaving it on our left, to the River Kapéta, and slaughtered a favourite kid to make a Christmas dinner. A trading-party came up from Ujiji; they said that we were ten camps from Tanganyika. They gave an erroneous report that a steamer with a boat in tow was on Lake Chowambé—an English one, too, with plenty of cloth and beads on board. A letter had come from Abdullah bin Salem, Moslem missionary at Mtésa's, to Ujiji three months ago with this news.

26th December, 1868.—We marched up an ascent 2-1/2 hours, and got on to the top of one of the mountain ridges, which generally run N. and S. Three hours along this level top brought us to the Kibawé River, a roaring rivulet beside villages. There were no people on the height over which we came, though the country is very fine—green and gay with varying shades of that colour. We passed through patches of brackens five feet high and gingers in flower, and were in a damp cloud all day. Now and then a drizzle falls in these parts, but it keeps all damp only, and does not show in the rain-gauge. Neither sun nor stars appear.

27th and 28th December, 1868.—Remain on Sunday, then march and cross five rivulets about four yards wide and knee deep, going to the Lofunso. The grass now begins to cover and hide the paths; its growth is very rapid: blobs of water lie on the leaves all day, and keep the feet constantly wet by falling as we pass.

29th December, 1868.—We kept well on the ridge between two ranges of hills; then went down, and found a partially-burned native stockade, and lodged in it; the fires of the Ujiji party had set the huts on fire after the party left. We are in the Itandé district at the Nswiba River.

30th December, 1868.—We now went due east, and made a good deal of easting too from Mount Katanga on the Lofunso, and crossed the River Lokivwa, twelve yards wide, and very deep, with villages all about. We ascended much as we went east. Very high mountains appeared on the N.W. The woods dark gieen, with large patches of a paler hue.

31st December, 1868.—We reached the Lofuko yesterday in a pelting rain; not knowing that the camp with huts was near, I stopped and put on a bernouse, got wet, and had no dry clothes. Remain to-day to buy food. Clouds cover all the sky from N.W. The river, thirty yards wide, goes to Tanganyika east of this. Scenery very lovely.

FOOTNOTES:

66. In 1827 Linant reached 13° 30' N. on the White Nile. In 1841 the second Egyptian, under D'Arnauld and Sabatier, explored the river to 4° 42' N., and Jomard published his work on Limmoo and the River Habaiah. Dr. Beke and Mr. D'Abbadie contributed their share to making the Nile better known. Brun Rollet established a trading station in 1854 at Belema on the Nile at 5° N. lat.

67. Miss Tinné succumbed to the dangers of African travelling before Livingstone penned these just words of appreciation.

68. Ezek. xxiv. 5.

END OF VOL. I.

BIBLIOBAZAAR

The essential book market!

Did you know that you can get any of our titles in large print?

Did you know that we have an ever-growing collection of books in many languages?

**Order online:
www.bibliobazaar.com**

Find all of your favorite classic books!

Stay up to date with the latest government reports!

At BiblioBazaar, we aim to make knowledge more accessible by making thousands of titles available to you- *quickly and affordably*.

Contact us:
BiblioBazaar
PO Box 21206
Charleston, SC 29413

Made in the USA
Lexington, KY
08 December 2010